D0522025

DENT'S MODERN TRIBES

Dent's Modern Tribes

The Secret Languages of Britain

Susie Dent

JOHN MURRAY

First published in Great Britain in 2016 by John Murray (Publishers)

An Hachette UK company

I

© Susie Dent 2016

A CIP catalogue record for this title is
available from the British Library

ISBN 978-1-473-62387-3
Ebook ISBN 978-1-473-62388-0

Typeset in Plantin Light by Palimpsest Book Production Limited,
Falkirk, Stirlingshire

Printed and bound by Clays Ltd, St Ives plc

John Murray policy is to use papers that are natural, renewable
and recyclable products and made from wood grown in sustainable
forests. The logging and manufacturing processes are expected to
conform to the environmental regulations of the country of origin.

John Murray (Publishers)
Carmelite House
50 Victoria Embankment
London EC4Y 0DZ

www.johnmurray.co.uk

For Nicky

Contents

Introduction

CLERK: Two lots of Sex, Miss. Old Bailey, tomorrow at ten?

MS X: Digitals?

CLERK: Yes, no briefs. Just quickies. You've been invited for both by Mr. Y.

MS X: Punters?

CLERK: Jimmy P and Bob H.

MS X: Okay. I'm up for that.

So runs a fairly routine chat between a clerk and a barrister of criminal law, one that could be spectacularly misinterpreted by anyone unversed in the language of Chambers. Coded exchanges like this one take place every day: private, encrypted messages that are used because they're expedient, fun, or designed to keep outsiders out; sometimes it's all three. This is tribal language, and we are all part of its conversation.

I like to think that being a word-watcher gives you an in-alienable right to eavesdrop. Dipping in and out of other people's conversations is in a lexicographer's job description. It's where you pick up the verbal curiosities that trip up your ear, and that you scribble down like a word detective for later investigation.

I've always been an eavesdropper. When I passed the age at which gawping at complete strangers was still forgiven, I turned to the ear strain. The first bit of 'nonsense' I remember puzzling through was the curiosity 'oh my giddy aunt', an expression that inevitably left me wondering precisely who, and why? When the vicar apparently lost his dog's collar, I decided it was time to write things down. I've gone through a lot of notebooks since then.

I still have some of those early scribblings. Many of them hint at the nerd I was to become. 'Why is pedestranians [sic] such a long word?' reads one, while another asks simply, 'Do wasps have knees?' (I imagine my thinking was, if bees can have them . . .). In one of my longer meanderings I pondered why the long plastic thing with which we drew lines at school was called a ruler, and whether the Queen liked to use one. In some ways I've been writing this book all my life.

The first tribe I belonged to was the convent crowd. We used to call school confession the 'spilling test' (because it was behind the curtain that we spilled the beans), while an H3 wasn't a type of lead pencil, but a three Hail Mary penance for a mid-table misdemeanour. (I have no doubt that the nuns had their own lexicon to draw on.)

Since then, I've belonged to many others, from the sculling and dictionary communities to the fellowships of writers and road cyclists. And, like every other member, I've dipped into each of their dialects, so that many of its expressions stay with me still. This is why whenever I try too hard and things go awry, I'll say I've 'caught a crab'; why I might ask a fellow linguist to 'gloss' a word rather than explain it, and why when I've stalled through a lack of energy or chocolate I will say I've 'bonked'.

I'm not alone in this. An IT engineer might talk about their private life being totally 'bogotified', or explain that they had to buy a new phone for 'hysterical reasons'. A surfer can be 'rag-dolled', 'harshed' or 'smoked' at any time of day; actors might excuse themselves to visit the 'honey wagon' in their local; a cabbie still enjoys a good 'Churchill' on a day off; and an air steward probably takes a 'plonkey kit' on holiday. Some words are identical across different groups, but mean vastly different things: a bird's 'jizz' is most certainly not the same as the one a chef slathers all over his chicken cacciatore. The language of each and every one of us is littered with tribal footprints.

That word 'tribe': it's shifted a lot in the past decade, shedding its dubious, imperialistic connotations and striding confidently into the anthropological world, in which groups are determined less by genes and more by the work they do, the clothes they wear, or the passions they pursue. Its ancestor is the Latin *tribus*, which first referred to the three divisions of the early people of Rome – the Latin, Sabine and Etruscan elements. From there it embraced the Greeks' notion of the tribes in Israel: each of the twelve peoples of Israel who claimed descent from the twelve sons of Jacob. Over the course of Roman history, 'tribe' took in politicians, countries and eventually entire races. In *The Merchant of Venice*, the Jewish Shylock speaks of 'suffrance' being 'the badge of all our Trybe'.

Today's tribes are no less identifiable, but they can take different forms. From football fans to undertakers, secret agents to bikers and, again, politicians, we all wear a badge – usually several. And of all the characteristics that unite us, one of the most significant will be language.

With the exception of the Klingons and the Elvishes – fictional (and beautiful) languages learned by heart – this shared lingo is rarely entirely new. Nor is it taken on wholesale: tribes are versatile code-switchers, able to flick from one tongue to another as the situation demands. The most obvious example of such instinctive skill is there in our local dialects. Most of us will recognize the shuffle we make into familiar vocabulary whenever we go home, slipping on our old words like a well-worn and slightly baggy jumper. Depending on where that home is, we might profess to be jiggered, knackerooned, paggered, pootled, razzored, spunned up, tewed out, bellowsed, ramfeezled, or wisht

3

as a winnard: all English dialect descriptors of being consumed by exhaustion and totally out of puff. 'Tired' doesn't cut it when we're with our clan.

Overlapping these local terms are thousands of other tribal dialects. Every sport, every profession, every group united by a single passion draws on a lexicon that is uniquely theirs, and theirs for a reason. These individual languages are the product of a group's needs, ambitions and personalities; for any linguistic anthropologist, they're richly informative (and every self-respecting tribe needs an anthropologist).

To gather such information is not just about eavesdropping – it also means facing a different way. Kate Fox, while researching her compelling study of *The Racing Tribe*, took her role as witness and chronicler so seriously that when she finally got to stand at the finishing post of the Epsom Derby, she failed to see the winner romp home: for the entire race she had her back to the horses in order to study the crowd. To catch a language takes a similar switch, a little like standing still in a sea of commuters at rush hour. You have to drown out the white noise to get to the sounds you need.

Which is why, in many ways, this book is not just about words that are lost in translation, but about ones that are sometimes lost altogether. We have a knack of filtering out the strange sounds surrounding us every day, because we're not part of the crowd they're intended for. Besides, we're too busy lobbing our own words over the same heads to get to the people who'll understand us. Hearing a twitcher talk about being 'gripped off by a mega-crippler' may momentarily raise an eyebrow, but it's not our world, and so we move on. Only we shouldn't, because these drops from the eaves are not just worth savouring themselves, they also offer us a little piece of wisdom about the group who uses them – in the case of the mega-crippler, you'll be learning that someone's entire year can be ruined by the failure to sight an extremely rare bird.

Why do we need such tribal language? If the coded lingo is our own, we often won't realize it's private at all, in the same way as we always see ourselves as the ones without an accent. When a paramedic 'blues' a patient into hospital with 'GCS 3' and possible 'EtOH', they are dipping into a standard protocol that is swift, succinct and painless (for them at least). It's also instinctive.

On other occasions, it is deliberate: we shield our private language in order to keep outsiders firmly out – none more so, as I've learned, than when we're dealing with customers. Ask a waiter what they really mean when they say they've been 'stiffed by a flea of a chimneyfish' and you may not want to know the answer (if you do, you'll find it on p225). Such codes can be turned on for fun too: vicar-to-vicar conversations about playing 'Fish and Chips' or 'Shoving Leopard' on a Sunday will always raise a smile, unless the 'Archdemon' is present.

Whatever our reason for using it, our lingo is our identity. Whether it's the craic of comedians or the verbal sidesteps of politicians, private languages are a loud marker of who we are or want to be, and where we fit (or don't) in society. Collectively, the languages of the tribes provide as composite a picture of the British set-up, mentality, and sense of humour as you will find anywhere. When lexicographers talk about 'eggcorns', or a builder laments the 'snotter' on Lionel Richie's dance floor, you glimpse a little bit of the people behind the dictionaries and the dust sheets. Our public faces are all well and good, but it's our private lips that do the talking.

In the course of researching *Modern Tribes*, I've marvelled at the verve of the lingo nonchalantly swapped by IT staff; I've stood on corners in Oxford Street and Oxford's streets to hone in on the banter of builders, the police, and Morris dancers; I've accosted retired admirals and club DJs, and I've even interviewed a Freemason or two. And of course I've quizzed every guest I've had the pleasure to sit next to in Dictionary Corner, who have unfailingly shared the words and phrases from their neck of the professional woods. Best of all, for this Arsenal fan, Arsène Wenger himself gave me a few glimpses into the argot of the football manager.

Throughout, the best material has been delivered unselfconsciously. The first thing I discovered in researching this book was that if you ask anyone about their lingo, you'll meet hesitation and a sudden blankness of memory. The real gems emerge in the pub afterwards – the best time to capture tribal language is when it's not looking.

Inevitably many more of these gems will have flown beneath my radar. I'm fully expecting each and every reader of *Modern Tribes* to say, 'But you haven't put in X and Y!' They'd be right, which can only be a good thing, following the rule that when it comes to people, there are no rules. This book reflects my own, highly personal, selections of words – those that made my skin prickle, that gave me a glimpse into the world they came from, and that their speakers clearly relished. What's more, to give each tribe their full linguistic due would mean a work the size of the *Oxford English Dictionary*. But if I've made any glaring omissions, I must apologize – it will have been entirely my own doing, or occasionally that of the extra pint in the pub. My original list of tribes was far, far longer than the seventy or so in this book, and I would welcome any suggestions on what I've missed or might have included. My supply of notebooks isn't exhausted yet.

As for that exchange in chambers, the translation goes something like this:

CLERK: You have been instructed in two cases, in which the defendants Jimmy P and Bob H are accused of sexual offences, at the Central Criminal Court, Old Bailey, London. Both hearings are tomorrow morning at ten o'clock. There are no separate papers for you to read; the details of the cases are stored on the Crown Court Digital Court System, which you will have to access yourself. Each is a pre-trial hearing so they will not take very long in court. Mr Y is your solicitor in both cases so you are representing the defendants, Jimmy P and Bob H. As you know, in order to be allowed to access the confidential case papers, you must be authorized online by Mr Y, which he says he will ensure is done.

MS X: Fine, I will be there. I'll access the material online and be ready for the hearings.

Between the private shorthand and the public translation, there is of course no contest.

1

The Great Outdoors

'I am at two with nature.'
Woody Allen

The British Isles are an archipelago in the North Atlantic. Go
up to the north of Scotland, to Aberdeen, say, and you are
further north than Moscow. Being cold literally comes with the
territory. English has duly obliged with an entire lexicon for
the state of being nithered, shrammed, nesh, or taters. And yet
the British love of the outdoors is both legendary and all-weather.
Whether we're grimly pursuing picnics beneath a thunderplump
(one for the 'wet' list: a sudden downpour accompanied by
distinct rumbling in the skies), or cheerfully spreading our
blankets and sandwiches on a soggy lawn at Glyndebourne, the
attraction of being at one with nature – or at two, in Woody
Allen's case – is clearly a compelling one.

It seems a little unromantic, then, that so many of our
outdoorsy tribes are focused on ways to quantify or tame the
terrain (Twitchers and Ramblers), plunder it (Anglers), or move
as fast as possible through it (Surfers and Runners). These are
people on a mission and like all good missions, it pays to know
the code. Unblocking the blocker may sound like a plumber's
emergency call-out, but it can be a twitcher's driving motivation;
carving a bluebird, on the other hand, most certainly isn't – that
belongs instead to the surfer.

Beyond the shared desire for a 'catch', be it a prize bass, a
Siberian chiffchaff, a running PB, or a gnarly wave, these are

often solitary pursuits. Some even allow time, for those who want it, for slow spells of gongoozling – staring idly into water, or space, as the rest of the world passes by.

When they do come together, you'll find shared admiration mixed in with a healthy dose of competition. The rivalry between twitchers for a rare sighting, the drive amongst anglers to find the best river spot, the race between groups of ramblers to get to the pub first, or the proud displays of 10K times on social media – all speak to contests that can be as intense as those of any sporting grudge match. But in races and competitions or simply in the wild, the appreciation of each other's efforts is as genuine as it is warm. None more so than amongst surfers, who may be losing the dudespeak of the fraternity, but whose common passion sits above all else. These are all tribes with a shared spirit of adventure and ambition – and their verbal dialects are an integral part of the ride.

Of course there's a fair bit of shared pain, too. Ramblers and runners can both bonk if they don't watch their sugar levels, while twitchers, surfers, and anglers will all recognize the frustration of a target missed. Each of their lexicons has vocabulary for the one that got away – but that keeps them coming back again and again.

TART'S TICKS AND SHOWING WELL

TWITCHERS

The very first lesson to be learned was that birdwatchers are a thing of the past. Today, the only terms that will do are **twitcher** and **birder**, and woe betide anyone who confuses the two.

A twitcher is one who travels around in search of rarities to add to his (or, more rarely, her) extensive 'life list'. These are the diehards, those who spend hours soaked to the skin, hands benumbed, poised for a glimpse of a shorelark or velvet scoter that another twitcher has announced on the Rare Bird Alert app. The adrenaline is in the chase: many twitchers will travel for hours in search of their target, watch it for a minute or two, tick it off the list or send a tweet (the virtual kind) and then move on. In many ways, a twitcher is a trainspotter in the wild.

Twitching is not a gentle pursuit. Don't expect warm camaraderie and note-swapping over a thermos. In Britain at least, the hunt can be brutal. It's said that other European twitchers, for whom the pursuit is a passionate pastime, look on their British equivalents as the most intense and bitterly competitive of the lot. Feathers often fly in the twitching world.

There is much speculation as to the origin of that word 'twitcher'. Some say it refers to the rumble of old motorbikes as rare birds are chased across rugged terrain. Others suggest that a rare sighting such as a rustic bunting or a short-toed treecreeper induces trembling and twitching in its observer (in which case they can be described as suitably 'betwittered', a useful word from the 1800s for being 'overcome with pleasing excitement').

On the other side of the ring are the birders – enthusiasts who actively seek out birds in order to gain as much intelligence as they can. The biggest distinction between the birdwatcher of old and the modern birder is that while the former watches birds, the latter looks for them.

Sitting on the loftiest branch of all is the **ornithologist**: a zoologist who doesn't just watch birds, but studies every aspect of their lives, including songs, flight patterns, physical appearance and migration patterns. And, crucially, droppings – for guano is the mirror to a bird's soul.

On the fringes of the bird-loving community are the novices, aka **dudes**, who inadvertently announce themselves to the world and its birds with their fluorescent green cagoules and noisy rustling through field guides. Dudes were previously known as

tyros, but whatever their name, true twitchers will always maintain few of them know their **white-arse** from their **egret**.

At the bottom end of the ladder are the **togs** and **greenies**. The first is a none-too-affectionate term for bird photographers, especially those who clog up a hide and block the view of others. A **greenie** is a beginner who buys all the right (green) clothes and expensive birding paraphernalia, but who tends to betray themselves by frantically flipping through their guide in order to identify a bird in the few vital seconds they could actually be watching it.

dip out: to miss a bird the twitcher has specifically gone to see.

gripped off: even worse than dipping out: this is where other observers see the bird, but you don't.

crippler: a rare and spectacular bird, the pinnacle of a twitcher's year. Richard Millington, author of *A Twitcher's Diary*, once famously called a red-eyed (a small American songbird) vireo that he saw on the Isles of Scilly a 'totally hyperzonky megacrippler'. Cripplers are also referred to as 'megas'.

blocker: a bird that proves perpetually elusive, especially a mega that is an integral part of a birder's life list. If and when the bird is finally spotted, this is known as 'unblocking the blocker', an event that brings on euphoria as well as a **tick.**

mega: a truly unusual feathered visitor.

show well: (of a crippler) to be easily seen.

grill: to watch a bird closely.

flog: to search an area intensely. Also known as **burning up**.

stunning: the catch-all adjective, applied liberally to birds that stir the birder's soul, aka a **stonker**. A 'stunning' bird is often less attractive to a non-birder than its more beautiful relatives, but has more cachet and rarity. Its use also handily compensates for a certain inarticulacy in its observer, too stunned to compose a real sentence of praise.

plastic: used to describe exotic birds that have escaped into the wild and are thus not accepted as naturalized.

elusive: hard-to-spot; a useful verbal nose-thumbing by one birder to another, and a word that carries overtones of triumphalism and an unspoken 'I managed to see it but I doubt you will'.

tick: a sighting that can be crossed off the list. A **life-tick** is a first-ever sighting in a twitcher's life, while a **tart's tick** is a relatively common sighting that is crossed off later than expected.

stringy: used of a fellow twitcher's tick list when it's considered to be slightly suspect.

All that jizz

Each bird has an indefinable set of characteristics that makes it identifiable. This is the **jizz**, a word whose origin has been lost over time but that has served as an indispensable catch-all for twitchers since the 1920s. If asked how they were able to spot an unusual bird at a single glance, the answer will come: 'by their jizz'. This could be a single characteristic, or a combination of many, but it will always be the intangible something that defies being put into words and just *is*. The word elicits an inevitable degree of humour. A favourite joke among birders involves two elderly ladies in a New York hide, trying in vain to identify distant sandpipers. They ask an experienced birder for help, who promptly names the birds without hesitation, much to their amazement. When asked how he is so sure, he replies that he checked out the bird's jizz. 'Well, young man,' they say, 'that sure must be a powerful telescope.'

Peeps and eggwhips: the spottees

Bird-naming enjoys a separate shorthand all of its own, one which handily reduces often long-named creatures to manageable syllables. Icterine warblers are known as **ickies** or **hippos** (from their scientific name *Hippolais*); a **gropper** is a grasshopper warbler; a peregrine falcon is a **pegger**; and **mipits** and **ripits** are meadow pipits and rock pipits respectively. A **sprawk** is a sparrowhawk, and a **stoddo** a stock dove.

Then there are the names based on the bird's call, or distinctive markings.

Chiswick flyover: a pied wagtail, from their calls as they fly overhead. They may also be heard in West London.

eggwhip: an Egyptian goose, on account of its white wing feathers that are only visible in flight.

peeps: a small sandpiper.

PG Tips: the Pallas's grasshopper warbler, which breeds in Siberia, Mongolia and China and that has white tips on its tail feathers.

Unclassifiable

Sometimes even the most committed twitcher must admit defeat:

Friday-night bird: the one that always gets away, intent on evading the flocks of weekend twitchers.

LBJ: any bird that remains resolutely unidentifiable – many birds become nondescript while moulting, for example. The abbreviation stands for 'Little Brown Job'.

ON SHANKS'S PONY

RAMBLERS

If much of the twitchers' life is spent in silent and suspended animation, ramblers are resolutely bent on forward (and chattier) momentum.

The verb 'hike' started to appear in the early years of the nineteenth century. Its origins are elusive, and early records suggest hiking wasn't seen as a good thing: one glossary of West Country dialect declares that to 'hike off' was 'to go off; used generally in a bad sense'; to this day, we tell people to 'take a hike'. 'Rambling', meanwhile, is some 400 years older, and has embraced many meanings, notably wandering off a subject as well as down a hill. As for the activity both verbs describe – walking vigorously, especially for pleasure – we've been doing that for a lot longer. Today, **riding Shanks's pony**, as walking was once known (the shanks being one's own legs), is more popular than ever.

There are many types of walker. Beyond the rambler and the hiker are the ambler, the stroller, the slackpacker, the Sherpa (now available in Britain on coast-to-coast walks), the roamer, and, for a brief period in the fourteenth century, the raver (in this case, one who wandered bodily rather than in the mind). Today's **racewalker** is the successor of the 'pedestrianist' – a participant in the nineteenth-century form of competitive walking, a hugely popular spectator sport that had seventeenth-century aristocrats pitting their footmen against one another alongside their masters' speeding carriages.

Motivations differ too: for most it's the physical benefits that attract, while others walk for inspiration – Charles Dickens' night-time walks through the sleeping streets of London helped him puzzle out his complicated plot lines. The hero of serious walkers is the **God AW**, namely Alfred Wainwright, author of the canonical guide to the Lakeland Fells and of some forty other guides to the walks of Britain.

Ramblers and seasoned walkers are easy to spot, and not just by their cagoules (those made out of anything ending with –Tex). They will be the ones sporting hefty walking boots, gaiters that zip around the ankles to keep said boots dry, a heavyweight rucksack, and a bar of Kendal mint cake for blood-sugar emergencies. Above all, they will have a map: whether it's Ordnance Survey, Landranger (amblers), Explorer (more serious walkers), or the plastic-covered Active maps (real pro). These are the people who know a blue line from a green dotted one, and who would never dream of asking directions anywhere.

That said, they're a friendly bunch, and it's an unspoken rule that all passers-by are greeted. Conversation amongst groups of ramblers might touch on such matters as the morality of disturbing cairns (the piles of little stones left as summit-markers and that may have archaeological value) or **Naismith's Rule** – the aficionado's rule of thumb for measuring time and distance when planning a walk, whereby one hour is allowed for every 5 km forward, plus one hour for every 600 metres of ascent. (There is an offshoot of this called **Tranter's Variations**, which allows hikers to measure their personal fitness and which marks out the truly dedicated.)

The day will always end at the furthest pub, whereupon pints of the local ale will be happily sipped as bearings are checked and the onward journey assessed. Talk may drift to the walks still on the bucket list, such as Glyndŵr's Way or Offa's Dyke Path, or of the desire to one day be a **Munro-bagger**. Munros are the Scottish mountains of at least 3,000 feet; the few people who have managed to 'bag' all 282, including the almost sheer In Pinn (Inaccessible Pinnacle) on Skye, are officially known as the **compleaters** (and unofficially as the **Munro-braggers**).

The lingo

RUPPs: Roads Used as a Public Path: routes that are often poorly maintained and that were once known as 'jumblegut lanes'. They tend to be used only by hikers and horse riders.

bothie: a labourer's hut or a mountain refuge, often used by hikers for a breather or for warmth.

geocaching: the same as treasure-hunting, but for hikers, and using GPS navigation. This has a lexicon all of its own, including **Ground Zero**: a term that once meant the hole left after a nuclear bomb before it became inextricably linked with the site of the Twin Towers; in geocaching terms, it is the site where the treasure, or cache, is hidden.

GORP: an acronym for 'granola, oats, raisins, peanuts' (or 'good old raisins and peanuts'): useful sustenance on the trail.

Vitamin I: ibuprofen, the hiker's painkiller of choice for everything from blisters to muscle ache. **Vitamin B** is the beer that washes it down.

permissive path: not one designed for flirting, but rather one that isn't technically legal, even though hikers will frequently take it. Adverse consequences are rare, but may include irascible landowners.

flip-flopper: a hiker who sets off in one direction, then at some point decides to hike back in the opposite one.

MacGyver: a verb meaning to build or repair hiking gear with flair and imagination. The name is from the old TV show where the eponymous hero would construct useful devices out of the materials to hand.

misery index: the scale of suffering on a difficult walk. Ten means full-on pain and intense longing for the pub; one means you're probably in the pub already.

bivvy bag: a sleeping bag expressly designed for use in the open air.

JOGLE: acronym for 'John o'Groats to Land's End'. **LEJOG** is the opposite way round.

What the blazes?

Trails used in hiking are often signposted with 'blazes' – a waymarking system that uses painted marks along the route.

Blaze was a term borrowed from the Vikings after they raided British shores. Their word was *blesi*, a white star on a horse's forehead, and the English version of it became 'blaze', a light-coloured mark or spot.

The practice of making a white mark on a tree by stripping off a piece of bark to mark a path or boundary in a forest is very old. Records made by the first settlers in Massachusetts include the note that 'the meetinge house shall be sett . . . by a small whit Oak, marked at the souwest side with two notches & a blaze'. These settlers would blaze roads through the woods, chipping the bark off the trees to indicate the path that would take the traveller to the other side. To blaze a trail was to be the first to take it, marking it out for others to follow.

FRUBES, SHUBIES AND HOTDOGGING

SURFERS

When it comes to surfers, we like to take stereotyping to a whole new level. If asked, few of us would look beyond the 'totally radical, duuude!' or 'most triumphant!' of *Bill and Ted*. But while bodacious adjectives still rule on the beaches of Malibu and Hawaii, most surf geeks and freaks prefer a lexicon equal to the proper challenges of their sport, albeit with a good smattering of surfari humour thrown in.

Still, English is not immune to the charms of surf-speak, which delights in terms for a good wave: one of the latest to slip into the mainstream is 'sick', now applied to anything 'excellent', while the recent explosion of so-called 'brocabulary' (bromance, brohemian, bro-hug etc.) has more than a tinge of dudeness about it too.

Terms of approval

Nothing is ever just 'good' in surfing terms: it all happens at the extremes of good and bad. A surfer is never simply excited; instead they will be **freaking, amped, buzzing, stoked, psyched,** or **frothing**. A dream of a wave, the be-all and end-all of the sport, will be **gnarly** (or **nar**), **beast, choka, kick-ass, explosive, hideous, rad, sick, hectic, harsh, killer, cooking, smoking, going off, insane,** and – of course – **totally awesome**.

Surfer types

These range from the beginner to the killer, with a few non-desirables in-between.

brah or **dude**: a fellow surfer.
barney: a complete beginner (also known as a **kook**).
gremmie/grommet/grom: a young and very inexperienced surfer.
frube: a surfer who doesn't catch a wave for the whole time they are in the water.

paddle-puss: someone who stays in the whitewater close to the beach.

Hellman: an extreme surfer of the big waves.

shubie: someone who buys all the surf gear, including a board, but never actually goes in the water.

blow-in: a non-local who moves in on other surfers' territory.

cluck: someone who is totally afraid of the waves.

hotdogger: a cool and expert surfer.

Melvin: a surfer whose shorts have ridden up the bottom very noticeably (the inspiration for the term has never been found).

waxhead: a real surfing enthusiast; a reference to the wax applied to surfboards to make the upper surface less slippery.

And then there are those who in the surfer's mind don't belong anywhere near them:

goat-boater: a kayaker or wave-skier.

hodad: anyone who annoys board-riders while they surf, or who is a non-surfing beach bum.

booger: a bodyboarder.

seapig: a fat surfer.

eggbeater: a surfer who gets in the way when you're trying to catch a wave.

Aloha

Hawaii is the home of modern surfing, and the local dialect has provided some staples for surfers everywhere, from **aloha** (greetings) to **maholo** (thank you), and **grinds** (food) to **da kine** (the best wave). Above all, it donated the **shaka**: the classic surfer greeting sign, made with a closed fist and the thumb and little finger extended, and alternatively known as the **hang loose**, the perfect summary of the surfing philosophy.

The moves

When a surfer takes one from their **quiver** – their collection of boards – they may choose from a **log** (a longboard), a **foamie** (a foam board for beginners), or a selection of fins (**singles, twinnies, thrusters, quads** and **bonzers,** 1–5 fins respectively). Donning their **wetty** (wetsuit), grabbing their **leggy** (the leash or cord that attaches them to the board) and heading out for a morning surf (fondly known as the **dawn patrol**), they'll hope to achieve at least some of the moves below. In the end, it's all about **ripping** – surfing like a dream. It won't however be about **riding on top of the wave**: a Hollywood misconception that started with early drawings of surfing dating as far back as 1769 and the voyages of Captain Cook. In the first European sighting of surfing, crew member Joseph Banks wrote of watching '10 or 12 Indians' diving in and out of the breakers on 'the stern of an old canoe . . . We stood admiring this very wonderfull scene for full half an hour, in which time no one of the actors atempted to come ashore but all seemd most highly entertaind with their strange diversion.'

drop in: to catch a wave and ride down the face of it.
hit the lip: to meet the top edge of a cresting wave as it's coming down. You can also **smash, crack** and **whack** the same wave.
shoot the curl: to trim with the breaking part of a wave.
fade: to position yourself deeper into the barrel of a wave.
take the backdoor: to enter the barrel of a wave behind its peak.
visit the green room: to be inside the tube or barrel of a wave.
Hail Mary: a term borrowed from American football, meaning an extreme (or desperate) manoeuvre of any kind.
reo: re-entry into the water.

chaka-khan: ripping super-hard.

pig dog: riding with your back to the wave.

hotdogging: making a radical turn on a wave; also known as **carving** and **shredding**.

hang ten: to ride a surfboard with all ten toes curled over the edge of the board. To **hang eleven** (if you're a man) is to surf naked.

stand Goofy: to stand with your right foot forward; apparently so called because of the way Disney's Goofy stands in an early cartoon. Goofy-footers are actually the minority in surfing, even among left-handers.

Going doughnuts

The **total wipeout**, the fall from the board, is when it all goes wrong. This may happen when a surfer is so **noodled** (arms so tired they've gone floppy) that they become any of the following: **drilled**, **flogged**, **smashed**, **beaten**, **served**, **rag-dolled**, **smoked**, **nailed**, **axed**, **tweeked**, **harshed**, **gruelled**, **hammered** or **mullered**.

Wipeouts (**going doughnut** or **taking dirty lickings**) take various forms. And while there is no equivalent to the French idiom for a wipeout, 'prendre la gamelle' (take the dog bowl), there is still colour aplenty.

take a railbang: to fall over and take the board between the legs.

go over the falls, or **pearl**: a wipeout when the nose of the surfboard buries itself in the wave.

bog a rail: to catch the edge of the board and trip yourself up.

endo: to nosedive, so that the board is standing straight up, nose into the air.

take a binger: the result of being run over by a bodyboarder.

locked in: the result of a wave crashing and trapping the surfer inside.

stuff it: to stay in the wave until you get pounded.

tombstoning: when, after a bad wipeout, the top half of the board sticks out of the water.

Let me count the waves

Buzzy Trent, the pioneer of big wave surfing, famously said, 'Waves are not measured in feet and inches, they are measured in increments of fear.' Most of all, they have nicknames, ranging from **flat, ankle busters, knee high, waist, head high, overhead, double overhead, big, huge,** or **massive** to **Code Red.**

victory at sea: choppy and windblown.

bone yard: the place where the waves break.

bluebird: a big wave breaking outside the normal breaking waves.

bomboras (bommies): big waves breaking further out.

corduroy: when a series of swells are stacking up as far as you can see.

party wave: one used by multiple surfers.

the soup: the white foam after the wave has broken.

avalanche: any big breaking wave.

pit: the trough of a very hollow wave, the closest to the lip that a surfer dares to go.

cruncher: a big hard wave that is almost impossible to ride.

shoredump: waves that are in shallow water, very close to the shore.

slab: a wave that breaks over a shallow slab of rock, giving the wave a thick, hollow form. Hard to surf, spectacular to watch.

BROTHERS-OF-THE-ANGLE

ANGLERS

Even the keenest angler would agree that the glamour of fishing is less immediate. Witness the solitary figures dotted along a soggy riverbank, silently staring at the water beneath a glowering sky with only a can of wriggling bait for company, and the inevitable question from the non-believer will be 'Why?' The angler's explanation might include 'It's the hunter in me', 'It gets me out of mischief', 'I love the peace and quiet', 'It brings me closer to nature', or 'I used to come here with my Dad'.

Far more unexpectedly, you might also hear 'It's the social side'. For, away from the silence of the river, the camaraderie within angling communities is tangible and noisy. Conversations between 'brothers of the angle', as Izaak Walton called them in his *Compleat Angler*, focus far less on the weight of their latest catch, and far more on poking and milk runs, stickworms and buzzbait: proof if you needed it of a widely shared community lexicon. Fishy jokes are always popular, the hoarier the better: 'What swims in the sea, carries a machine gun, and makes you an offer you can't refuse?'* (See below)

Within such gatherings, the one thing you won't get is mixed company. It's estimated that only five per cent of all recreational anglers are female, a statistic that's unlikely to change at least within syndicates, said by some (i.e. those outside them) to operate like secret societies, in which new syndicate members are recruited with a hushed whisper and a celebratory shoulder clap over dinner.

---

* Answer: the Codfather

Those wanting to avoid club or private waters tend to be left with the **free** ones, classed as 'family-friendly' and consequently overfished and underwhelming. And yet as any angler (with the notable exception of the trophy or big-game variety) will tell you, fishing is not just about the fish: it's also about the journey. Sometimes that journey is a disappointing one: fishermen are so famous for their tall tales that 'the one that got away' has entered common usage. Anglers will always have their personal nemesis: mythical, huge and ever-elusive fish that lurk in the depths and taunt anyone who presumes to look for them.

Piscators (the technical term) can choose to categorize themselves in various ways. At the most leisurely end of the spectrum are the pleasure anglers, those who take to the day-ticket waters with a thermos and a smile, and the occasional child or dog. These are the dilettantes of the river, who come and go as they please. That's not to say they won't bring their 'stuff': any angler worth his salt will carry to his **beat** or fishing spot a lot of gear, variously consisting of **disgorgers**, **swivels**, **clips**, **rod rests**, and **landing nets**, not to mention a sleeping bag and Styrofoam cup. If he's heading for a longer session, the **bivvy** will come too: the small domed tent used for over-nighting.

Playing for 'proper' stakes are the match anglers, competitors racing to catch their weight in fish and carry home the prize (plus said fish). Their ambition is matched only by the trophy angler, out to find a **totem fish** (think of weighing scales, and of glass cabinets housing huge bass or **wall-hangers**). Finally there is the 'serious' angler, a hardy out-in-all-weathers type who is always fully across new techniques, tackle and territories.

It's all about that bait

There are dozens of types of fishing rods available to the angler, including **feeders, wagglers** and **quivers**. To go with them are a myriad of baits, jigs and lures (designed to look like a small fish and so attract the attention of a larger one). Most boast zappy names that seem to be variously inspired by dubious sports (**rump the stump**), children's games (**jig-and-frog, stickworm, rubby-dubby**) or excellent daytime quiz shows (the **Countdown lure**). Baits themselves go by names such as the **Flaming Booby, Millennium Bug, Aggravator**, and **Hairy Mary. Gozzers** are the maggots bred at home, while anglers in Devon and Cornwall like to call the earthworm the **angletwitch**.

Fishy personalities

fingerling: an immature fish (in terms of youth rather than behaviour).

fishproud: applied to an angler who is proud of the results of their fishing season.

hole-jumper: someone who knowingly fishes a productive location previously discovered by someone else; regarded as a low tactic in competitions.

yaffuller: an angler carrying an armful (yaffull) of fish.

Reeling you in

do-nothing: a technique in which a plastic lure is cast out, often to the bottom of the river, and then reeled in at a steady pace when a fish bites.

broggle: to fish for eels by thrusting a sharp baited stick into the riverbed.

bulging: using a lure just below the surface so that it 'bulges' the water without breaking the surface.

bump the stump: a technique in which a lure is brought into contact with another object such as a log or rock, ricocheting off and so provoking a reaction strike from fish.

milk run: the strategy of running a few casts in one spot to tempt active fish, and then quickly moving on to the next.

ripping: a technique whereby the lure is rapidly pulled forward ('ripped') before being dropped again as a way of making lethargic fish react.

walking the dog: moving the lure in a zigzag pattern, in the way a dog might pull back and forth on its lead.

How to tickle a trout

There are two types of tickling: **gargalesis**, the heavy, laughter-inducing kind, and **knismesis**, the lighter, stroked-by-a-feather, itchy kind. If you ask a trout, there's a third way: one that enduces a zen-like state of calm.

The art of **trout-tickling** is centuries old, mentioned as far back as in *Twelfth Night*: 'for here comes the trout that must be caught with tickling'. This is the mystical act of stroking a trout's underbelly until it enters a trance, whereupon it can be scooped up onto dry land. A manual from 1901 instructs the angler to slowly run his forefinger along the fish's belly, moving further and further towards the gills until a full hypnotic state is reached. It makes no mention of any application to humans.

CHUB-RUBBING ON THE DREADMILL

RUNNERS

It's easy to spot a seasoned runner across a crowded room. There's an unmistakable energy about them, even when they're standing still – which they don't do all that often.

If you ask someone who *lives* with a runner, the telltale signs are rather different. They describe toenails that are black, broken, or ready to drop off altogether; phone apps or Polar watches that measure a resting heart rate; a spare pair of trainers in a work bag; computer bookmarks of great running playlists; and a training manual or ten under the bed. These runner widows and widowers complain that they always come second best to a personal best, are frequently woken up by a ludicrously early alarm, and have a daily battle with sweaty kit in the bathroom. They are also expected to converse freely about the number of 'K' their partner has put in ('kilometres' rather than anything narcotic), and to have their kitchen stocked with goji berries, bananas, peanut butter, pre-race carb-loaders, recovery drinks, and tubes and tubes of energy gels.

Like cyclists, runners will usually acknowledge fellow members of the tribe while they're out. But unlike cyclists, this acknowledgement will take the form of a panting 'hello' or fatigued raise of the hand rather than any cheery good morning or helpful warnings of impending obstacles. Most runners will be lost in playlisted reverie, broken only to check their distance and heart rate or to pop another gel. Although running clubs are becoming increasingly popular, in essence, runners are a tribe of individuals. And they like it that way. As one runner puts it: 'You need to be running away from something to get better.'

Such solitude-seeking disappears on race day, when fraternal endorphins start to flow long before the physical ones. In marathon-running in particular, high-fiving is compulsory, both of fellow participants and the friends and family gathered for support. If you're wearing a tiger suit or a pink Lycra unitard, high fives tend to outnumber the metres run by a ratio of 5:1.

As for the lingo, much of it is shared with other sporting types, save for the **junks, LSD** and the occasional **chunky Elvis**.

The strategies

the Elvis: the traditional pre-marathon fuel of peanut butter and a banana, usually on some kind of bread; a snack famously loved by Elvis Presley.

negative splits: achieved when you run the second half of a marathon faster than the first; the mark of an elite runner.

LSD: Long Slow Distance: a type of aerobic training designed to build endurance and to burn fat.

junk miles (or **junks**): miles run at a steady pace to achieve a specific mileage target rather than any physical benefit.

dreadmill: the semi-affectionate name for the treadmill in the gym, and often featured in a humblebrag: 'It was tipping it down outside, so I put in a good 20K on the dreadmill.'

The pitfalls

mountain dew: a sweaty cleavage.

chub rub: painful chafing caused by the friction between a runner's inner thighs.

lac attack: the sort of fatigue brought on by a painful excess of lactic acid that has been built up in the course of a run.

sandbagger: a runner who deliberately holds back in order to seem slower or more tired at the beginning of a run, only to pass everyone later on.

bonk: a total lack of energy experienced by a runner when they burn through all their glycogen stores.

hitting the wall: this is when the bonk becomes a psychological state, often around the 20-mile mark of a marathon. All the body's energy supplies have been used up, and carrying on requires formidable willpower.

. . . and the rush

runner's high: the dangerous feeling of euphoria on completing a race that makes the runner immediately sign up for another. This has been likened to the temporary elation a woman experiences after giving birth, tricking her into believing she could easily have another baby straight away.

2

Modern Life

'Change is inevitable. Except from a vending machine.'
Robert C. Gallagher, attributed

'All the best words are disappearing.' Lexicographers hear this a lot. It's a sadness expressed by many that some of the jewels of our language are being replaced by the on-fleek selfies and emojis of today's vernacular. Lamented above all else are our local vocabularies – the dialects we grew up with and that we all fear will disappear under a single, garish blanket of mono-talk. Happily, the end of the word as we knew it is no longer looming – in fact, it never really threatened at all. The BBC's *Voices*, an ambitious project that set out to gauge the health of Britain's local lexicons, proved that not only are old dialect words still alive, they are kicking too, thanks to new generations mixing up their own versions of their parents' and grandparents' vocabulary.

This is more proof, if we needed it, that language is both endlessly regenerative and curiously circular. There is much to recognize in the language of even the most recent cultural arrivals, among the baristas and the gamers, the IT crowd and the rippers performing their alley-oops at the skate park, or the home bakers riding the stiff peaks of their meringues.

Take 'geek', a term that is still very much in vogue. The partnership of geekdom and fashionability would have astonished visitors to the circuses and freak shows of the 1900s. At that time, a 'geck' was a local word for 'fool', one who would pull grotesque stunts to shock and entertain the crowds. Today we even have 'geek chic', sported by those whose Bluetooth technology is also rooted in the past, taking its unlikely name from a unifying Viking king.

Take the 'zarf', too: the cardboard cupholder dispensed with every barista-brewed cappuccino. This throwaway symbol of modern life could not have had a more prestigious beginning. Zarfs in the Ottoman Empire were honed out of precious metal and encrusted with emeralds and diamonds.

Alongside such reconfigured relics there is of course much that is new, which is just as it should be. As technology marches on, linguistic gaps emerge and are just as quickly filled. Some are more inventive than others – the 'crapplets' of our computers and 'quadzillas' on the gym bench speak cheekily for themselves, while a 'flat white' sits at the blander end of the scale, in language at least. Meanwhile the lexicon of the 'couch co-ops' and 'RPGs' is as full of fun and inventiveness as befits the notion of a game: here we find wordplay at its best.

THE GREAT BRITISH LOVE AFFAIR

HOME BAKERS

Forget shopkeepers. We are a nation of home bakers. All talk of bread and cake today (and there is lots of it) generally falls into two categories: BGBBO and AGBBO – *Before* or *After The Great British Bake Off*. Few TV programmes have had such a pronounced effect on both the popularity of a pastime and its language. 'Soggy bottom' looks set to enter today's dictionaries as a byword not just for an overly moist cake, but for all sorts of other misfortunes that life might throw at us. Meanwhile, we are tossing around terms such as 'bavarois' and 'îles flottantes' like they're going out of fashion. Except they're most decidedly not, and their sudden hipness looks set to last a lot longer than jeggings and flatforms.

Before Mary Berry, Paul Hollywood, and that incident with the stolen custard, baking had been an integral part of our domestic lives for centuries, quietly shaping our culture as well as our cities (the Great Fire of London famously sprang from a bakery in Pudding Lane), and even our tax laws – a VAT tribunal in 1991 ruled that Jaffa Cakes are exempt from VAT as they harden when stale, and are consequently cakes not biscuits. We might even throw fornication in there too, a word rooted in the Latin *fornix*, meaning 'arch', and apparently associated with prostitutes huddling under Roman arches near the warmth of the city's bakeries. (Perhaps this is why bakers can occasionally come over all *Carry On*. From 'ganaching our buns' to 'rigid egg whites', baking and bawdiness clearly go together.)

Evidence of baking dates back to 4000 BC in Egypt. The Romans boasted an impressive repertoire of pastries, cakes and breads (unappetizingly, the word 'placenta' originates from the Latin word for a flat cake). In the Middle Ages, baked goods were a luxury – the rich ate fine, floured wheat bread, while the poor were left to eat the chewy and black kind. The industry was tightly regulated, with draconian consequences waiting for any who flouted the rules, unwittingly or otherwise: any baker selling bread that was underweight could be fined, pilloried or flogged. The only way to avoid this was to give each customer a little extra – known as an 'inbread' – a practice which gave birth to the famous phrase **a baker's dozen** for a rough count that errs on the generous side.

Today, the word 'cake' has ousted 'chicken' in recipe searches, and supermarket shelves continue to groan under the weight of cake-making equipment. *GBBO* produced a marked spike in the usage of words like **showstopper** and **vol-au-vent** during its airing. **Croquembouche** (literally, 'crunches in the mouth') and **millefeuille** ('a thousand leaves') now positively trip off the tongue (if it's not swallowed immediately) and even the **profiteroles** and **syllabubs** of eighties' dinner parties are making a comeback. Baking has hit the mainstream, and a sweet tooth plus the right jargon can be the makings of the amateur cake-maker. Beyond the aforesaid overly moist bottom, and talk of **soft peaks**, **stiff peaks**, **ribbon stages**, **crumb**, **creaming**, **folding**, **rubbing in**, **proofing**, and **baking blind**, it seems there is no limit to the advance of baking chat.

HAVING THE LAST ZARF

BARISTAS

The language of coffee belongs to Italy. The first record in the *Oxford English Dictionary* for the word **barista** is from 1982 and a book by Paul Hofman on life in modern Rome: 'A good barista can simultaneously keep an eye on the coffee oozing from the espresso machine into a battery of cups, pour vermouth and bitters, and discuss the miserable showing of the Lazio soccer team.' In other words, those Roman bartenders dispensed alcohol as well as cappuccino and chat – today's breed is far more focused. 'Coffee' as a single entity has ceased to exist, and on the menu instead is a dazzling array of shots/milk/syrup combinations that promise to dramatically improve our quality of life. Whatever the historians say, for the devoted fan BC will always mean 'before coffee'.

The precise history of coffee is a mystery. The legend attached to it tells of a goatherd named Kaldi, who noticed his animals running around in excitement after munching on the berries and leaves of a particular plant. We took the modern word 'coffee' from the Arabic *qahwah*, said to be rooted in a term for 'having no appetite' and to refer to coffee's stimulating properties. In the seventeenth century, when coffee was introduced into Christian Europe, it was promptly condemned by the Councilmen of Pope Clement VIII as being 'the bitter invention of Satan'. The Pope himself rather liked it, declaring the satanic drink to be so delicious that 'we should cheat the devil by baptizing it'. There were many who dissented, including those signing a 'Women's Petition Against Coffee' from 1674, which declared that 'the Excessive use of that Newfangled, Abominable, Heathenish Liquor called *COFFEE* . . . has so *Eunucht* our Husbands, and Crippled our more kind *Gallants*, that they are become as *Impotent* as Age'.

As it spread to English coffee houses, the drink acquired various names, including 'devil's brew', 'coals of the evil one', 'puddle water', 'go-juice' and 'ninny-broth'. A far cry from today's half-caf–skinny-light-whip-no-foam-mocha.

Coffee also played a hand in the battle for American independence. It was during a protest against the British by the Sons of Liberty that many crates of tea were destroyed inside ships at Boston Harbour, and the bay was turned into the largest and most unappealing cup of tea ever made. As other ports followed suit, patriotic Americans denounced tea and turned instead to coffee.

Most baristas see coffee-making as a means to an end rather than a vocation in life. It's not unusual to find baristas with a degree in astrophysics or a PhD. For the time being, though, they have to get up hours before their customers, survive on the minimum wage and too much coffee, and yet still come out smiling.

To become a member of the baristahood requires skill, dexterity and the patience of Job. When asked what they'd *really* like to say to their customers, top of the baristas' lists were 'Get off the phone', 'Be nice to us; we have a decaf button', and 'When we greet you with "Hi, how are you?", don't snap back "grande latte"'.

Today's coffee giants continue to stir up both lattes and venti-sized controversy, as they exert their dominance into every chink of the British landscape. Their kingdom is vast – not for nothing is Starbucks a name taken from a character in *Moby Dick*. Legend has it that the founders initially considered naming their company after Ahab's boat in the same novel, the *Pequod*, but changed their mind when they realized the first syllable of that name conjured up images of a less appetizing liquid.

The vocabulary of the baristahood remains predominantly Italian. It began with the **espresso** (*not* 'expresso'), from the Italian meaning 'pressed-out (coffee)', though of course most of us think it has everything to do with how fast the coffee is either served or hits the bloodstream – for the latter you might want to go for a **redeye** with one or two extra shots.

The **cappuccino**, famously, was named after the Capuchins, friars of the order of St Francis. The name was chosen, back in the 1940s, not on account of the monks' love of caffeine, but because the colour of the frothy drink was thought to resemble the colour of their habits.

A **caffè latte** means simply 'coffee with milk'; the first record of it dates back to a travelogue from Italy from 1847. If your beverage of choice is a **caffè macchiato**, you are drinking 'stained coffee' thanks to the very small amount of hot or foamed milk. Mocha, meanwhile, is named after the port in Yemen near the entrance of the Red Sea, from where it was first shipped for export.

Most other drinks on the coffee menu are riffs on these Italian names, whether it's the **frappuccino**, the **babyccino**, or even the **Frankencaf** (barista-speak for a half-decaf espresso). And so when something else comes along, and it sounds resolutely

English in its making, it makes an impact. In 2015, America jumped on the blandwagon of the flat white, a double espresso 'hit' with microfoam and a smooth milky finish, and once the sole preserve of Australia. According to reports, the moment the flat white hit the coffee bars of Vegas, the Australians washed their hands of it. The British show no signs of doing the same.

Education at barista schools involves such matters as latte art and cupping skills, as well as recognition of a coffee's 'nose'. When work starts for real, it's inevitable the new recruits will devise a vocabulary of their own. The writer Ben Schott rounded up the 'Java Jive' of some US coffee shops for the *New York Times*. He discovered a nifty lexicon for different types of customer, including a **fresh pot** (a flirtatious one); **nice weather for shoes** (hot); a **snaggler** (disagreeable); a **sweaty Susan** (impatient); and a **Falstaff** (drunk or stressed). **Demitasse**, meanwhile, in at least one coffee shop, is barista-code for 'celebrity in the house', for whom a barista might linger over the preparation of a special **alpaccino**.

Then there is that 'zarf', the cardboard sleeve that's travelled a very long way since its ornamental and golden beginnings in the Far East. Perhaps with that in mind, some chains have decided to add other embellishments to their coffee with flourishes such as the 'latte art dot', or the cappuccino dusting of a chocolate heart. The Capuchin monks would surely approve.

JUDI DENCH AND THE QUADZILLA

GYM-GOERS

Grunts, the thundering crash of metal and a low, quiet moaning noise: not the ear-assault of an action movie, but an average session in the weights area for the **curlbro** – the slightly snarly term for the gym rat whose life ambition is to look shredded. Such is the prevailing stereotype of the muscle-seeker – one that, like most snapshot reductions, is largely true. But not all weightlifters are grunting Popeyes with a low IQ: for many the inspiration is simply good health and a toned mind as well as body. Moreover, the gym is home to many personalities, from the frenetic spinners to the gentle treadmill-strollers, and the yogis in their logoed spandex to the flailers on a balance ball. Each of these groups will peak in number in the early part of the year, when guilty resolution pushes membership to its highest. Those still breaking a sweat in the summer months are the diehards of the gym, whose lingo speaks to the passion, determination, and occasional obsession that you'll find there. You may also pick up some **broscience**: the word-of-mouth 'knowledge' passed on from bro to bro that, like all good whispers, somehow always ends up as the 'truth'.

Gym etiquette is not a bad basis for daily life. Never leave your sweat on anything, respect the desire of others to be left alone, and studiously ignore any kind of bodily noise. These alone will serve you far better than **yogatude**: the dismissiveness occasionally shown by serious yoga practitioners towards amateur yogis (even if they reserve their real scorn for carbs, dairy and any material other than organic cotton). Above all, the smart gym-goer should avoid **miring**: posing post-workout in front of the mirror while taking the obligatory selfie. These scantily clad mirers might be heartened by the knowledge that the word 'gymnasium' comes from the ancient Greek for 'exercising naked'.

The players

gymhead (or **gymbot**): an automaton who has little or no life beyond the weight room or training mat.

newbie: the novice, one who can be spotted injuring themselves by using equipment in entirely the wrong way.

cardio bunny: a female gym-goer who spends her entire workout on cardio equipment.

iron maiden: one who dispels the myth that women shouldn't lift.

quadzilla: a gym-goer whose quadriceps are so enormous that their jeans look as though they might rip at any moment.

hard gainer: one who finds it difficult to gain muscle in spite of doing everything possible to achieve it. Usually applied to lean and lanky ectomorphs, who remain skinny even after double protein shakes and endless jars of peanut butter.

Judi Dench: rhyming slang for 'hench', i.e. someone strong-looking or muscular.

power couple: partners who work out together. Giveaways can be matching gym gear and a shared grimacing intensity.

spinhead: a passionate pedaller at a high-intensity spinning (stationary bike) class.

weekend warrior: one who, come Saturday, carries out a range of intense, strenuous workouts having been unable to/disinclined to do anything during the week.

yogi/yogini: a lover of the purple mat and such positions as the **cow face**, **firefly** or **camel**.

freak: a bodybuilder with almost unnatural muscle development. Some see this as an extreme compliment.

The training

burpee: a type of squat thrust with an extra push-up and silly-looking jump at the finish.

planks: the core-building exercise that keeps those training literally on their toes (and forearms, and in pain).

stacking: the strategy of adding more weights to your workout in order to build strength and increase muscle.

beast it up: to go for the max with intense effort in order to look as shredded (SEE BELOW) as possible.

maxing out: lifting extremely heavy weights for just one rep.

go to failure: to be unable to do even one more rep without sending the weight crashing to the floor or achieving total body collapse. Training to failure is a badge of honour for some, though only the pros can go to failure on an overhead move without dire consequences.

cheap reps: the imperfect kind that come after having gone to failure.

cut up: to become as lean as possible.

bulking: the process of adding muscle mass to your body through strength training and nutrition.

Vitamin S: anabolic steroids. Also known as **gym candy**.

DOMS: delayed onset muscle soreness. The kind that hits two days after training and prevents you from walking up the stairs.

The body

shredded: having ridiculously/admirably defined muscles. ('Muscle' itself is from the Latin for 'little mouse', thanks to the apparent resemblance between the small rodents and shredded biceps.)

guns: pumped biceps and triceps.

jacked: well-defined or muscular. Also known as **swollen, swole, ripped, cut** or **gunny**.

boulders: shoulders that are solid as rock.

V taper: the ultimate bodybuilding look of wide shoulders, a huge back, and a small mid-section.

vascular: displaying visible veins as a result of exercise and low body fat.

The equipment

pies/wheels/plates: nicknames for various weights.

pec deck: the machine alternative to free weights.

power rack/power cage: a four-posted rack with safety bars, the venue for heavy lifting.

skull crusher: the floor press, in which the trainee lowers a barbell from a full extension above their head.

YOU ARE NOT EXPECTED TO UNDERSTAND THIS

THE IT CROWD

To the outsider, 'working in IT' will generally conjure up images of company help desks and technological SWAT teams who descend whenever a system breaks down – i.e. often. In reality, information technology is a vast and continually growing field, one that encompasses as diverse a range of jobs as you might find in the armed forces. Which is not a throwaway comparison: this is the geek army, and they are advancing all the time.

Ask a programmer for their favourite joke and you'll do well to follow it. This applies in particular to Unix programmers, who are among the industry's biggest nerds. Take one of their jokes involving the Unix command line prompt 'less', which denotes the ability for a user to scroll backwards in a text. Programmers are fond of the formula less > more, implying that less has greater functionality than more – they find this very funny. At some point the joke will also involve the phrase 'more or less', but the outsider may not have stuck around to hear it.

The lingo of the IT crowd is a curious mix of inventive nicknames, slick acronyms, references from literature, and shortcuts that really aren't shortcuts at all (just as WWW takes longer to say than 'World Wide Web'). Elsewhere, the strange stories and sheer serendipity behind the coining of terms helps them lodge in the mind. Even 'Google' is said to have been a spur-of-the-moment riff on 'googol', a fanciful term for ten raised to the hundredth power and an allusion to the volume of information contained on the Net. 'Bluetooth', meanwhile, was named for King Blåtand (real name Harald Gormsson) who ruled over Scandinavia in the tenth century and who apparently had a conspicuously dead and blue-tinged tooth. Whatever his dental arrangements, Harald was credited with uniting Denmark and Norway, and so seemed a fitting choice for a technology that unifies the telecommunications and computing industries (and certainly a catchier one than 'Personal Area Network' or PAN).

The good

hackish: characteristic of a hacker. For the IT team, 'hacker' often denotes an expert, either in a certain program or in all things technical. True hackers, however, will never use this name of themselves: those that do are considered to be **bogus** or **wannabees**.

bang: a common programming name for the exclamation mark.

black art: the collection of mostly improvised techniques developed for a particular application. When they are so arcane they can only have been developed by a wizard, they are known as **deep magic**, and when they require an intimate knowledge of a particular system, they are known as **heavy wizardry**.

foo: a sample name for absolutely anything, especially temporary scratch files that can be deleted. These are markers of individual hackers and programmers, or of particular countries, ranging from **fred** and **barney** in Britain, to **blarg** and **wibble** in New Zealand.

moby: large, complex or impressive. Also used as a title of address that conveys admiration or respect to a competent hacker. The allusion is to the whale in *Moby Dick*.

HAL: a letter sequence believed by some to represent being 'one step ahead of IBM', but officially the acronym for 'Heuristically programmed ALgorithmic computer'.

hello, world: the canonical first program that a programmer writes in a new programming language.

The bad

Blue Screen of Death (BSOD): the white-on-blue text screen that appears whenever Microsoft Windows crashes. The acronym **BSOD** is sometimes used as a verb, e.g. 'Windoze [sic] BSO'D on me twice today'.

donut of death/doom: an American term for the spinning cursor in Windows telling you to wait (indefinitely). The Apple version is known as the **beach ball of death**.

crapplet: an applet (a small application program performing a simple function) that's not worth much.

angry fruit salad: a flashy visual-interface design that uses too many colours; a reference to the unnaturally lurid colours found in tinned fruit salad.

bogotify: to make or become bad. A program that has been changed so many times that it becomes a complete mess has been 'bogotified'. The term is a riff on 'bogus', a useless program.

Higgs Bugson: a hypothetical bug that's cited when the problem is generally unknown.

hysterical reasons: a variant on the stock phrase 'for historical reasons' and signalling that, because of a bad design, something must be done in a particularly stupid way for a system to work.

The ugly

baklava code: a code with too many layers. 'Spaghetti code' is one that's too complex and tangled.

sausage code: one which, once you know how it was made, you never want to use again.

voodoo programming: a technique in which the programmer guesses blind at making a system work; if it doesn't work, no one will understand why.

thinko: a momentary, correctable glitch in memory. Also known as a **braino**.

glork: used as a verb when a computer has a temporary lapse, as in 'my program keeps glorking itself'.

mouse arrest: getting caught out for violating an online service's rule of conducts.

And the customers

known lazy bastard: used by technical support staff for 'repeat offenders', i.e. users who repeatedly ask for help with problems whose solutions are clearly explained in the documentation if they'd only read it, i.e. **RTFM** = 'read the f***ing manual'. IT abounds in acronyms such as this, with probably the most famous one being **PICNIC** – problem in chair, not in computer.

NATO: no action, talk only. A popular strategy when all else fails.

AIRING ON THE DARKSIDE

SKATEBOARDERS

A US magazine from 1964 noted the arrival in California the previous summer of the 'skateboard'. It told its readers that 'skateboarding requires only a tapered piece of wood, flexibly mounted on roller-skate wheels, and a stretch of pavement'. The array of words and expressions that have since grown up around this 'tapered piece of wood' would astound the skaters of the early sixties.

Most skateboarders will tell you that their sport began as a hobby and ended up an obsession, where the world is divided into what's skateable and what's not. A seasoned skateboarder can't walk down a set of steps without imagining what they, or the bankrail alongside them, would be like to skate, while a swim in a pool will always have them wondering if the bottom would propel a good 'airwalk'. These are the people who feel butterflies just looking at a marble ledge or a long smooth hill.

Skateboarding was initially tied to the culture of surfing before it found a life, and venues, of its own: many even skateboarded barefoot. And like their surfing brothers and sisters, skaters favour a distinct look rather than a single uniform – one that's as expressive as the designs on the decks of their boards. Nevertheless, fashion plays an important role in tribal identity, and today's skaters tend to embrace either the hip-hop style of baggy jeans, an XL T-shirt, necklace, earring, beanie, hoodie, and well-kept skate shoes, or Metal and Punk gear, with its tight black or grey jeans, an even tighter, graphic T-shirt beneath a loose shirt, and a distinctly tired pair of shoes. There are a fair few sub-styles too, ranging from the well-kempt, bearded hipster to the old-school skaters who resolutely stick to old skull and crossbones shirts, glasses, and the iconic skateboarding emblems of the 70s and 80s: checkered slip-on Vans shoes.

Alongside the dress code is the non-verbal one, such as the banging of a skateboard on the ground to show approval for another skater's trick. The ritual may look aggressive to outsiders, but it's really just the skating equivalent of tapping the table after a good shot on the snooker table.

Similarly, most serious skateboarders would baulk at hearing their passion called a sport. They might practise over and over, fall down, bruise hard, and pick themselves up again, but there are no rules, and nobody wins. If they use any term, skaters like 'dance', since the best moves look natural and fluid rather than premeditated.

The following represents just a taster of the skateboarding glossary. Entire books have been devoted to **bonks** and **drops**. **Flips** may come as **ghetto birds, diamond flip, Ninja flip, hospital flip, gazelle flip, nerd flip,** or a **psycho white boy,** while **grinds** come in all sorts of shapes and sizes, including the **anchor, nose** and **hurricane**. Collectively they are all part of what the Toronto *Globe and Mail* once foolishly described as 'the latest fad'. As fads go, it's never looked back.

The skaters

goofy-footer: a skateboarder who rides with the right foot leading. The opposite of a 'regular footer'.

grommet or **grom**: a child skater or novice.

ripper: a consistently good skater.

snake: a skateboarder who steals your space at a park, or cuts you off.

tech dog: a skater who enjoys plenty of technical moves, particularly in combinations, e.g. a flip and a grind together.

The moves

acid drop: skating off the end of an object without touching the board with your hands, or running with the skateboard in hand and landing on the board as you drop it.

air: a jump, i.e. riding the skateboard with all four wheels in the air.

airwalk: a technique whereby the front foot is kicked out and the back foot is kicked back to give the appearance of walking on air.

alley-oop: a spinning trick on the board.

ollie: the basis of most skateboarding tricks, whereby the tail of the board is 'popped' and the front wheels take off first (as opposed to a **nollie**, where the back wheels take off first). Named after Alan 'Ollie' Gelfand, the originator of the move.

backside grab: the act of grabbing the board's edge with your front hand while airing forward. Also known as a **melongrab** or **mosquito**.

bonk: to hit something with the front wheels of the skateboard.

nose pick: 'stalling' the board while the nose of the skateboard is grinding along the ground.

shove-it: a trick that involves spinning the skateboard 180 degrees beneath the feet while the skater remains in the same position.

fakie: riding backwards with the tail facing in the direction that the skater is moving.

darkside: describes a board that is upside down.

sex change: a body turn of 180 degrees while the board is doing a tight spiral or 'kickflip'.

walking the dog: a freestyling trick in which the board is spun around one foot that's positioned in the centre of the board.

SO HYPE

GAMERS

'I finally hit Ander's Overpass wallbang!'; 'FNC defeat H2K in dynamic queue with lulu jungle' – so run the titles of two posts on the social news site *Reddit*, which offers an intriguing and, to the outsider, fairly perplexing peek behind the curtain of gaming's most insular tribes.

The word 'gamer' is a slippery one, encompassing solo individuals, vast communities, and an array of motivations. Of the latter, number one is of course entertainment. Video games offer unparalleled immersion in escapism: a safe space for adrenaline junkies who can trick their mind into being thrilled without risk. Here we explore our fantasies. 'What if I could score goals like Messi?' 'What if I could fly like Superman?' 'What if I could go on a murderous rampage with no real consequences?': these are some of the questions survival games ask, and duly answer.

The most formal representation of tribalism in video games can be found in the guilds and clans of online gaming. A **clan** is a group of gamers who play the same online competitive game together. The set-up provides different benefits to different people. A group of time-strapped gaming parents, for example, may form a clan to synchronize their hectic schedules, finding time to play when the kids are in bed. In the age of e-sports, many clans become even professional sponsored teams, to the extent of living in the same house to maximize training time.

Guilds, meanwhile, represent a group with a shared in-game objective – usually to best an opponent in short bursts of combat. Here the hierarchy can be almost military; the position of guild leader is given to the most skilled, knowledgeable and respected player, and can be as involved as any full-time job.

Gaming has distinct analogies with the film industry. In its early days, creation was handled by those with the expertise to wield the tools, just as the first films were made by the few who could operate a camera. Today, while most games can be pigeon-holed into broad categories such as **Platformer** (in which the player moves through an environment), **Strategy**, or **RPG** (role-playing games), the cool, edgy material is often to be found in the niches. As a result, a divide is emerging between the big-budget, blockbuster **AAA** games, and the modest but artistically creative **indies**. And, just as a music fan will call themselves a rocker or bluesman, most gamers will stay in their lanes. Music exerts an influence on vocabulary, too: take **gank**, for example, an overwhelming attack by one player or group of players on another in a competitive online game, and a term that has its roots in early 90s West Coast hip-hop, where it was a byword for ripping someone off.

Community and tribalism are integral to gaming – a fact that was amply borne out during what have become known as the **console wars**. Because console iterations have generally been released in groups of two or three, because the hardware is an expensive luxury for most consumers, and because one platform usually edges out the others in terms of technical specs and performance, there has always been rivalry between owners of competing systems. During the **seventh generation**, the longest generation in gaming history, the competition for market share between the SNES (Super Nintendo Entertainment System) and the Sega Mega Drive produced a war between opposing fans which rages to this day. Online forum denizens coined mocking nicknames to describe their gaming rivals: PlayStation 3 owners were **cows** because they were willing to be milked by Sony for expensive accessories and add-ons; Xbox 360 fans were **lemmings**, since they would blindly follow Microsoft to its death; Nintendo's dedicated followers were **sheep**, as

Nintendo could lead them down any path; and PC owners, the outsiders in the console wars, were **hermits**, because they'd always stay inside. These epithets endure to this day, even if those same hermits have since adopted the much less modest title of **PC Master Race**.

The idea of a higher power is there in the word **avatar**, too: the visual representation of a player in the online world which comes from the Sanskrit for the incarnation of a deity when it descends to earth. A **smashtag**, meanwhile, is the player's linguistic identity – their chosen moniker for the game. Both avatars and smashtags operate as secret identities for the gamer, who may be a 9–5 office worker by day, but the winged rider of an Imperial speeder bike by night. Smashtags are frequently used in real life – players may have long-time friends, in or out of **smashfests**, without ever knowing their real name.

There is a distinct kind of morality in gaming. Defeat must be accepted gracefully rather than with the type of bitterness that makes players **salty**. The phrase **No Johns** ('no excuses') captures the importance of sportsmanship in this world: it's poor form to blame one's defeat on any external factors. In the same vein, typing **GG** for 'good game' at the end of a match is the digital equivalent of a handshake. Win or lose, it demonstrates a respect for the opponent. Neglecting to GG an opponent is the gamer's equivalent of thumbing your nose.

Like the games themselves, the gaming field operates at many levels and has its own **tierlist**, from the casual to the hardcore, the **couch co-op** and **Pass the Pad** to strategy games and **MOBAs** (Multiplayer Online Battle Arena; the closest gaming has come to a real sport). At the highest level, gamers will apply themselves with all the dedication and hard work of a prize-fighter: training, studying and striving to be the best.

The best involves knowing the lingo as well as the moves. Gamers are as intense about their language as they are about their sport. They love to argue over the origin of a gaming term like **pwn**. Pronounced like 'own' and used in the same sense, to 'pwn an opponent' is to completely dominate them in online play. The accepted history of this word is that it's a typo for 'own' in the popular strategy game *Warcraft*; plenty of gamers, however, will argue that it stems from 'pawn' and the early days of the Internet, when chess was played over message boards.

hype: used to express excitement by players and fans. It can be used as a noun: 'Hype is building for the next tournament'; an adjective: 'That last match was so hype!'; a verb: 'I'm so hyped for the finals'; and even just a repeated chant by a particularly overzealous crowd.

spacing: the act of keeping your opponent at a specific range from your character; one which limits their option to attack but maximizes your own.

rush-down: an all-out attack strategy, employed to confuse and overwhelm your opponent.

salty runback: a rematch, usually quickly after defeat, because the defeated player is bitter about their loss.

fightstick: a controller that emulates the joystick and button layout of original arcade machines; the only serious way to play some fighting games.

AFK: Away From Keyboard, describing a player who has turned their attention away from an online match, leaving their character motionless and vulnerable to attack.

frag: slang for a kill from the early days of online shooting games. The term has largely fallen out of popular use but is still used by older players.

respawn: reincarnation, used in online first-person shooting games that revolve around killing, dying, and coming back to life to do it all over again. The defeated player is returned to a specific location of the play area, called a **spawn point**.

OP: short for overpowered, and describing a weapon, character or item that is considered far stronger than all other options in a game (not always a good thing – balance is important in competitive video games). OP has made its way to the playground to describe anything cool or awesome.

The characters

Online gamers have a variety of slang terms for the various character classes within a game, and their abilities:

boss: a special class of enemy that is stronger, smarter, or simply more important than others. The big, bad leader of all the bad guys.

nerf: a character that loses strength or ability for a patch in a game (an allusion to Nerf plastic toys).

buff: a character with increased strength, or an item in a game that gives that strength (e.g. a mushroom in Super Mario).

tank: one of the heavily armoured fighting classes who relies on muscle rather than magic. The tanks' motto: **hold the aggro**.

caster: any of the wide variety of magical spell-casting classes such as mages, wizards, enchanters, shamans etc. Casters have their own lexicon for their magic, including **freezing** an opponent or **mezzing** (mesmerizing) them.

stealther: a character that can become invisible and is therefore lethal to their enemies.

healer: the best loved, yet also most maligned, of any class in group play. As one gamer puts it, 'when the group lives, the healer is the greatest thing since sliced bread. When the group dies, the healer takes the blame. You need a thick skin to be a healer.'

rezzer: one of a class that has the ability to 'rez' (resurrect) the dead.

snowflake: a character whose abilities are unique or very rare, e.g. a good version of a typically evil race. From the popularly held belief that all snowflakes are unique.

PUG: an acronym for Pick-Up Group, a set of players who come together in order to accomplish a particular quest.

Christmas tree: a character whose power comes from their equipment rather than personal skills or muscle.

The foes

MOB: a dangerous monster.

INC: when said the MOB is coming your way (short for 'incoming').

BAF: used when the monster has brought a friend.

PAT: a patrol of monsters. To **pull** is to attack the PAT.

hackfactor: the degree of danger in an adventure or dungeon.

speed bump: an easily defeated enemy.

3

Getting Somewhere

'Walk! Not bloody likely. I am going in a taxi.'
Eliza Doolittle in George Bernard Shaw's *Pygmalion*

Boatman: 'I 'ad that Christopher Marlowe in the back of my boat once' – a favourite line from the 1998 film *Shakespeare in Love* that dishes out the traditional formula of cabbies up and down the land. Like most traditions, it's reassuring in its familiarity, and of all the lexicons in this book you might assume that those of the trainspotters and the taxi drivers, the pilots and the truckers would be the most predictable – not boringly predictable, but comfortably so.

You'd be wrong. The world of the cabbie is turning in unexpected and not entirely welcomed ways, and the demographic of the average trainspotter is also shifting. As for truckers, you can forget about CB radio: only the veterans dip into it on special occasions. Hot-rodding has even become glamorous.

The result of such change is a mix of influences amongst the languages of each group. Drivers of black cabs may draw on rhyming slang and destination nicknames that are generations old, while their Uber counterparts will let the satnav do the talking. The modern trucker, more likely to go by the name of Paul than Jawbone, must now know his 'tramper' from his 'gooseneck' and, in a world where time is everything, be ever willing to 'pull a ten'. Today's trainspotter is more likely to be a 'Baglet' than a 'kettle-basher'.

There is much secrecy here too: after all, passengers are involved. Among cabbies and cabin crew there's a need for entirely private codes to discuss those who use their services, and who are both the be-all and the bane of their existence. Terms like 'spinners', 'mangoes', 'bilkers', and 'single pins' are transparent only to the initiated few, who clearly sometimes wish that we travellers would stay at home. Then again, if you're a one-percenter in a biker gang, the road belongs entirely to you.

THE KNOWLEDGE BOYS

CABBIES

In 1636, King Charles I launched the world's oldest taxi service by granting permission for fifty hackney carriages to ply their trade on the streets of London. Some three hundred years before, the grassland of Hackney Marshes northeast of the city became renowned for the horses that were bred there. These were riding horses as opposed to those used for war or labour, and hackney horses were often made available for hire, pulling hackney carriages across London and becoming so commonplace that the journalistic term 'hack' was born. Hackney Carriage remains the official name for the black cabs that are, for locals and tourists, as synonymous with London as double-deckers, Beefeaters, and traffic jams, and which became one of our national icons during the 2012 Olympics.

Cabbies, whether in London or elsewhere, are amongst the hardest workers in the land. It's not unusual for a driver to clock up seventy hours a week. Along the way, he or she gains a unique insight into the lives of those they carry. They pick you up from your home, swap confidences along your journey, and will almost always discover the reason for your trip, whether legitimate or louche. They also run the risk of violence, verbal abuse, and the unsavoury consequences of drink. It's estimated that between one and five per cent of cab drivers are women – an advance at least on the six you'd have found behind the wheel of a London cab twenty-five years ago. ('We keep ourselves to ourselves,' one female cabbie told me. 'Many of the older drivers still don't want to admit we can do it.')

Whether a lifer or part-timer, cab-speak goes a lot further than 'you'll never guess who I picked up yesterday', though it is always worth asking about notable passengers – the answer is invariably worth it. But today, almost unthinkably, the black cab is under threat. We have become all über Uber and other online, on-demand taxi companies, those that can offer cheaper services from freelancers armed with little more than enthusiasm and a satnav. In 2015 the number of minicabs on London's streets was estimated to be 40,000. One year later, the number has risen to 100,000. The capital could become a very different place, and yet the traditional cabbie has one supreme trump card: a memorized map of an entire city.

Dismayed by complaints from visitors to the Great Exhibition of 1851 that London cabbies were frequently incapable of getting to their destination, Victorian Police Commissioner Sir Richard Mayne put in place a requirement that a taxi licence could only be granted if the driver was an expert on the capital's geography. From that day on all cabbies, including those of the Victorian hansom cabs so beloved of Sherlock Holmes, had to learn **The Knowledge** (capital T and K, always).

If you're in any doubt of the commitment required by a cabbie to 'learn' an entire city, neurologists have discovered that the part of our brain responsible for spatial awareness and navigation, the hippocampus, is significantly larger in the brain of a London cabbie than the rest of the population. They attribute this to the intense work undertaken while preparing for The Knowledge.

Only one in five make the grade. There is no limit to how many attempts a would-be cabbie can make, but the majority of candidates drop out after just a few tries at the series of tests known as the **Appearances**. Those who persevere, even after being **redlined** multiple times (i.e. they are bumped back from their next possible appearance by a month or more) can be easily spotted from the **Blue Book** in their hand: the ultimate guide of 'knowledge runs', all 320 of them. The Blue Book is actually pink, and provides the framework from which all other knowledge and Knowledge will spring. Add that to a magnifying glass plus pins and pens to link the routes on their oversized maps, and the would-be cabbie's arsenal is complete.

A Knowledge-seeker will need to commit to memory some 25,000 streets, avenues, mews, crescents, courts, high roads, and alleys within a six-mile radius of Charing Cross. On top of that come all the landmark destinations of London, as well as restaurants, theatres, embassies, even cemeteries: nothing must be beyond the cabbie's ken if asked.

If you were to eavesdrop on a tense practice run you'd probably hear some of the aides-memoire handed down from generations of **Knowledge boys**. A **good pull** is the correct identification of a particularly tricky route, while a **bad drop** is one in which the driver forgets the correct **point.** A **whoosher** is a particularly skilled **caller** of routes, able to reel off landmarks as they plot the journey in their head.

The cabology

Knowledge gained, the fun (and the headaches) begin. Cabbies have a finely honed lexicon to express the pleasures and tribulations of a life on the **hickory.**

brooming (or **brushing**): the practice of declining a job on the rank and leaving it for the cabbie behind you, usually because the passenger is only travelling a short distance. This is much frowned upon and is usually accompanied by an excuse like 'I've got a booking in ten minutes, mate'.

hickory (dickory dock): the meter, rhyming slang for 'clock'.

binder: a very long wait at the rank.

sherbet: a cab, rhyming slang based on the popular sweet 'sherbet dab'.

LBT: Life Before Taxi-driving.

pole: pole position, the first taxi available for hire, at the front of the rank. Also referred to as **1/1**, or **on point**.

Churchill: a meal. Churchill gave cabbies the right to refuse a fare while they were eating.

butterboy: a novice cabbie, one who is 'but a boy'. A **butterfly**, on the other hand, is one who only works in the summer.

leather-arse: a cabbie who's worked particularly long hours.

kipper season: slow season in taxi terms, apparently from the days when cabbies could only afford to eat kippers.

legal-off: the meter fare without a tip (and a tip is always expected).

musher: a cabbie who owns their cab as opposed to renting it, as most do.

on the cotton: the shortest distance between two points, as straight as a thread of cotton between the starting and finishing points on a map. If the route you took is close to the straight line, it's described as being 'on the cotton'.

putting on foul: joining a taxi rank that is already full.

The passengers

Most cabbies will tell you that the variety of passengers and their individual stories is what makes the job. Of course, there are exceptions, especially if a fare **casts up their accounts**, a popular euphemism for what is more bluntly known as a **puker**.

When it comes to passenger etiquette, there are a few surprises. Technically, shouting 'Taxi!' to hail a cab is illegal; the correct gesture is to stick out your arm. It is also illegal to flag down a taxi if you are suffering from a notifiable disease, such as the bubonic plague. Bowler hats are to be encouraged; in fact, the ceiling height of hackney cabs was originally calculated to allow a passenger wearing one to fit with ease.

the cage: the passenger area.

cock and hen: a male and female passenger.

single pin: a solo passenger.

Billy Bunter: rhyming slang for a punter/passenger.

bilker: a passenger who runs off without paying.

flyer: a fare to an airport – much sought after amongst cabbies.

a golden roader: a long journey out to the suburbs or even further afield – a cabbie's dream job.

the burst: a mass exodus from a venue, e.g. once a film or show has finished.

London landmarks, cabbie-style: the insider's guide

The landscape of our capital city is notoriously labyrinthine. As the *NY Times* journalist Jody Rosen puts it: 'To be in London is, at least half the time, to have no idea where the hell you are. Every London journey, even the most banal, holds the threat of taking an epic turn.' For every visitor (and local) scratching their head, there is a cabbie who will show them the way. To outsiders, their directions will use only the official names of roads and landmarks. Amongst themselves, however, it's a different matter. Sitting in the **Kremlin**, they might lament the snarl-up in **Kangaroo Valley**, or the chaos **Down the Wasp**. From such tribal conversations come, as ever, both camaraderie and consolation.

Den of Thieves/Fagin's Kitchen: the Stock Exchange.

American Workhouse: Park Lane Hotel, particularly popular with American tourists.

Dirty Dozen: twelve roads through Soho running between Regent Street and Charing Cross Road.

Down the Wasp: Walpole Street, Anderson Street, Sloane Avenue and Pelham Street.

Gasworks: the Houses of Parliament.

Kangaroo Valley: Earl's Court.

Magic Circle: the area around Piccadilly Circus, which provides a lot of custom.

Dead Zoo: the Natural History Museum.

The Kremlin: the cab shelter by Albert Bridge.

Rathole: the rank at Embankment station. The rank at Waterloo station is the **Rat Run**.

The Resistance: Harley Street – so called because its private doctors once opposed the formation of the NHS.

The Scent Box: the rank at King's Cross station.

The Tripe Shop: Broadcasting House.

The Wedding Cake: The white Queen Victoria Memorial outside Buckingham Palace.

The Flower Pot: Covent Garden, home of London's famous flower market.

The Pipe: the Blackwall Tunnel, often clogged with traffic.

GASH BAGS AND PLONKEY KITS

CABIN CREW

Flight attendants are full of secrets. Their private cabins are home to an equally private language, one that both replaces complex technical terms and communicates situations that they don't want passengers to know about.

To take one example, in the unlikely event that an attendant finds a fire on board, protocol dictates that they grab another crew member and say, in a hushed but urgent whisper, 'I'm the firefighter, you're the communicator,' thereby instructing them to pass the message on while they themselves tackle the blaze.

Of course code is also good for private commentary, particularly when it comes to passengers. Mostly this is non-verbal – a roll of the eyes at a demanding passenger, a quick, meaningful look when someone is rude, or a wink across the aisle to indicate an attractive traveller. But beyond the body language there is a pocket of slang reserved for the sharing of passenger (or pax) assessments. **BOB**, Best On Board, has nothing to do with the wine in First Class.

The dynamic between the crew and its passengers is a curious one. Flight attendants essentially preside over a plane full of captives who for whole suspended hours are entirely at their mercy. But with power, as the cliché runs, goes responsibility, and keeping those captives both happy and docile can be a mammoth task. In-flight brouhaha is no rarity, as any attendant will tell you. Airlinese is the language of calm and reassurance, and it needs to be. The standard list of troublemakers includes recalcitrant children and/or their parents, one or more aggressive drunks demanding yet more alcohol, and petulant business travellers who don't like the menu – let's not even mention wannabe members of the Mile High Club. All such flare-ups must of course be handled with aplomb; in extremis, there's always the air-rage restraint kit, with its hand-cuffs and extremely strong plastic tape. Meanwhile, some things need to be learned quickly, including the length of time that the froth of a Diet Coke takes to settle at 35,000 feet (35 seconds).

In the 1960s and 70s, female cabin crew were required to wear girdles, have weekly weigh-ins, and give up their job the moment they had children. The reward was the freedom of the Sky Girl, a 'swinger' of ground and sky. Novels of the time promised such delights as 'a mile-high frolic with the playgirls of the air!' while the glossy smiles and lips of promo-tional brochures emphasized the supreme importance of looks. Since then, thankfully, the flight path has changed course quite considerably. Moreover, roughly twenty-five per cent of flight attendants are male.

To this day however, far from being a term used against them, 'trolley dolly' is the career description you'll hear from any member of a cabin crew, whatever their gender. 'Stewardess' you will hear rarely (and 'hostess' almost never).

For all the ups and downs and trudging of the aisles, the glamour of the airborne life is of course still there: the exotic destinations, the hotels, even the uniform. A 1960s manual entitled *How to be an Airline Stewardess* promises 'breakfast in New York on a winter morning, and lunch in Miami under the palm trees'. If you ask today's trolley dolly whether the potential for sunshine and partying is sufficient pay-off for turbulence and tempers, you'll probably get a different answer after every flight.

The crew

flying mattresses/tarts with carts/sky hostesses: the terms, alongside trolley dolly, used by female flight attendants for themselves. If you're a passenger, any such moniker should be used with extreme caution.

bidding: the monthly process of telling the airline which shifts you'd like; a competition based on seniority.

slam-clicker: a crew member who goes straight to the hotel on landing and doesn't emerge again until it's time to leave.

Delsey dining: taking your own food in your suitcase so you don't have to fork out at a hotel; Delsey being a popular brand of cabin luggage.

coach roach: any flight attendant who prefers working in the main cabin as opposed to First or Business Class.

crop-dusting: (allegedly) when an attendant suffering from wind walks up and down the aisle to distribute it evenly amongst the passengers.

Pax

pax: passengers collectively.

crumb-crunchers: child passengers.

gate lice: the crowd of people who rush to the gate eager to board.

spinner: an undesirable or annoying passenger, e.g. one who boards late and then 'spins' (looks around helplessly) in an effort to locate their seat.

mango: a male passenger considered to be hot by the flight attendants.

BOB: Best On Board. Awarded to the best mango of all.

cling-on: a family member of the cabin or flight crew.

illegal: a working member of an aircraft, cabin or flight crew, who crosses over the maximum amount of hours allowed to work per flight.

um: an unaccompanied minor.

inad: an inadmissible passenger, either a deportee or one who doesn't have the required visa status.

The necessaries

gash bag: the rubbish bag. A term borrowed from the navy, where the gash man is the recipient of the 'rubbish' jobs.

plonkey kit: the small bag of essential things that flight attendants carry on their flights. This might include clippers, a sewing kit, perfume or aftershave, toothbrush and toothpaste, a clothes brush, and even oven gloves.

blue juice: the water in the plane's toilet, aka the 'blue room'.

bus/crew juice: a welcome drink at the end of a long-haul flight.

bottle to throttle: the period during which a crew member is not permitted to drink before their next flight, usually twelve hours.

Sharon Stone jumpseat: the fold-down chair used by crew for landing and take-off, and that may be over-revealing for any female attendant.

The chores

starburst: a trolley service that starts in the middle of the cabin and then works out towards the galleys.

wagon train: two services that follow each other, e.g. drinks immediately followed by food.

'We've met': said by one member of the crew to another when meeting in the middle after carrying out safety checks from each end.

top of the drop: the point at which the plane begins its descent before landing.

crotch watch: the walk-through of the cabin when carrying out a seatbelt check. Also known as a **groin scan**.

WHEELS-UP TIME

PILOTS

There are few professionals in life to whom we relinquish all control. Doctors, lawyers and taxi drivers are among them, but top of the life-and-death list must surely be the commercial pilot. This is the person in whom we trust as surely as they themselves trust in the air they fly.

The official language of the pilot follows a heavily scripted protocol. Each airline will have its own extensive manuals on every aspect of the flying process, known as **SOPs** (standard operating procedures). Utterances like 'Pull Hd9/090 FL 190' from a **director** (air traffic controller) will be crystal clear to every pilot. Some codes may appear transparent to the outsider, but if you were to hear about a **deadhead** in Aisle 17, there's no need to panic.

The codes

EAT: expected approach time.

EFC time: expected further clearance time, i.e. the point at which the crew expects to be set free from a holding pattern.

FOD: foreign object debris, caused by objects or birds that are sucked in by the propellers or rotors and that may damage the engine.

area of weather: the bad kind, the one that may cause turbulence.

souls on board: the plane's headcount.

65

Code Bravo: Security alert.

7500: hijack situation.

7600: a radio failure.

7700: general emergency.

The flyers

deadhead: a crew member travelling as a passenger to their eventual place of work.

heavy pilot: an additional pilot on a long-haul flight.

the director: the air traffic controller, the true master of the airways.

The flying

wheels-up time: a surprisingly childlike term for the moment when a plane is expected to be fully airborne.

alley: a taxiway between terminals.

apron: the area of tarmac that is neither a runway nor a taxiway, and where planes are parked.

Zulu time: the international standardized time in aviation, no matter what the time zone.

squawk: the transponder code which identifies each plane on air traffic control radar.

the jets: the jet streams – high, fast winds that can speed or impede the aircraft's journey.

sin-bin: the area in which a plane must wait to make room for other aircraft.

The planes

Pilots like giving nicknames to their machines – particularly those flown by other people, for which mocking epithets abound:

the light twin: the 777 (so called by pilots of 747s).

the en-suite fleet: the 747 aircraft collectively, which provide cosy bunks and a toilet inside the cockpit.

wanker-tanker: the double-decker Airbus A380. Also known as the **Fugly Bus**.

Plastic Jet: the 787 Dreamliner, made of a hundred per cent composite material.

BEDPANS AND GURGLERS

TRAINSPOTTERS

Go to most large stations and at the end of platforms you'll see small knots of men in anoraks earnestly clutching note-books, pens, and a bible – in this case the much annotated latest edition of the *Spotter's Companion*. They aren't rushing to catch a train or to meet someone; instead they're here to tick off the serial number of every engine listed. Meet the trainspotter.

Trainspotting was formalized as a hobby in 1942 by Ian Allan, a young trainee in the Public Relations office of the Southern Railway at London's Waterloo. Bored by constant letters from railway enthusiasts seeking every piece of information about the company's locomotives, and having to write identical responses, Allan suggested that the company should write a booklet on the vital statistics of each train. When the idea was rejected by his boss, he took on the task himself.

One of the first duties Allan decided upon was to teach an awareness of railway safety, the lack of which had prompted both accidents and scandalous headlines. His Locospotters' Club expanded dramatically, and by the 1950s roughly one million 'ABC' guides were being sold every year. Since then, while its attraction has ebbed and flowed, trainspotting has kept its head of steam.

Part of that ebb and flow is the spotter stereotype. Search any language database and you'll find that the majority of adjectives used for the railway fan follow a typical trajectory of 'sad', 'nerdy', or 'loser'. Even the word **anorak** itself, born on the chilly platforms of Britain's networks, has become a scathing shorthand for a tedious obsessive. And yet the pull of the outdoors, the mental challenge of ticking off a wish list, and the romance of railway history keep the pursuit very much alive. Not only that, but as today's railway industry receives the biggest investment since Victorian times, spotters are updating their image. Gone or going are the notebooks and pencils, and coming in are the digital cameras and tablets. Trainspotters are even getting younger.

One thing hasn't changed much: the trainspotting demographic remains resolutely male, even though the earliest proponent of the hobby was a 14-year-old girl named Fanny Johnson, who kept a notebook of the trains that boomed through London's Westbourne Park in the 1860s. Looking at the names she recorded in her journal, including Firefly, Eclipse, and Morning Star, it's easy to see how trains romanced the teenage imagination. The drama and anticipation, and the pull of adventure, must have been hard to resist. Today, ticking off trains on a locomotive bucket list is not vastly dissimilar to a seasoned music fan taking in every festival.

The romance has always been greatest with steam trains, whose enthusiasts are often at odds with the buffs of the **iron horse**. But the compulsion is the same, and much of that is down to atmosphere – the warmth of the station waiting room on a dank winter day, the odd egg sandwich, and the heady smell of diesel.

Doing the locomotion

In 1959, the *Junior Radio Times* gave a quick guide to any budding rail enthusiasts. 'The object of loco-spotting,' it explained, 'is to see – or "cop" – all the engines in a particular class, marking off the number of each engine as it is observed.' Few train lovers would call themselves 'loco-spotters' these days, but there are plenty more epithets to choose from.

gunzel: a highly enthusiastic railway fan, particularly one who's so intent on taking a good photo that they become reckless. Originally derogatory, the name is now a badge of pride, and may be rooted in 'gunsel', US slang for a gunslinger.

gricer: a fanatical railway enthusiast. Possibly a humorous representation of the upper-class pronunciation of 'grouser', because a railway fan 'bags' trains as a grouser bags birds. Another theory holds that it comes from Richard Grice, a trainspotter who became legendary for having travelled the entire British Rail network.

festoon: an older gricer who brings along tape recorders and other gadgets.

ferroequinologist: a fanciful creation for someone who studies trains; literally, an observer of 'iron horses'.

crank: an old-style rail fan who shoves people out of the way when boarding a train in order to get the best window position. Also known as a member of the **coach A crew**.

basher: a collector of train numbers and mileage statistics. When certain milestone numbers are reached, such as 10,000 miles by one engine, the basher will observe certain rituals, including the swearing of oaths (and a fair amount of alcohol).

trackbasher: this subset of bashers may be the most dedicated of all: their aim is to travel over every inch of track on the railway system, taking in every loop, siding and crossing – a process that's also known as **complete riding**. Trackbashers will even alight a train and walk the last few yards should the stock not make it all the way down the line.

Hell is other people

There is one more term for the railfan, this time an excessively enthusiastic one. US railway workers know them as **foamers** – a prickly suggestion that they foam at the mouth in their excitement. Unsurprisingly, however, gricers may have the last laugh, for they've developed an equally vivid vocabulary to describe those who don't fit in.

normal: a non-enthusiast of trains and railways.

bert: the average traveller, who is only interested in getting from A to B.

insects: occasional railway enthusiasts who tend to swarm at certain times of year.

kettle-basher: one who is obsessed with steam engines and is thus looked on as overly sentimental.

baglet: a woman, traditionally looked upon with disdain. **The Baglet** was one of many nicknames for Margaret Thatcher, who was notoriously reluctant to travel by train, and who began the privatization of British Rail.

Blood on the tracks

Trainspotters may look as though they wouldn't say boo to a goose, but appearances can be deceptive. Many exist in a state of constant tension, thanks to the rail authorities' efforts to enforce health and safety regulations and ticket fares. New anti-terrorist legislation can even keep spotters off platforms altogether. Most of them carry on defiantly. Some, like the artist Andrew Cross, see trainspotting as part of a long tradition of English radicalism: 'Trainspotting demonstrates the ability of individuals to act freely in pursuit of their interests, simply because they are not influenced by fashion or social expectation.' These are Hells Angels, but in anoraks.

flailing: hanging as far as possible out of the window of old-style train windows as you race through the countryside.

cess: the safe area either side of the track where spotters can stand when trains approach.

cabbing: the illegal activity of climbing on the train's footplate (following which 'C' for 'cabbed' can be written in your spotter's guide).

bunking sheds: trespassing without a permit into the train sheds in the hope of finding a train not yet ticked off the list.

effing it: riding without a ticket.

Hellfire! and **Dreadful!**: traditional exclamations of delight at spotting a desired train.

The train crew

The yin to the trainspotters' yang are those whose dedicated hard work and unsociable working hours keep the trains running. Many members of our train crews are almost as passionate about trains, but if the trainspotter (whom they call **neds**) play the field, these are the serial monogamists.

The crew from my local line, the Great Western Railway (or, as they like to call it, **Grub Water Relief**), have been working there for generations. There is a real folklore to the way they talk about the railways: the metal tracks that the trains run on are still called **the Permanent Way**. They reminisce about pranks played upon new staff in the 1950s that involved them being thrown sticks of water softener resembling dynamite, or being asked to fetch a 'bucket of steam'. Should you ever hear a guard ask another member of staff to check on the whereabouts of **Mr Sidmouth**, they are actually requesting back-up.

Liveries

Barbie: the purple and pink of First Group's bus and rail companies pre-2006.

ferret and dartboard: a British Railways emblem introduced in 1956 featuring a heraldic rampant lion (resembling a ferret) holding a wheel that, from a distance, resembles a dartboard. The previous British Railways emblem was known as the 'bicycling lion'.

Blood and Custard: the Crimson and Cream livery used on BR's coaches during the 1950s and 60s.

flying banana: the first livery of GWR diesel trains, and subsequently applied to Network Rail's New Measurement train as well as the High Speed Train.

toothpaste: the red, white and blue stripes chosen by Network SouthEast.

SPINNER OR SQUIRREL

CYCLISTS

Cycling, like Lionel Richie and vinyl, is back in fashion. Whether you're a **MAMIL** ('middle-aged man in Lycra') or a professional roadie, the appeal of the bicycle is both timeless and utterly of the moment. 'Cycle tracks will abound in Utopia' said H.G. Wells in 1905. It's a sentiment millions of us would agree with today.

In the same year that Wells wrote *A Modern Utopia*, the Tour de France was just two years old, and cycling for most was of the gentle-paced and sit-up variety, with an abundance of 'breeks' (tucked-in suit trousers) for the men and, for the women, perilously long skirts and highly elaborate hats. Such resplendent fashion could be witnessed in its full collective glory in Hyde Park, London, where spectators would gather to watch the bustle (and bustles, if a woman was particularly daring) on two wheels. At the same time, 'Ellimans Universal Embrocation' offered the soothing equivalent of today's chamois cream for saddle-soreness, euphemistically declaring its use for 'aches, pains, and bruises'. (Other riders, particularly those on older bone-shakers, resorted to sitting on a raw steak, which it is said would be fully tenderized by the end of the ride.)

Images of cycling these days include families happily cruising down tree-lined country lanes, of women cycling with bars of chocolate and bunches of flowers in their baskets, or of hard-fought battles in a steely velodrome. The reality, as any persistent cyclist will know, can be very different. Mending a puncture in a downpour beside the A34 can test the desire of the heartiest rider. But despite the daily run-ins with buses and feisty car drivers, plus some close encounters of the puddle kind, cycling can quickly become a compulsion. Very soon, the motive has nothing to do with getting from A to B, and everything to do with reaching the top of a hill and freewheeling down the other side, or the sheer satisfaction of cycling past a mile-long traffic jam. It is also very much about the tribe.

Roadies will always acknowledge each other with a quick wave and a blurry smile. They are the two-wheeled equivalent of the split-screened camper-van driver, except there are far more of them around. As a result, it's not unusual to have a hand held high in perpetual greeting for miles on end. Sometimes roadies even hold a **tea party**, at which other cyclists stop to chat. This sense of community, of being the 'special ones', is integral to the joy of modern cycling.

Within such a vast tribe, rivalries still exist. Many lone cyclists will have experienced the onslaught of a twenty-fold peloton of club riders, who sweep past and then sit confidently two or three abreast on a busy road before moving into each other's slipstream. These are the **racers,** who revel in steep climbs and who can be seen sucking vigorously on their energy gel to make them faster, better, stronger. Back at home, they will studiously note their heart rate during the ride, and compare themselves online with other riders who've taken the same route. Like the roadies, racers will always acknowledge each other, though the facial expression may be more grimacing than grinning.

Next come the **weekend warriors**, also known as **Fred** and **Doris**. These are the amateurs who step out of their suits and smarts on a Saturday morning and eagerly climb into dazzling bright Lycra tights and high-vis windproof jackets. This is generally where the MAMIL lives: he who took to cycling at the turn of a big birthday when he noticed The Bulge, and who tends to love the gear more than the riding: in other words, they are all mouth and no padded shorts.

Conversations between serious cyclists tend to focus on equipment ('I've had my Ortlieb pannier over ten years and it's still going strong'), cycling facilities (always better on the Continent) or routes ('Is it on Strava?'). Occasionally you might hear a serious conversation about road tax, the laws of highways and byways (cyclists have an automatic right to use roads; car users can use them only under licence), or **naked streets**: ones with no signage and no road markings.

There are many more categories of cyclists, from the commuters with their foldaway cycles and backpacks stuffed with shower gel and toiletries, to the happy tourer or the rider of a recumbent (an armchair on wheels). Death-dicing couriers, Boris-bikers and plain old utility cyclists are in there too. BMX and track cyclists, however, are definitely not: for roadies and racers, these come under what they call **NPB** – 'not proper bikes'. That doesn't prevent conversation turning to the Keirin, Team Pursuit or Omnium races of track cycling teams that now transfix the nation thanks to Britain's dominance in the sport.

The players

roadie: a devoted road cyclist.

chaser: a competitive cyclist whose main mission is to accelerate past riders ahead.

Clydesdale/Athena: a cyclist on the large side.

Fred and **Doris**: cycling newbies, often identifiable by their blinking lights and abundance of water bottles, even if they are only out for 5K.

RLJ: a red-light jumper. Generally frowned upon unless it avoids a hostile run-in with a car or lorry.

spinner: a cyclist who pedals at a very fast cadence in smaller (**granny**) gears, relying on pedal RPM (revolutions per minute) for speed. Spinning up a hill requires grit and the occasional quick suck on an energy gel.

pusher: the opposite of a spinner, a cyclist that pedals at a slow cadence in large gears. Psychologically easier but less efficient than spinning.

squirrel: a newbie on a road bike or simply an unstable one who is unable to keep a straight line, particularly on a climb.

turkey: a novice.

The gear

clip-ins or **cleats**: a type of pedal that locks onto the studs of a special cycling shoe, so that the rider is firmly attached.

This may result in a spectacular tumble if the pedal is not released in good time before stopping (and in a good deal of waddling around off-bike).

spuds: Shimano-branded cleated shoes, also known as **SPDs**.

aerobars: not a chocolate snack, but rather handlebar extensions that allow a racer to fully extend their arms for a highly streamlined riding position.

brain bucket: a helmet. Also known as a **skid lid**.

chamois: used both for padded cycling shorts and for the wonder-cream that prevents chafing. Chamois, or **shammies**, should never be worn with underwear – this is a total cycling faux pas.

jersey: cyclists speak of jerseys rather than T-shirts or tops. The term is taken from major races such as the Tour de France, where coloured jerseys are the prize swag.

supersuit: a fully-accessorized cycling outfit featuring matchy-matchy shorts, jersey and socks. Supersuits are often highly branded, and modelled on the gear of particularly famous riders.

lube in a tube: lubricant to help the bike run smoothly.

The aches and pains

bonk: as with running, this is hitting the wall of cycling – a state of utter exhaustion. Many cyclists use this as slang for being very hungry. Outsiders don't always get why 'bonking' should ever be a problem.

biff: a crash.

road rash: the result of a biff.

endo: a forward flip over the handlebars.

Vitamin I: Ibuprofen, the pain reliever of choice for racers.

chain-ring tattoo: the patterned grease spots left on a cyclist's leg after accidentally pressing against the chain ring. Also known as a **rookie mark**.

rockectomy: the removal of stones and debris from the body after a biff.

tombstone: a small rock protruding from a path that may take a cyclist by surprise and have undesirable consequences.

The moves

peloton: the main pack of riders in a road race; it is French for 'little ball'. Riding in a bunch allows riders to take advantage of **slipstreaming** behind each other's wheels to conserve energy.

crank: to pedal fast by kicking up the RPMs.

jam: a period of hard, high-speed cycling.

hammering it: pedalling hard in the big gears and big chain to achieve some sustained power.

full tuck: a full crouch down on a road bike towards the handlebars, to achieve maximum speeds on descents.

bushman's hankie: a clearing of the nose with the hand while pedalling. (Also know as a **snot rocket**.)

KEEPING THE SHINY SIDE UP

TRUCKERS

Giving a call-out for truckers on social media gets you an interesting response. The instinctive chip-ins from non-truckers tend to involve two things: chocolate and CB radio. 'Just put your name on a car registration plate and put it in the windscreen, buy a Yorkie bar, job done', '10–4 Smokey on the back door. Ten Ten till we do it again. Anyone give me a ten thirteen on the Mickey One?'

Today's reality is rather different. Mobile phones have brought about the slow decline of CB shorthand, although the veteran truckers still like to indulge in it when they get together. They are the **friends of Charlie Brown**, who will wish fellow roadsters a safe trip with formulations like **keep the shiny side up and the greasy side down**, or **keep your nose between the ditches and smokey out of your britches**. Phrases like these may be a hundred per cent American, but they are alive and kicking in a fair few of Britain's **tractors** too.

Other CB codes have slipped into mainstream trucker talk, including **catch ya on the flip**, 'see you on the way back', and **clean and green**, a signal that there is no traffic in a fellow driver's way. Being **on a red light** for hours, meanwhile, indicates that a driver is stuck on the unloading bay. **Rojo** means okay, a **breaker** is another user, and a **bobtail** a tractor-unit without a trailer.

But while just twenty years ago any new driver hitting the road would be searching for their CB handle – be it Smoky Dog, Big Mack or Hell's Bells – today's handles are more likely to belong to Twitter, and the need to check on weather or traffic ahead is easily answered by an app or GPS.

Such fundamental shifts in technology may have brought about big changes in language, but trucker etiquette remains constant. The rules of trucking dictate that one driver must always help another, no matter what the cost to the schedule. This is why drivers will unfailingly let each other out at junctions or slip roads, and see each other out when reversing. Such friendliness within the tribe is everywhere, and conversations between complete strangers at truck stops and services are commonplace. Meanwhile, if any driver hears of an **Alice in Wonderland** (a lost driver), one with **fresh air in the tank** (no fuel), or **bubble trouble** (a tyre problem), trucker's law means they will go out of their way to help.

The term 'truck' takes its name from the Latin *trochus*, a Roman hoop used as a toy and in athletic sports. From there it evolved to mean a small wooden solid wheel or roller, especially one at sea for the mounting of a ship's gun carriages. The first record of the modern truck is from a British Columbian newspaper, reporting on how 'the iron-shod war horse of former days has evolved into the padded wheel motor car, motor truck, and motor cycle of 1916'. The early truckers would be boggle-eyed over the shiny customized vehicles on the tarmac today with their bright lights, slick interiors, and paint jobs, as well as fridges, cookers, and flat-screen TVs. The **Trucker's Pride**, as any visitor to a truck show will tell you, is taken very seriously.

Ask any trucker about their bugbears and the answer is twofold: cyclists, aka **organ donors**, and car drivers (including the foreign ones, known as **Johnny flip-flops**). The antics of the latter are notorious, usually involving the failure to give enough room, being oblivious to the fact that a 44-tonne truck needs a lot of distance to stop, or coming down the inside when a trucker moves over to allow for the trailer when turning. Truckers see this as a combination of poor judgement and impatience, plus a severe lack of appreciation for the long hours and time they spend away from their **YLs** (Young Ladies, aka girlfriends), and their **XYLs** (ex-young-ladies, i.e. wives), all in order to deliver the things the rest of us demand from our shops. **Sick horses** (slow drivers) and **willy weavers** (drunk ones) complete the list.

Moreover, a trucker's job is rigidly governed, and drivers face heavy fines for breaking the rules if they work too many hours or forgo the required breaks. So large do these penalties loom that there's a whole lexicon to cover them. To **pull a ten** is to have an extra break so that a driver can keep going for ten hours instead of nine (usually on a tank full of **battery acid** or **road tar**, i.e. coffee), while a **reducer** is a day in which they will have fewer than eleven hours' rest. On a **fifteen-hour day** the total duty time exceeds thirteen hours and one minute precisely. All such events must be meticulously recorded in the truckers' driving log, the **comic book**. When drivers do eventually **cut the coax** (turn off the rig) to cut some Zs, you'll know they will have earned it.

As for the vehicles themselves, a trailer that's been dropped without winding the legs down is **on its knees**, while the **fifth wheel** is the large metal plate that attaches a unit to a trailer (**fifth wheel grease** is used to lubricate it; it gets everywhere). **Dolly knots** tie goods down with rope; trucks with cranes on them are **hi-ab**, and those with forklifts are **moffets**. Big trailer tyres are **supersingles** (as opposed to the old tyres that were doubled up); a **full bus** is a truck fully loaded at 44 tonnes; a **sloper** or **lift-off** is a trailer used to carry **multimodal** equipment (carried on more than one means of transport), and a low-loader is a **gooseneck**. A **tramper truck** is one that can be happily slept in, as opposed to a **day cab**, which can't.

The police inevitably feature large in Trucker Tongue. They are variously known as **bluebottles**, **blue lights**, **plain wrappers** (the unmarked kind) or **Kojaks with Kodaks** (the speeding police, who issue **Christmas cards** or **invitations**, or might ask you to blow into the **green balloon**). **Brush your teeth and comb your hair** is a standard trucker's warning that there's a radar ahead, while for those same friends of Charlie Brown, **Smokey** is a regular. A **Smokey on rubber** is a police vehicle, a **Smokey with ears** is police with CB, and a **Smokey report** is a friendly inter-trucker warning of police up ahead, who may be accompanied by **bubble gum machines** (emergency services or other vehicles with flashing lights). Finally, **flag wavers** are motorway maintenance workers, and **yellow Erics** the men from the AA.

Those Roman athletes who loved to play with their *trochi* would be amazed at what they started.

TWISTERS OF THE WICK

BIKERS

'Four wheels move the body; two wheels move the soul': a saying that adorns many a poster showing a long desert road and a lone bike speeding ahead into the distance. The belief that motorbiking frees the spirit is a totemic one in one of the most tightly knit brotherhoods there is. So much so that the biker term for a car is a **cage** (apart from their own cars, which are **grocery getters**).

According to some studies, the desire to ride is in a biker's DNA. It seems they have a novelty-seeking predisposition to adventure and risk. Owners of such genes will also share a low boredom threshold, a desire for change, and a dominant impulsive streak. Motorcycling is in the blood, and there's little anyone can do about it. Then again, few, if any, bikers would want to.

The riders

In *Zen and the Art of Motorcycle Maintenance*, Robert M. Pirsig explores two types of rider: the 'Romantic', who knows nothing about bike mechanics and simply hopes for the best, and the 'Classical', who is able to diagnose and repair the machine himself through logical and rational thought.

Pirsig could have added more, including the **waxer**, a motorcycle owner who is more likely to spend time washing and waxing their bike than actually riding it; the **BOB** or 'born again biker' who's returned to riding in middle age, and the **front** and **back door**: the leader of the pack and the last rider (aka the **sweep** or **tail gunner**) in a group respectively.

The equipment

The bikers' own arsenal for their kit and Kawasakis is even more varied.

sled: a slang term for a bike.

crotch rocket: a sport bike, optimized for speed and acceleration.

ape hangers: high motorcycle handlebars, often with handgrips at or above the shoulders that make the rider look like a monkey hanging from a branch.

blown: (of a bike) supercharged.

binders: motorcycle brakes.

rainbows: motor oil.

pasta rocket: an Italian-made motorbike.

rice rocket: a Japanese-made bike.

sissy bar: a passenger backrest that allows a biker to recline while riding. Also known as a **sister** or **bitch bar**.

skid lid: an open-faced half-helmet.

skin: a bike's paint job.

slammed: having a lowered suspension, sometimes for performance but often just for looks.

road rash: chipped paint on a bike.

chicken strips: the remaining tread on a sport bike. The greater the tread, the more of a 'chicken' the rider is.

The techniques

blip: to rev quickly, then release the throttle.

burnout: the act of spinning the rear wheel with the front brake locked, performed either to warm up the tyre or as a display of bravado.

carve: to ride extremely fast around corners, so that the bike is almost horizontal with the ground.

stoppie: stopping with the rear wheel off the ground (as opposed to the front one, which is a **wheelie** or **catwalk**). Also known as an **endo**.

grab a handful: to apply the brakes or apply the throttle quickly and hard.

stitch a line: to weave skilfully through traffic.

stay vertical: an expression used by bikers on departing, meaning 'ride safely'.

tuck: the most aerodynamic riding position, whereby the biker lowers their head and torso.

twisting the wick: accelerating through rolling on the throttle.

tank slapper: a particularly bad fall at high speed, when the tyre used for steering skids, and the handlebars bend backwards on the fuel tank.

big slab: the motorway.

crash mushrooms: plastic bumpers bolted onto a motorcycle frame in order to protect its bodywork and engine. Also known as **bungs**.

When it goes wrong

pavement surfing: the act of sliding down a road after **laying down** a bike at high speed.

fat: having too much fuel, resulting in thick black exhaust and a lot of wear and tear.

static: a code word signalling trouble of some kind, particularly from the police.

tar snakes: the erratic – and slippery – black lines caused by the repair of road surface cracks.

SQUID: an acronym for Stupidly Quick, Underdressed, Imminently Dead, and used for reckless riders who ride without the proper gear and/or respect for others.

THE ONE-PERCENTERS

HELLS ANGELS

It is a truth universally acknowledged that a single biker in possession of a Harley-Davidson must be in want of a club. While this certainly doesn't cover everyone in the motorcycling tribe, it remains very much part of the stereotype of the **lone wolf**. Popular belief will tell you that a hard-core biker, boasting a name such as Hambone or Bald Eagle, will always aspire to join a **one-percenter** club – an outlaw biker gang, identifiable through the '1%' patch worn on their clothes, whose name is said to derive from the American Motorcyclist Organization's judgement that ninety-nine per cent of bikers are law-abiding citizens. The remainder belong to **MCs** like the Pagans, Bandidos and the Hells Angels (no apostrophe, it's official).

Founded in 1948 and representing a new breed of rebel, the romantic view of the Angels is of free-spirited, roaming adventurists who go where they please and want nothing more than to be left alone. The contrasting view is of a violent subculture that revels in dangerous situations and bloodshed. In the US, it's clear on which side the judgement falls: the Department of Justice regards the gang as an organized crime syndicate.

Photos of the Angels, most famously from California in the sixties, capture bearded figures in shades and studs, laughing with exhilaration as they speed past blurry landscapes, or swarming into small towns. Then, as now, the Club will always come first. Membership is a lifelong commitment, and leaving it is unthinkable. This might explain the serious, quasi-religious language Angels use, including **chapter**, a local group, and **church** or the clubhouse where members meet to discuss club business. Each Angel must adhere to the club's **by-laws**: its written code, and one held so sacred that members are expected to honour it above the laws of their government.

The prospective Hells Angel candidate (always male) must pass through three phases before becoming a **Full Patch**. The first step is to be a **hang-around**, meeting club members and doing little more than observing. From there, he will become an **Associate**, participating in some club events, but still as an outsider. If he is granted the right to be a **Prospect**, he is almost there, but only as a **Full Patch** can he wear the insignia of the tribe, including the **Death's Head**. Like those on a boy scout's uniform, every patch means something, including a pair of wings, a symbol that is steeped in mystery: historically 'earning your wings (or patch)' meant committing a murder for the club.

81: shorthand for Hells Angels – H is the eighth letter in the alphabet and A the first.

GBNF: Gone But Not Forgotten – a patch used in remembrance of dead brothers.

FTW: F★★k The World.

OFFO: Outlaws Forever, Forever Outlaws.

It's said that society needs its rebels. Hunter S. Thompson would agree: in his book exploring the Hells Angels he wrote: 'In a nation of frightened dullards there is a sorry shortage of outlaws, and those few who make the grade are always welcome.' Not quite always. As the Angels themselves might say: 'When we do right, nobody remembers. When we do wrong, no one forgets.'

4

That's Entertainment

'Part of show business is magic.
You don't know how it happens.'
Sammy Davis Jr

You'd expect the entertainers to be a chatty lot, and they rarely disappoint. Talking, singing or, in the case of Morris dancers, running jingly rings around the rest of us, is their job, and so it goes that they provide rich pickings for the eavesdropper.

Given that performance is everything, you might also expect the distinctions between the private and the public to be slightly fuzzier than in other groups. And yet you will still find the encrypted chat, the exchanges that are markers of the tribe and that deliberately keep outsiders at bay. Perhaps the greatest example of this is Polari, a pidgin language created by traders but taken up and honed by the acting community as the basis for a showy but coded exchange.

The language of the carnies and circus workers goes back further still, to the travelling communities viewed by mainstream society as dark outsiders. Their vocabulary both speaks of a life on the margins and also, in its secrecy, reinforces it, to the extent that an anthropologist may be hard pushed to decide which came first, the language or the ostracism. Whichever it was, the shills, spielers, and ballies offer some of the best tribal lexicons in the business.

Those three words 'in the business' mean something very specific in the entertainment world. This is showbiz, and the thrills are in the execution. The actor's line 'See you on the green' packs a sense of fluttering excitement and pre-show adrenaline, emotions that are also captured in the 'pearlies' of the orchestra: those moments of extreme fear and vulnerability in a performance. And yet it's the graft and grist required before the curtain opens or the camera rolls that generates the most vocabulary. This is the language of preparation and expectation, whether it's the actor's 'swallowing a cackle', the musician's endless rehearsals of the 'smack in the face', or the sound engineer's lining up of the 'fairy dust'.

Those sound engineers provide some of the biggest surprises of the book. We may see them as the silent workers in a TV studio or concert arena, who move unobtrusively among the 'talent', but their vocabulary is one of the flashiest of the lot. This is a group for whom 'donkey's dongers', 'squelchers', 'stickies', and 'dead cats' are daily currency. Not only that, but plugs (and butt plugs) are always male or female according to their shape. The sound team, it turns out, are the dark horses of the entertainment industry.

As for comedians, I've worked with a few. Whether or not the stereotype of neurotic extrovert is borne out, these are the true solo artists, who may dip in and out of a collective language but who are just as happy in their own heads until it's time to get into those of their audiences. When they do come together, their language is strangely preoccupied with images of death and destruction, no matter if they 'died on their arse' or 'blew the roof off'. Yet even they can't rival the Morris dancers when it comes to sombre alter egos: today's village japers were once thought to be messengers from Satan.

Perhaps entertainment will always have a dark underbelly, the mark of the outsiders who, since the time of the Shakespearean fool, have been viewed as both madmen and soothsayers. It may be fitting that 'zany' was born on stage and in comedy, and that the word 'funny' looks both ways. Whatever the ingredients, they certainly work: life would be a lot duller without the entertainers.

WHEN THE GHOST WALKS

ACTORS

Waiting for you here, Godot – one of the oldest theatrical jokes, chalked upon many a backstage door. It contains an essential truth about actors: they wait. Not just in the wings, but for any work at all. In fact, most can expect to spend a lot of their time economically insecure, short of work, and having a second job. Yet the adrenaline, the pull of the lights, and the anxious pleasure of being scrutinized by hundreds of strangers, are the hallmarks of a life of strange hours and an irresistible passion for being someone else. Benedict Cumberbatch put it this way: 'I want to do it all. I want to climb mountains, go through jungles, fight wars in space, get the girl, shoot the bad-guy full of lead, have all the zippy one liners, bulge muscles out of a singlet, drip sweat and blood. All of that.'

Steeped in over two millennia of history, the argot of the theatre is vibrant, sumptuous, and as gnarly as a Shakespearean plot. Much of it has also found its way into the mainstream. English has borrowed an immense number of terms from the stage, from 'stealing the limelight' to 'waiting in the wings'. Some you would never guess at. The first explosions took place in the theatre: the Romans' *explaudere* described the slow hand-clapping that accompanied a poor performance and harassed the offending actor off stage because they had 'bombed': 'explode' is linked to 'applaud'. Enough to make any actor 'histrionic', a term for a player in an ancient Roman farce, and subsequently for anyone showing excessive emotion.

Meanwhile from the *commedia dell'arte*, the improvised popular comedy of Italian theatres in the 1600s, we take both 'zany' (from Zani, a pet name for Gianni and the moniker of the stock character of the ludicrous servant), and 'pantaloon' (from Pantalone, the old buffoon with the bright red trousers).

But many more terms remain tightly bound to **the boards** (a nod to the wooden planks used as a stage in medieval mystery plays), and to the place known by actors as **the factory**. To outsiders, the theatre has been known variously through the centuries as the **bloodtub** (home of violent melodramas), the **bughouse** (the theatrical equivalent of the fleapit), the **gaff** ('low-class'), the **honky-tonk** (for cheap musicals) and the **grind-house** (for burlesque comedy).

The players

Dive into a historical thesaurus and you'll find some telling synonyms for the actor 'type'. Among the most prominent is 'bohemian', a word applied to an actor or artist who 'leads a free, vagabond, or irregular life, not being particular as to the society he frequents', and so called because such mavericks were thought to enter the West through Bohemia. But for the most part, the outsider's expectation of unconventionality goes along with one of openness, affability, empathy, and fun – with perhaps a dash of neuroticism for good measure.

Actors are (usually) extremely nice to each other; the word **luvvie**, now permanently attached to the acting type, was once a standard endearment for anyone held in great affection. Not that all epithets are positive; ultimately, performance is all, and some labels for the thespian are not for the squeamish.

fluffer: a person employed to prepare or warm up an audience for another act. The term was borrowed from the porn industry where a fluffer ensures the actor is 'ready' to perform.
spouter: an amateur actor.

stick: a wooden actor.

skin act: an animal impersonator.

rhubarber: an extra, who repeats the word 'rhubarb' to imitate background chatter.

scenery-chewer: an actor who performs in an exaggerated, hammy manner.

twirlies: the chorus dancers.

oyster part: an actor who appears or speaks only once, in the manner of an oyster that opens up just one time.

Come back Tuesday: said by a director to an unwanted actor as a way of fobbing them off.

star-queller: a supporting actor who performs so badly that he or she undoes all the good work put in by the leads.

The critics

Actors dread a **damp blanket** (a bad review), but not quite as much as **fremescence** and **exsibilation**, terms for the collective murmuring of a growingly dissatisfied crowd, and disapproval of the hissing kind respectively. Worst of all is **getting the bird**: drawing boos from the audience, a cruel phrase said to refer to the aggressive behaviour of an angry goose.

The audience

papered: used of a theatre with a largely non-paying audience.

claque: a body of hired applauders.

handcuffed: used of an audience who refuse to clap.

gravy: easy laughs.

baskets are in: a full house, referring to the once traditional practice of leaving prop baskets as security with the management in case a play didn't succeed.

plush family: rows of empty seats in the auditorium.

stage-door Johnny: a nineteenth-century term for an audience member who hangs around the stage door after a performance for autographs.

vomitorium: one of the many passages for access to and from the seats, originating in Roman amphitheatres and descriptive of the way in which spectators suddenly 'spewed' in or out when the doors were opened.

The method

pong: to give maximum projection or exaggerated emphasis. This is as opposed to **pinging,** speaking lines softly and without intonation.

gag: to add lines that aren't in the original text. ('Ad lib' is from the Latin *ad libitum* meaning 'for pleasure', while 'winging it' originally referred to studying a part at very short notice, even while in the wings.)

learn the dickies: to memorize a script.

pratfall: a comedy fall onto the buttocks.

step on a line: when an actor inadvertently speaks over another. To **step on a laugh** is to throw away a laugh line through bad timing.

tag: the last line of a play, also known as a **curtain line**. In some companies it's considered unlucky to deliver this line before the opening night.

Props to you

wafters: blunt swords made especially for the theatre.

bronteon: a means of producing the sound of thunder. In Greek architecture, vessels containing stones were placed under the floor of a theatre; when shaken, they would imitate the sound of thunder. The expression 'steal my thunder' looks back to the invention of a thunder-making machine, poached by one theatre company from another in 1704.

fly (verb): to raise or lower scenery, by means of a counter-weight system operated by **flymen** from an area known as **the flies**.

legs: the curtains that cover the wings.

tabs: stage curtains. Those that close across the proscenium arch are the 'house tabs'. The backdrop is the **cyc** (short for 'cyclorama').

banjo: a rail along which a curtain runs.

tormentors: semi-permanent wings used to mask the offstage area, so called because they can obstruct the view of those audience members sitting at the side.

ballyhoo (verb): to create a spectacular lighting effect with the use of swirling **follow-spots** (the movable beams of spotlight), often preceding the arrival of the star performer.

tut: an actor's term for make-up, as in 'I really need to top up my tut'.

The code

the half: half an hour before the first actors are due on stage and the time by which they must be in their dressing rooms.

Mr Sands: theatrical code to warn theatre employees of a fire without frightening the audience. 'Mr Sands is in the foyer' means that fire has broken out there.

between engagements: also known as 'resting', this is the ageless euphemism for the time spent by an actor between jobs.

the ghost walks: 'It's payday'. The expression is said to be a reference to a nineteenth-century theatre company who hadn't been paid for over a month, prompting the player of Hamlet to refuse to come on stage until all salaries were met.

stagger-through: the run-through before the 'proper' run-through, when things may not go too smoothly.

Varda your bona batts:* the creation of Polari

Parlyaree, an anglicization of the Italian *parlare* meaning 'to talk', was originally a trader's language brought back by sailors who'd picked up a working pidgin on their trips abroad. As they found jobs on shore in travelling fairs, circuses, and theatres, their lingua franca was soon picked up by the show-people and entertainers they mixed with. The draw of the theatre was an obvious one: with their fearless ability to climb to precarious heights, sailors became much in demand behind the scenes. Not for nothing do both professions refer to 'rigging', 'flying', 'working a show' and 'striking' a set.

A little later, the language found a new home in the gay community, one perhaps so marginalized that a new tribal language felt not only fitting but essential. Here it gained a new title, Polari, and was made famous by the ostentatiously camp crosstalk of Julian and Sandy (Hugh Paddick and Kenneth Williams), the unashamedly queeny duo created for BBC Radio's *Round the Horne* and *Beyond Our Ken* who became staples of the 1960s' airwaves.

Polari is not a true language in that it has no grammar or syntax. But its vocabulary, from **zhooshing the riah** (fixing your hair) and **shaving the lallies** (legs) to **fluttering your ogleriahs** (eyelashes) or **powdering our eeks** (faces), found a natural home in the glitz and chatter of showbusiness.

*Look at your nice shoes

SPANISH ARCHERS AND CHERRY PICKERS

TV AND FILM CREW

There is an unspoken pecking order amongst performers. George Clooney described it thus: 'Theatre actors look down on film actors, who look down on TV actors. Thank God for reality shows, or we wouldn't have anybody to look down on.' There are distinct differences in tribal language – those who tread the boards will invariably sniff when they hear their TV counterparts called **the talent**, while a soap star might not immediately grasp a film crew's request for a **four-bagger** and **Martini**. Total outsiders may be rightly puzzled by a presenter being 'on the floor' (to say nothing of 'looking hot').

As with their theatrical counterparts, the TV and film actor can experience large chunks of unemployment. As the old joke goes, actors don't look out of the window in the morning, because they'd have nothing to do in the afternoon. For them, 'fake it until you make it' may be a truism, but it's also true. Their language is consequently sprinkled with the glitter of Hollywood, full of sumptuous Yiddish chutzpah and phraseology such as **meshugaas** for craziness (in Hollywood, *everything* is meshugaas) or **bupkis** (nothing, nada, and hence heard a lot). Conversation between actors will probably include the lines **I'm on a pencil** (translation: 'I might have a job'), **I'm on a heavy pencil** ('I'm down to the last two') and **Are you busy?** (subtext: 'Let me gauge my success based on what you're doing').

At the other end of the spectrum are the runners, those on the first rung of the mighty TV and film ladder who see the world stretching before them like a giant red carpet. More often than not, these are freelancers working for diminishing pay in an industry where job security is virtually non-existent. Not only that, but any initial enthusiasm will be dampened by the fourth round of teas they're asked to make for the talent and crew that morning, and further crushed by the realization that the closest they've got to any celebrity-schmoozing is organizing the repair of the loo in a Z-lister's Portakabin.

As for the rest of the team, whether on set or in the studio, the roles are vast and complex ranking from floor managers and directors, to **cable-bashers** and **D-girls** ('development girls', an insulting title used for both men and women in the lower ranks of a film company or crew). It's probably unsurprising that there is no adequate collective noun for such a diverse set. Certainly not 'the media', which, as Tom Stoppard put it, 'sounds like a convention of spiritualists'.

Cameras (a term that embodies those behind them) and talent have their own distinct dialects, too. When the actor Henry Fonda was asked what the pencilled exclamations 'AH!' and 'DAH!' in the margins of his script meant, he replied simply: 'Act here', and 'Don't act here'.

Between the groups there is much crossover, particularly when it comes to universal behaviours, such as the dash to get things done at the end of the day, when phrases like **KBS** (kick bollocks scramble) are pantingly delivered. These aren't the only phrases that turn the air blue. The film lexicon delights in terms such as **blow job** (cleaning the camera lens with a blow of compressed air), the aforementioned **four-banger** (in the US, a trailer with four dressing rooms), and **Lewinskys** (knee pads used for camera operators).

It's all worth it, of course. To borrow the words of Alan Coren, TV and film are much more interesting than people. If they weren't, we'd have people standing in the corners of our rooms.

Ready

cold read: a piece of dialogue presented to an actor at an audition that they must act out without any preparation.

blocking: part of the rehearsals that involve staging the actors and camera positions, and plotting their moves.

day out of days: the chart that tells the crew and talent when each actor is needed for filming.

blondes, **brunettes**, and **brutes:** different types of set-lamps.

off book: (of an actor) knowing your lines during rehearsals.

DLP: actor's term for being dead-letter perfect, i.e. match fit for the scene.

White noise, white noise, my line: 'Other people's dialogue and then me.'

I knew it in the bath: 'I have learned these lines, honestly.'

the floor: the studio where the action is taking place.

bunny: the script, from the rhyming slang: (bunny) rabbit + pork = talk.

butty wagon: the location catering truck.

honey wagon: the location toilet facilities.

winnie: the location dressing room (short for Winnebago).

See you on the green: said by one actor to another before meeting on stage/set.

beginners (or **big dinners**): show time.

Get set

nervous: a final check of the set by the crew.

last checks: used to call in hair/make-up to give a final touch-up to actors before a scene is filmed. The first touch-up is sometimes known as **buff and puff**.

look hot: said of an actor who looks overlit or shiny on set.

cherry picker: a crane or tower, with lights if needed for night scenes. Also used as high-angle camera platforms at sporting events.

cable basher: someone who keeps the cables tidy and out of the way of a camera as it moves.

best boy: the second in command in the electrical department (below the **gaffer**).

gantry: a grid area above the studio, from which lights are hung and positioned.

gallery: the control area of the studio from which the director and producer can shout via talkback. Also known as **The Box**.

dolly: a camera mount on wheels that allows the camera to move smoothly as part of the action.

Clear the lens!: the polite way of telling someone to get out of the f***ing way.

Number Ones: direction to take positions for the show.

Where's dead?': An enquiry as to the outer limits of a shot.

Roll!

roll up: start the recording machine.

at speed: an anachronism that harks back to the days when tape was first used to record, and the machines involved had to run for a while to make sure the recording was stable. Nowadays everything is recorded digitally onto cards and the picture quality is instantly good, but technicians and operators will still say 'at speed'.

noddy: a shot of a presenter listening to a guest.

Norman Hunter it: to walk or move backwards (in the style of the 1960s and 70s Leeds United and England defender).

jib: any kind of crane that has a camera at one end and is counterbalanced with weights at the other. The camera may be fixed to the jib via a **hothead**, which can then be remotely controlled by the operator. He can **pan**, **tilt**, **zoom** and **focus** while watching the picture on a monitor.

Steadicam: a hand-held camera that is often anything but steady, and that will inevitably get some viewers complaining of vertigo.

magic hour: the time right before sunrise or after sunset in which the sky is darkening but still illuminated. Perfect for atmospheric shots.

wild track: not the Sex Pistols, but a sound-only recording that will be used as part of the edit or dubbing process.

cod corpse: to pretend to laugh as if not directed, in order to make the audience believe they're part of an inside joke.

Lord Privy Seal: the unnecessary over-illustration of an idea to the audience. Amateur film-makers tend to illustrate every significant word in the dialogue by cutting to a picture of it. The Lord Privy Seal is an antiquated title in Britain's heraldic tradition: the joke implies that a novice or poor film director will illustrate it by cutting to a picture of a lord, followed by a privy, followed by a seal.

One Take Wendy: an actor who gets it right straight off.

It's a wrap

one more for Lloyds: one more take to be banked.

KBS: Kick Bollocks Scramble. Used at the end of the day when headless chickens are the main talent.

Martini: the last shot of the day.

in the can: scene finished.

in the bag: a performance worthy of a BAFTA.

print: to 'print a take' is to be happy with it. The term originates from the time of physical film, referring to a take printed from the negative so it could be viewed.

fix it in post: sort it in the edit.

rushes: from the days of physical film, when it would be processed overnight to allow the director/producer to view the unedited tape the following day.

Spanish archer: used for anything that's been elbowed.

DFI: the 'director's final instruction' officially, but is more often used to mean 'daft f***ing idea' (as in, 'No, DFI that, do this instead')or 'different f***ing idea' or, just occasionally, 'director's a f***ing idiot'.

That's a wrap

. . . the canonical phrase for the end of the shoot, the origin of which is of some debate. The most popular suggestion is that it's an acronym for 'Wind Roll And Print', that came directly from Hollywood. However, it may simply be another use of the phrase 'wrapping things up'. The film and TV team love to debate this.

The radio presenter

Pilots of the airwaves turn to a different lexicon. It seems that talk radio, which can encompass serious newscasting, sports commentary, call-ins, and everything in-between, likes nothing better than a doughnut and a disco.

have a disco: a discussion between two people on air.

sneaky disco: a conversation between guests who had previously insisted on talking only to the presenter, but who can't help interrupting each other once the debate gets under way.

doughnut: a format in which a DJ introduces a correspondent on the road, who then interviews a guest before handing back to the studio (i.e. the jam is in the middle).

up and down: an unexciting but prominent news item that the show must lead on. The presenter will duly cover it but move quickly on to the juicier stories, which will be 'given time to breathe'.

on it like Rob Bonnet: shorthand in some studios for 'I'm there' – Rob Bonnet being a BBC sports journalist and clearly useful for rhyming slang.

WOOFERS, DEAD CATS AND FAIRY DUST

SOUND ENGINEERS

Butt plugs, **donkey's dongers**, and **sex changers**. You'd be forgiven for thinking you'd wandered into a branch of Ann Summers rather than a room of technicians. But the scientists of sound, it turns out, are as rock 'n' roll as you will find anywhere, and their language follows their (insulated) lead.

The job of the sound team is to assemble, operate and maintain the technical equipment used to record and mix sound. They work in a range of industries, from film and broadcasting to advertising and live performance. It's at the latter that most of us will encounter them: the geeky roadie combos who, according to gender, tend to sport two out of three on the list of long hair, beard, and black T-shirt emblazoned with the logo of Led Zeppelin or other iconic rock band. Plus shorts, no matter what the weather, from which will dangle huge bunches of keys.

Every department knows how their own equipment works, but only sound people know how everyone's equipment works. These are the ones who, to quote one member, took their toys apart as kids, and who looked at laser guns wondering if they had a stun setting. They are the people who nobody cares about until something goes wrong, and then *everyone* cares.

If you go to a gig or watch TV with a sound engineer, it's inevitable that they will at some point mention how bad the sound is, and how they could do it better. They will also probably take a good look at your home music system, and promptly fall silent for a few minutes.

Sound engineers are noted (not just by themselves) for their sense of humour. More often than not, this will wander or dive head first into *Carry On* territory. All sound cables, for example, have pins at one end and holes at the other. Pins are outputs, and are consequently known in the sound industry as **males**. Holes, meanwhile, are **female**, and receive the input from the male. If two similar cables need to be joined, you need little adapters that are called **sex changers**. The **coil** and **diaphragm** refer to components of speakers and microphones respectively. Sound technicians find all of this hilarious.

They are pranksters at heart, too. The traditional items that every new apprentice is sent out for are a **long stand** and a **long weight**. The newbie will return much later having asked for both items at the sound shop and being left standing and waiting for a considerable length of time.

As for their tribal lingo, this one is surely one of the best and bawdiest in the business.

The equipment

butt plug: the plug on a radio transmitter, which can turn any microphone into a radio mic; an obvious reference to the shape (but not to be googled for verification).

donkey's donger: a mic used for voiceover work, one that is long-ribbed and phallic.

fish pole: the long stick used on film shoots that holds the microphone. Referred to more loosely as the **boom**.

snakes and spiders: long cables with many connectors for use in large studios.

cat-o'-nine tails: the connector at the end of a snake/spider that carries all the connectors. (Not all of them have exactly nine tails, but it sounds impressive.)

tweeter/woofer: a small/large speaker that carries high and low frequencies respectively.

cans: headphones.

dog/dead cat/Woolly/Kevin/Dougal/Furry: various terms for the fluffy windshield used on outdoor mics.

stickies: small sticky pads used to secure microphones under clothing, usually in drama productions. These inevitably stick to the body and are discovered in strange places by the actor when they next shower.

gram: a person who plays the music for a show; a shortening of 'gramophone' and still used even in the digital age.

The sounds

fairy dust: effects such as echo and reverberation, for use in a music mix.

wet/dry: (in sound effects and fairy dust), the processed sound and the original sound, respectively.

snoop: a pre-hear of a presenter's microphone, allowing the director to hear their conversation on the **floor** (on set).

wow and **flutter**: terms from the days of vinyl and tape, describing speed errors with the sound. Wow is for slooooooooowly varying speed, flutter is very quick.

shash: white noise, such as you used to hear on an untuned TV.

birdying and **squegging**: radio mic faults, usually caused by outside interference, and imitative of their sound.

deadroom: a totally silent room with zero reverberation, used for equipment testing and in radio drama to simulate outside environments. Also called an 'anechoic chamber'. If you stand in one for too long, the sound of the blood in your ears will apparently drive you insane.

hot: a sound that is too loud. Sound technicians don't recognize this concept.

buzz track/chatter track: background sound recorded to cover edits on location. In the Rover's Return on *Coronation Street*, the chatter you hear in the background is this.

The phrases

One two, one two: the traditional words used when testing sound gear. Leads to the assumption that sound technicians generally can't count any higher.

It's all right leaving me: a regular refrain meaning that if there's a sound problem, the sound engineers are not responsible.

ROCKING THE JIB

CARNIES AND CIRCUS FOLK

There's a saying that the circus collects outsiders like a light seduces moths. There is a magic to the idea of a life on the road that is both mysterious and bewitching, and part of it is undoubtedly the chance to escape 'normal' society. Yet carnies and circus crew will tell you that being an outsider is a mixed blessing.

The Roma people have contributed enormously to outdoor public entertainment, but they are often scorned by larger society, which likes to use 'Gypsy' as a catch-all identifier, a term that originally arose because the nomadic people were thought to come from Egypt. Theirs is a tight-knit community for a reason. Indeed, central to the Roma world is fellowship with others: its members rarely share the **gadgie** (non-Roma) need for privacy: instead, theirs is a life of noise, bustle and the spirit of the group.

The most obvious question to start with is 'Who are they?' Carnies and circus folk are traditionally cast as black sheep, escapees from the chains of an anchored existence in favour of one that's footloose and fancy-free. For many, it's a lifelong commitment. These are the second-, third-, even fourth-generation carnies, sporting names like Boxcar Bill or Tornado Tam, and for whom erecting 300-piece rollercoasters, buffing up the dodgems, pitching the Big Top, or rigging up the ghost train is in the blood. The work is hard, requiring sixteen-hour days, little time off, and even less sleep – what there is happens in cramped trailers where everyone bunks down together. Before long it will be time to take off again, a ritual that even has its own word within carnie and circus communities: to **jal** is to set up and derig at speed.

Yet complaints are few, and those you do hear focus on two topics: ignorant customers (who come in many guises), and the dreaded 'Health and Safety', an ever-looming presence that carnies see as the biggest threat to the thrills and spills of the fair.

It's carnie law that these thrills, like their owners, must have a nickname, this time one straight from either a superhero comic (Condor, FlowRider, Gravitron, Omnimover, the Flying Zedoras) or the section in the thesaurus marked 'speed' (Velocity, Vortex, Hurricane, Rotor, El Niño). Such rides sit alongside the traditional **joints** (games) and attractions, including the **dukker slanger,** the fortune-teller's tent.

Given their history, it's unsurprising that carnivals and fair-grounds are home to a vibrantly motley code. And a code it is, one of the oldest 'cants' or secret jargons ever collected. Part of it is steeped in a subset of the Roma language known as Parlyaree (see POLARI, p93), so that the ubiquitous terms of approval are **bona** and **cushty**, while **having a dekko** is taking a look, **dinari** is money, and **jarry** (from the Italian *mangiare,* to eat) is food. One word can carry multiple meanings: a **gaff**, for example, can mean a fairground; music hall or brothel; ride operator; fake sideshow exhibit; subterfuge used in a trick; or the underwear that male cross-dressers wear to conceal their tackle. Exhibitionism runs through language as well as performance.

To crack the carnies' shorthand or, as they would put it, **rock the jib**, is to snatch a glimpse of a tribe whose otherness we both cherish, and keep at arms' length.

The operators

ride monkey or **ride jock**: a ride operator.

shill: an accomplice who masquerades as an audience member to facilitate a sale or a trick.

spieler: a voluble talker who delivers the sales pitch to prospective visitors, and who **makes the opening**, including the traditional 'Roll up! Roll up!' Also known amongst street-entertainers as the **spruiker**, who **spruiks things up**.

broad tosser: the operator of a three-card monte game, popular at travelling fairs and carnivals.

jogah: a queue entertainer.

razorback: showmen's slang for a circus hand who loads and unloads the wagons. Also known as a **roustabout**.

The bally

blind opening: a general sales pitch for a raft of attractions inside the tent or fair.

bally or **ballyhoo**: the spieler's sales pitch.

freeze the tip: to gather onlookers into such a tightly packed crowd that it's hard for anyone to leave. Devices used may involve a semi-naked performer with a snake, or a fire-eater.

jam: the ratcheting-up of the urgency of a sales pitch, often delivered by the **grindman**.

blow a tip: to lose the interest of an audience.

blow-off: the extra 'attraction' promised by the performer at an additional cost. In freak shows of old this might have been a peep behind the curtain at an 'unspeakable human'. Today, it might involve a special show of legerdemain by a magician.

scarper the tober: to run off without paying the rent. The tober is the site occupied by a circus, fair or market. It first featured in the form 'toby', from *tobar*, Irish tinker slang for road, and was used by thieves for the highways they 'worked' at night, when they would 'ply the toby'. The **tober omi** is the circus owner, aka the boss.

. . . and their customers

jossers: non-circus people. Also known as **flatties**.

gadge (also **gadgie**, **gadje** or **gorgio**): a non-Romany.

rube: an outsider or non-carnie. The term is from the name Reuben, a byword for a country yokel.

pal: a friend, whether inside or outside the community. The word, now mainstream, originated in the Romany for 'brother' or 'mate'.

rakli: a non-Romany girl (**raklo** for a boy).

Mr & Mrs Wood & All the Little Woods: code for empty seats in a house.

Chav: a word born in the fairground?

The precise origin of **chav** is a matter of debate, but most people agree on its geography, namely that it probably began in Chatham, Kent, where it was best known until it gained its recent high profile. It seems that the term began there as a derogatory label for Gypsies, many of whom have lived in that area for generations. Its beginnings, however, may well be entirely innocent, and come from the Roma word for a child, *chavi*, recorded from the middle of the nineteenth century. To this day carnies and fairground workers refer to children as 'chavi', though 'chava' has very different connotations meaning either sex or a promiscuous woman.

The performances

aerialist: a performer who operates suspended in the air, such as a trapeze artist.

kinker: a contortionist, once known as a **frog**, **bender** or **Limber Jim**. Now a general (but not always complimentary) word for any circus performer.

ponger: an acrobat.

roper: a cowboy.

buffer: a performing dog.

grai: a horse.

dukker: a fortune teller.

run-in: a short piece performed by a clown to fill a pause in the performance.

slanger: the tent.

desultor: a circus performer who leaps from horse to horse. The term originated in the dramatic performances at circuses of ancient Rome. The 'desultor' is linked to our word 'desultory', describing someone who drifts from one thing to another.

charivari (also known as **shivaree**): a noisy entrance by a troupe of clowns.

windjammer: a member of a circus band.

ORCHESTRAL MANOEUVRES IN THE PARK

CLASSICAL MUSICIANS

'The money's terrible, the stress is awful, and the music is plain boring': a quote from a *Guardian* article headlined 'Pit of Despair', which explored the realities of the orchestra musician. It's a despair that springs from long hours, poor prospects, and the pay – especially the pay. More than half of all classical musicians – many of them professionals at the top of their game – supplement their income through other means, such as taxi-driving, nannying, or cleaning.

As for the stress, part of the problem, it seems, is that it's difficult to relax. Even in an amateur orchestra, a player must be consistently note-perfect if they're to avoid censure from colleagues sitting just inches away. Every member can tell at least one story of how a single player wrecked a performance by coming in at the wrong moment or, worse still, by blowing the wrong (alcoholic) kind of wind. The dynamic of the team becomes even trickier when a soloist enters the fold: accustomed to high praise for themselves alone, they suddenly find themselves in a sea of other 'soloists' and with as many line managers as you'd find in a large commercial business.

Beyond the politics, other musicians speak of the boredom of waiting – waiting to go on, waiting to go home, and waiting for other sections to get it right. It's not at all unheard of for the flutes to imitate the sound of a kettle when they decide it's time for tea, or to whistle out the tune of laughter when a hapless outsider walks across the hall. It's all part of the humour of the pit, and it's a chance to liven things up a bit too.

And yet, despite the squabbles and stresses, when this big family finally gets to perform the charge is electrifying. It's the time when the players will tell you they are at one with their instrument as well as the entire body of the eighty-piece ensemble. This is musical alchemy, and it's addictive.

There are no sure-fire giveaways when it comes to identifying the orchestral musician. They largely defy physical typecasting: double bass players can be tiny, while fiddle players can be huge. Violin and viola players sometimes sport a small strawberry mark on the neck, like a welt, where the instrument makes contact. But more telling are the different personalities, which can often match their instruments. Thus brass players can be loud and brash; bassoonists cultured and introvert; clarinet players eccentric; oboists nervous or wound up; flute players flighty and capricious; French horn players philosophical and heroic; percussionists manic; viola players philosophical and downtrodden; cello players classy; bass players down to earth; and violinists neurotic. Of course, these are overly neat stereotypes, but most orchestra members will give a sage nod when they hear them. Then there are the collective nouns, which can be revealing as well as funny: they include **a flatulence of bassoonists**, **a melody of harpists**, and **a backache of cellists**.

There are tribes within tribes here, too. Trumpet players stick solidly together, occasionally widening their social circle to include a trombone or a tuba but rarely a horn player. Oboes, basses, violas and clarinets will form groups when out hunting for food between rehearsal and concert. The percussionists are an especially tightly knit social group, one with distinct protocols, such as seeking the highest-quality watering-holes when on tour.

Nicknames are popular in the orchestra, particularly when it comes to composers. Thus **Shosty**, **Proke**, and **Rock** are Shostakovich, Prokofiev, and Rachmaninov respectively (and **Rocky II** is Rachmaninov's Symphony No. 2). The Russian conductor Gennady Rozhdestvensky is known throughout the industry simply as **Noddy**.

The tribal tendency to have enemies is also here if you look for it. The second violins don't much like the piccolo, whose seating in the orchestra frequently threatens to deafen those around them, and there is little love lost between violas and trumpets. Oboists, above all, dislike their reed, a good example of which is for many the impossible dream, even if some players do say they fondly remember once having had one. The universal enemy is the conductor.

Finally, whatever you do, don't mention Berlioz's *Symphonie Fantastique* which, thanks to the number of historic offstage percussion disasters associated with it, should always be referred to as **The French Piece**. As with the unmentionable Shakespeare play, all indirect references are intended to ward off catastrophe, or a meltdown of the trombones.

Meet the team

breakfast bandit: the musician on tour abroad who packs their lunch and dinner into a carrier bag at the hotel breakfast, in order to save on expenses.

carver: a conductor of any ability.

bang bang: the percussion section.

stone-agers: musicians who play baroque music with period instruments.

deskie: a music stand partner in a string section.

wrecker: a string that can be heard above the others, thereby spoiling the ensemble and disturbing the delicate sound of the entire section.

A life in the day

duff gig: an engagement to play with a choral society, almost invariably amateur, usually in a cold church somewhere, and often involving Elgar or Mendelssohn (or worse still, Stanford Robinson).

the pearlies: a term that describes the feeling, particularly in string players, of extreme fear in the performance of a solo or otherwise exposed piece, likely to induce tremors.

spare: a note that a player unintentionally plays in a gap in the music. Rarely more extended than a single note as the perpetrator will shrink into a small hole immediately. Also known as a **domino**.

scrub: a tremolo in string music, in which the player repeats a single note with a rapid 'scrubbing' motion.

squeaky gate: contemporary music of a particularly unpleasant nature.

smack in the face: a programme or piece that is especially demanding of wind and brass players.

red mist: what trumpet players experience while performing a very loud passage inducing a loss of vision from oxygen deprivation.

The essentials

grit: rosin used to treat the bows of stringed instruments.

liquorice stick: a clarinet.

hooter: a French horn.

stick: the conductor's baton (but never, ever referred to as such).

cheating: practice.

a roasting: what occurs when a conductor unfairly singles out a player during rehearsal and asks them to play a small passage, solo, over and over until the performer is reduced to wreckage.

gig spanner: the bottle opener used on the coach coming back from a venue.

'99': the pub; originating from the fact that there are ninety-eight practice rooms at the Royal College of Music.

FISH-FEEDERS AND CABLE MONKIES: THE ROADIES

ROADIES

Ask any roadie about the single most important job on arriving at a venue, and you'll get the same answer: the kettle. Despite catching some of rock 'n' roll's reputation for drugs, drinks, and all-round hellraising, roadies are the self-confessed tea-makers of the highways. They may prefer Alice Cooper T-shirts to overalls, but they are the hard grafters of a tour, ensuring that not only is there a brew on hand, but that almost every other aspect of a gig goes to plan.

All of which makes them (alongside SOUND ENGINEERS, pp100–103) the unsung heroes of a tour. (Unsung, that is, until they actually turn up in songs, such as Jackson Browne's 'The Load-Out', which charts the roadies' rituals after the audience has gone.) And yet the spark genies and masters of the gaffer tape often acquire as mythic a status as the performers they serve; they are the unnamed member of the band, without the ego. When Tom Hanks played Barry the Roadie alongside Aerosmith in *Wayne's World*, uttering the line 'Check. Check. Check 1. Sibilance. Sibilance. Check. Check. Check 2. Sibilance. Sibilance,' he stole the show – something a real roadie would never do.

Linguistically, on the other hand, they are allowed to make a splash, and this they do. From feeding the fish to the notorious DFA knob, to borrow from those Jackson Browne lyrics, these guys are champs.

feeding the fish: throwing the band's plectrums into the crowd at the end of a gig.

clown nose: a foam microphone cover.

neck-down: any member of the stage crew who isn't required to think, and simply takes orders from those above.

P45 button: the button on a mixing desk that must only be touched in extreme circumstances. Any accidental push could bring instant unemployment.

DFA: a mythical fake knob on a mixing desk that can be turned as required to appease the 'talent' (a word described by some roadies as a 'one-word oxymoron') whenever they demand 'more bass/treble' etc. The term is an acronym for 'Does F★★k All'.

LB: 'lucky bastard'; a power adapter with one male and two female sockets.

VLB: as above, only with three female sockets, thus 'very lucky bastard'.

snake case: the box that tidies all the different cables running across the stage.

113

toast rack: a multiple guitar stand.

percussive maintenance: hitting something in order to mend
it.

SILLY FOOLS AND SKIRMISHES

MORRIS DANCERS

We all love Morris dancers, but few of us would want to be
one. At least, that's the way it's seemed for the past few decades.
The tankard-clinkers and jingly-belled flourishers of hankies,
have tended to invite curiosity and affection, but not a great
desire to join them.

All of that might be starting to change. Recent years have
seen an upsurge in membership, particularly among the young.
Go to a university Freshers' Fair and you might even find a
stand of dancers clamouring for your attention. Few other
university pursuits can boast a history of some 500 years or
more, or ribboned shoes.

Some historians believe that the roots of Morris dancing may
be older still, originating in pre-Christian fertility rites: the higher
the dancers leapt, the higher the crops would grow. Its name
suggests that it was a Moorish dance brought back by the
Crusaders, with links to the Spanish *Morisca* dances of the
1500s. What we do know is that the first record of the tradition
in England is from 1458, when it featured in the will of a lady
of means named Alice Wetenhale. In it she bequeathed various
items of value to her daughter Katherine, including gilded and
silver cups bearing splendid engravings of Morris dancers.

If Morris dancing began as a pursuit of the gentility, it soon
became popular as a folk tradition in the parishes of England.
In 1600, the Shakespearean comic actor Will Kemp recorded

in his *Nine Daies Wonder* the feat of dancing all the way from London to Norwich. By the reign of Charles II, Morris dancing had become inextricably linked with the Whitsun Ales – celebrations at Eastertide which welcomed in the beginning of spring (an ale was a general festivity at which ale was drunk alongside other amusements and general merriment; our word 'bridal' began as a wedding feast, or 'bride-ale').

The key date in the modern history of Morris dancing, however, must be Boxing Day 1899, when Cecil Sharp, the instigator of the folk-song revival in Britain, witnessed some dancers in Headington, Oxford. He was later to note: 'When he is dancing, the true Morris-man is serious of countenance, yet gay of heart; vigorous, yet restrained; a strong man rejoicing in his strength, yet graceful, controlled, and perfectly dignified withal.' Sharp was to become one of the most active promoters of the tradition at a time when it was in serious need of popularity.

That need was born in the Industrial Age when folk traditions were being replaced by squeaky-new ones. It wasn't the first time Morris dancing had fallen out of favour. The Puritans had held little love for its joy and abandon, while in the sixteenth century it was even associated with satanic rituals. It takes some stretch of the imagination to associate a pastime that we now rank among the cuddliest with dancing to the Devil's tune, but that was exactly how it was seen by Philip Stubbs, a sixteenth-century pamphleteer. Denouncing the moral depravity of Elizabethan society, he decried the Morris dancers through clearly clenched teeth: '. . . then march this heathen company towards the church and churchyards, their pypers pyping, the drummers thundering, their stumpes dancing, their belles jyngling, their hankercheefes fluttering about their heads like madde men.' Sharp's contemporary Sir Thomas Beecham would have agreed. His verdict on the art became notorious: 'Try everything once, except incest and Morris dancing.'

Undeterred, the proponents of the tradition established multiple styles of music and dance, often associated with their area of origin. Variations include **Cotswold Morris**, **Border Morris**, **Molly Morris** (in which one dancer is dressed as a woman), and the **Northumbrian Rapper**, short for 'Rapper Sword' and a variation on the sword dance once popular with the mining families of the pit villages of Tyneside.

Sword or no, Morris dancing is not for the faint-hearted. It is, in effect, the equivalent of a contact sport, and far from the odd hanky-burn, its practitioners frequently sport bashed limbs and crunched bones. Dances such as the aptly named **Skirmish** involve as much stick-waving as the angriest of shepherds, and in multiples of ten. Perhaps the required levels of aerobic fitness explain its growing appeal among the young.

Very Moorish

The 'Morris' part of the equation sounds exceedingly British and thus entirely fitting. In reality it is anything but, having begun as 'Moorish' in a nod to the dance's beginnings. The exotic flavour of the dance and its occasional fantastical representations were a firm part of its appeal. The *Great London Chronicle* records the vivacious performance of 'spangled Spanish dancers' before Henry VII in the Christmas of 1494, whose repertoire may have been close to some of the dancing we see today.

In the end, 'The Morris' clearly tripped more easily off the British tongue.

The language of the Morris dancer is steeped in this long and rich tradition, one in which each side or **team** will have their own shorthand. More than anything, the lingo delineates the roles within each dance, for like the Italian *commedia dell'arte* and modern English pantomime, stock characters are all-important. Especially the fool.

fool: with his painted face and garish trousers, the Morris fool follows in the tradition of the Shakespearean soothsayer, and is the counterpart to the buffoon of the street fairs of eighteenth-century London, and to today's circus clown. The fool's role is to communicate directly with the audience through speech or gestures, commentating on the story unfolding in the dance. As in drama, the fool is the one who, through silliness and madness, dares to speak the truth.

squire: the squire will normally call the dances and take the lead.

bagman: the keeper of the team's purse, i.e. its funds and necessary equipment.

ragman: the keeper of the all-important Morris accessories, including hats, ribbons, sashes, and bells.

foreman: the team instructor, held responsible for the overall performance on the day.

hobby: a dancer dressed to resemble an animal. Also known as **the beast**.

JANGLERS, JAPERS AND JONGLEURS

COMEDIANS

The oldest English joke found to date is from Anglo-Saxon times, recorded in a tenth-century anthology of poetry that is still held in Exeter Cathedral. It goes something like this: 'What hangs at a man's thigh and wants to poke the hole that it's often poked before?' Answer: A key. Admittedly the punchline's not great, but it underscores the fact that we've been laughing about the same things, and especially sex, for over a millennium. Perhaps even longer: the oldest surviving joke book, dating back to the fourth or fifth century AD and entitled the *Philogelos* (or 'Laughter-Lover'), features an early incarnation of the absent-minded professor (the *scholastikos*). On a sea voyage with his slaves a severe storm hits, causing them all to wail in terror. The professor attempts to console them with humour: 'Don't cry, I have freed you all in my will.' Clearly the ancient Greeks loved dark humour as much as Jimmy Carr.

A few centuries later, the clown, the fool, and the court jester were each given permission to test the limits of public acceptance. Today's stand-ups rely on that same licence, with the difference that threats of royal banishment or a day in the stocks have become the wagging finger of legislation and, if they've made it big, Ofcom. Broadcasting authorities have been deciding what's funny since the 1940s, when the BBC formalized its categories of banned jokes in a series of documents aimed at avoiding offence. The censorship code of 1948 imposed 'an absolute ban' on the following: 'Lavatories, Pre-Natal influences, Marital Infidelity, Effeminacy in Men, Immorality of any kind, suggestive references to Honeymoon couples, Chambermaids, Fig-leaves, Prostitution, Ladies Underwear, Lodgers and Commercial Travellers, and Animal Habits'. Since then, every one of those taboos has been systematically dismantled, and even the strongest profanities have their own watershed ('f**k' is all systems go after 9 p.m., while 'c**t' must wait until at least ten o'clock).

However successfully they come to navigate these waters, most comedians will have tested their gags on small audiences (or, if they started young, their parents). If they're over forty, these will probably have included working men's clubs, one of the most hostile, and therefore 'character-building', environments there is. Before they get on stage, most will have put in a day on a 'second' job to pay the bills. The rest of the time, if there is any, is spent promoting shows, distributing flyers, writing material, or thinking about writing material. Each joke must seem fresh to its audience, no matter how many times it's been perfected, or how tired its performer.

While TV and radio comedy is largely scripted and – crucially for broadcasters and regulatory boards – pre-recorded (each *8 out of 10 Cats Does Countdown*, for example, runs for a good two hours before being edited back), the language of stand-up is inevitably more reactive. Around the pre-planned jokes and props, a live act has to alter its text on the spot, not least to respond to hecklers. However rehearsed, the impression of spontaneity is key, hence the abundant use of conversational fillers such as 'y'know' and 'right', and standard tropes like 'there was this bloke . . .'. Formulae like these enhance both intimacy and recognition.

Comedy is a risky business. According to Arthur Smith, there are three basic rules – unfortunately no one can remember what they are. One of them is surely to 'know thy audience'. The comic Andrea Henry recalls how, at one gig, the comic preceding her did a long routine about taking revenge on his ex-girlfriend's cat, before being told that the night was being hosted by an animal shelter charity. Awareness of your entertainees must be coupled with the ability to push away hecklers with a single sentence. Comedy nights on a Friday, when the pack mentality is strong, can be the trickiest to navigate. If the comedian's set is after midnight, the audience can turn sadistic. Jo Brand is one of the best at dealing with (or **slamming**) a heckling customer, with lines like 'Why don't you put some jam on your shoes and invite your trousers to tea?' Sometimes, of course, the heckler wins, and most comedians will acknowledge the funny ones.

As for subject-matter, fashions in humour come and go as surely as beards and leggings, and nothing says more about a society's state of mind than its comedians – or, as they've been known through history, its harlots, ribalds, ape-wards, janglers and japers. A recognition of those mutual preoccupations is a key ingredient of success. Some of the best comedians, like Eddie Izzard, focus on the minutiae of every day and the absurdities hidden within them. The result is a kind of observational comedy based on the delight of a shared human experience, one that gives its audience the endorphins of belonging to the same team. For Izzard, this is comedy's distinct advantage: 'Music is a feel gig, and comedy is a mind gig.'

This mind gig requires rhythm, timing and good wordplay, from slapstick puns to subtle subversion and a mastery of double-entendre. You only need to have known Richard Whiteley ('Did the inventor of the door knocker win the no-bell prize?') for the former, and witness the 'Fork Handles' sketch by the *Two Ronnies* to appreciate the latter.

There is no collective noun for professional funny men and women, which speaks perhaps to their inherently solo existence: for all their touring and festival gigs, they are never more alone than when on stage. When they do get together, their conversation makes for strange listening. For a business designed to make people laugh, the terminology of comedy is curiously black. **I died on my arse** is standard comic-speak for 'no one laughed', while, on the other hand, if an audience **almost died** they were laughing uncontrollably (yet if they were a **bunch of stiffs**, they didn't crack a smile). A comedian who storms the evening is said to have **killed it**, the opposite of **bombed**. The acme of excellence is of course the **killer joke**, an image taken to its literal brilliance by Monty Python in 'The Funniest Joke in the World', which kills off anyone who hears it, including its inventor. Joining this violent lexicon is **taking the roof off**, now such a hackneyed phrase that comedians will riff on it to each other along the lines of 'I need to phone last night's venue and offer to pay for their new roof'.

Lines like the last hide a level of insecurity that hangs around like the comedy partner you never asked for. It runs through apparently blasé enquiries such as '**Where are you at the weekend?**', comedian-speak for 'How are you?' and designed to gauge the other comic's popularity – as club comics take their money at the weekend, any successful member in the comedy tribe will be gigging. If they are **doing the Store**, you're talking big success: this is the Comedy Store, one of the oldest and most famous venues in the profession. It sits at the opposite end to the **open mic**: a gig that allows amateurs to have a go at stand-up in which a typical audience total is about four or five.

Finally, if you happen to be backstage before a gig, you might pick up some surreal exchanges between comedians warming up for their turn – such as 'Got anything on wizards?' for example. Meanwhile the trading of jokes can take on a very literal sense, as in one overheard exchange which went: 'Tell you what, I'll take unicorns, and you can have bats'.

What the heckle

A heckle, in the sixteenth century, was a comb used in the textile industry for removing knots and dirt from flax or hemp fibres. Heckling was no easy task, requiring concentration and grind. It also attracted a belligerent workforce. It's sad that the Scottish town of Dundee became known for its particularly antagonistic workers, who dictated wages and working conditions through strength in numbers and a lot of shouting. When others in the industry followed suit, the heckling shop gained a reputation for activism and general haranguing. From there the move to politics and comedy must have seemed quite straightforward.

SO SELECTOR

DJS

'I am amazed at DJs today. I am firmly convinced that AM stands for Absolute Moron. I will not begin to tell you what FM stands for': this was Jasper Carrott's verdict on the **pancake turners** of the 1980s. If events have since proven that some of those DJs were rather more than morons, his comedy jibes against those who fill the emptiness of our homes and cars found their audience even then. Deejaying can be a thankless task: as the saying goes, 'Friends never let friends get into radio.'

First the word 'disc jockey': a strange combination born in the 1940s and a follow-on from the slightly earlier 'record jockeys' who **rode herd** over (i.e. supervised) the music. At this point, the discs in question were meant to provide the illusion of live music, the staple of radio broadcasting at the time. Martin Block, the first radio announcer to become a celebrity in his own right, would pretend his music was being performed live in a huge dance studio, as opposed to a singly-manned one full of spinning discs.

As the profession developed, so did the personalities. DJs became as much the show as the music, and the ratio of chat to songs changed accordingly. Catchphrases were born, from Alan Freeman's 'Not 'arf!' to Zoe Ball's 'It's a pile of pants!' (which duly propelled the underwear into the British lexicon as a byword for 'rubbish'). Today's DJs will often share their banter not just with the listener, but with a team of others for conversation and applause.

Those conversations might involve anything from a sausage sandwich to the vibe of this year's Glasto. It's all a far cry from the tropes of old, where show openers would include such lines as 'I trust you're fit and well and in fine fettle. Let's get the show on the road . . . Yes indeedy!' Memes such as these, ones you would never hear in real life, would become the lingua franca of comfort radio, copied up and down the land in local stations. Today, it's an acknowledged truth within the industry that the best DJs are those in whom the line between real and radio self is paper-thin. It makes the difference between the person you have on in the background and the one you actually listen to. With those that get it right, the DJ's tribe includes the audience, too. From Terry's Togs to Team Grimmy, the frequency you tune into is a marker of more than just your musical taste.

Outside the studio, DJs can be hard to spot, save perhaps for the ability to talk a lot without the ums and ahs of conversational white noise. Had you put John Peel and Timmy Mallett in the same room, you'd never have guessed they were from the same world: as one seasoned presenter puts it, while Peel could have passed for a philosophy professor, Mallett might be an entertainer from Butlins.

The club DJs are a different breed. Their trailblazers were the jockeys who found their home in the nightclubs and discos of the 60s and 70s, when specialized equipment began to appear and the art of **beat-matching** and **slip-cueing** pulled in the crowds. These were the shapers who witnessed the birth of disco, hip-hop, house, and techno, in clubs as legendary as the Peppermint Lounge and the Ministry of Sound. Today's club DJs can attract as much celebrity as any pop star, drawing followings that make pilgrimages from Ibiza to Zagreb to hear them turn the music.

Ultimately, the aim of these DJs is to **shut the club down**: not a Health and Safety directive, but the skill of elevating the party to such heights that people will be exhausted by the end of it. For the music makers themselves, the euphoria of the shutdown might have its edge taken off by the notorious **DJ flu**: an illness resulting from excessive late nights and the occasional ingestion of party-related products, some of which may not be entirely legal.

The DJ's lexicon, on the other hand, is never tired. From **mash-ups** to the **Middle 8**, it's one to listen to.

Turntablism

scribbling: the basic scratch technique whereby the DJ moves backwards and forwards around a sound. Scratching itself is the manipulation of a record under a needle to produce the characteristic **wicky-wicky-wah** sound.

boom-bap: the hard bass and snare sound that is the signature of classic hip-hop.

cut 'n' shut: stopping one song while starting the other simultaneously, rather than mixing two tracks into one another. This must be done on the first beat of the preceding bar.

pots and pans: the result of a terrible mix between two tracks, making the beats clash together rather than seamlessly mix into each other.

selector: a master craftsman of the art of DJ'ing, one who can select and build a musical narrative without necessarily having mixing ability. Picking the right song is not about how popular it is is nor its **BPM** (beats per minute); instead the selector listens more deeply for what links two tracks together. These days, everyone can be a DJ, but not everyone is a selector.

biting: copying the techniques that another DJ has applied to a particular track.

SORTED!

THE RAVERS

The club DJs would be nowhere without their committed audience. The earliest sense of the French word *raver* was to be mad, or to behave as if delirious; it's related to *rêver* 'to dream'. Modern ravers would probably recognize this feeling of being **tranced out**, particularly as the **beat drops**, that all-important moment when, as one post in the *Urban Dictionary* puts it, 'a song goes from being slow to being really intense and WOAHHH'.

Under the Criminal Justice and Public Order Act 1994, the definition of the music played at a rave is defined as one that is 'wholly or predominantly characterised by the emission of a succession of repetitive beats'. Today the movement that started in free parties in squats, disused warehouses, and random fields has joined the mainstream and become a highly profitable concern, and the definition has become a little more complicated. As any expert raver would agree, there are more genres of **EDM** (Electronic Dance Music) than a desk DJ has buttons, and they are even harder for an outsider to pin down. Among those on offer to today's raver are **house**, **acid house** or **techno**, **hardcore**, **gabba** (from the Dutch slang for 'friend') **electroclash**, **speedcore**, **garage**, **dubstep**, and **jungle**. Each has its disciples: as the novelist Jodi Picoult put it 'The music we listen to may not define who we are. But it's a damn good start.'

Beyond musical taste, there is much that unifies. The mantra of the rave is **PLUR**: peace, love, unity, respect, while the tribal badge is **kandi**: colourful bracelets made out of chunky beads (and not the same as **candy**, the drugs that might also feature, such as **E** or **Molly**). The aspiration of every raver is to **rinse** (dance) so hard they become **turnt up, plurnt,** or **crunk**: high on alcohol, drugs or music – especially in response to **the banger**: the one song that makes a raver go wild.

5

Playing the Game

'I remain of the opinion that there is no game from bridge to
cricket that is not improved by a little light conversation.'
Osbert Lancaster, English writer and cartoonist

The British pride themselves on having invented pretty much
every sport from cricket to baseball (which Jane Austen wrote
about forty years before its official American invention).
Whatever their heritage, each game has its own rich vocabulary
to go with its complicated rules.

The word 'game' encompasses many areas of human play.
The original meaning of the word, dating back to Old English,
was 'amusement, fun, or pleasure' – Shakespeare's *Love's
Labour's Lost* includes the musing 'We have had pastimes here
and pleasant game'. Today's sports, to borrow from Bill Shankly,
are a lot more serious than that.

You'd expect, for example, the players and fans of a marbles
championship to be full of polite applause and fellow feeling,
occupying a world designed for those like the American
humorist Erma Bombeck, who once professed: 'I do not partic-
ipate in any sport with ambulances at the bottom of the hill.'
Yet the presenter Chris Packham, researching the life of the
'mibster' some years ago, recalls being staggered by the victo-
rious blasting of horns and waving of flags as the winners
lapped the pub car park. This world may offer a different kind
of jeopardy, less physical than rugby or football, but it's just
as intense. In contests like these, concentration and tactics are

everything – it's where games for the mind and mind games come together.

Far less shouty, other than the occasional 'Fore!', is the golfer's lexicon. This doesn't signify a reduction in competitiveness: indeed, whether professional or amateur, it's said that nothing speaks to a man's personality more than his behaviour on the golf course. The rules of play are matched by a set of firm linguistic codes, but while transgressions of the former entail stiff penalties (including ostracism), verbal sparring is par for the course. It's deemed perfectly acceptable amongst golfing partners to (literally) call the shots of other players, with such jesting jibes as 'Arthur Scargill' or 'O.J. Simpson' ('good strike, bad result', and 'got away with it', respectively). For cricketers, the sledging arsenal might include such curiosities as 'agricultural'.

Each player of every tribe will of course think their own game as the best. Bias is necessary for success, as one writer on the craft of baseball, George F. Will, demonstrated: 'Baseball, it is said, is only a game. True. And the Grand Canyon is only a hole in Arizona. Not all holes, or games, are created equal.' A shared language, you might think, could even up the playing field. But from what I've learned, and as the following lexicons will testify, this is what a darts player would call a 'scud': a shot that's a little bit wide of the mark.

KEEPING 'EM ON THE ISLAND

DARTERS

The British, George Orwell famously noted, 'are a nation of flower-lovers, but also a nation of stamp-collectors, pigeon-fanciers, amateur carpenters, coupon-snippers, darts-players, crossword-puzzle fans'. As ever, Orwell was on the money. But while coupon-snippers may be turning to lottery tickets, and pigeon fanciers to the 2.10 at Sandown, darts stand solid in British culture. As do its players – often quite literally, for darts is singular in not requiring any kind of fitness from its participants. Indeed there are many who consider it not to be a sport at all, the maximum effort required being walking the distance of the oche (7 ft 9 ¼ in precisely). The player Andy Fordham once notoriously boasted: 'Before a match I like to relax with twenty-five bottles of Holsten Pils and six steak 'n' kidney pies.' Not for nothing had Fordham embraced the nickname 'The Viking'.

And there the stereotype remains: darts is first and foremost a pub game, and drinking is in its blood. When The Viking returned from a serious illness some nine years later, it was, he explained, a new experience for both him and his fans: 'First time I've done it sober.'

Return to the present day, and an article on a day in the life of Phil 'The Power' Taylor relates how, for breakfast, the former champion will have porridge with water, egg whites, and blueberries. He's lost four stone and the weight is still dropping off. Like most of his contemporaries, Taylor discovered the game by going to the community pub darts for entertainment. Spotted and subsequently mentored by Eric Bristow, he became the entertainment. Taylor's journey from the boozer to the gym, and from a team game in the pub to annual prize money in excess of £1.5 million, neatly sums up what's been happening in the sport over the last decade. No longer does the fug of smoke kiss the ceiling above the crowd at Lakeside, and the relatively new kid on the block, the PDC (Professional Darts Championship), prefers the razmatazz, pounding music and chants from the 'terraces' over the traditional silence of the Crucible.

Darts may be smartening up its act, but, in the words of one commentator, it remains 'resolutely Essex'. The professional game is known for its larger-than-life characters, like the 'King of Bling' Bobby George, who throws excellent banter as well as arrows. Nor has drink disappeared entirely: most darts pros will tell you that when the beer stops flowing, so will the 180s, and that would never do.

The language of darts is suitably steeped, if not in beer, then in the atmosphere of the pub and bingo hall. Like the fashion of its players, whose Hawaiian shirts still rock the vibe of 1980s pop videos, the lingo doesn't change much. And that is a big part of its appeal.

Whether a player is a **bullshitter**, adept at hitting bullseyes, or a **chucker**, who throws the darts willy-nilly and hopes for the best, the pull of the oche is the same. **Oche** itself has inspired many theories as to its origin. Some believe it to stem from the time when the throwing line was marked by a line of three beer crates, branded with the logo of the brewery Hockey & Sons. The *Oxford English Dictionary*, meanwhile, suggests that 'oche' may be a corruption of the 'hog line' used in curling that a stone must cross in order to count (and originally a stone that failed to go the distance, perhaps a reference to the traditional laziness of the pig). After that, the rest of the names for the darters' essentials are easy.

The equipment

arrows: darts. Also known as **nails** and **1s**.
bed: any scoring segment of the board, such as the 19s segment.
clock: the dartboard.
downstairs: the lower half of the board.
house: the double or triple zone.

Kit in place the game begins, with the thrower closest to the bull going first – in other words, **diddle for the middle, middle for the diddle**.

The scores

The lexicon of scoring in darts is probably the best-known aspect of the sport. Clever, colourful, and frequently irreverent, much of it is echoed in the bingo hall (and the bedroom – where else but darts would a rubber, the final game of a match, be called **the prophylactic**?). Much of the lingo comes from London's East End and its home-grown rhyming slang. Thus a **Big Ben** is a 10, **beehives** a double 5, **chopsticks** a 6, **dinky doo** a 22, **old hens** a double 10, and **two whores** a double 4. Bedrooms crop up again in **bed and breakfast**: 26 from three darts, based on the standard price of B&B in England in the early twentieth century: namely two shillings and sixpence. The bull, meanwhile, is variously known as the **bugbutton**, **bunghole** (referring to the bunghole of a beer barrel, said to have been used in early darts matches), **cherry**, **dosser**, **middle**, and **tit**.

all the varieties: a score of 57, from the advertising slogan of Heinz.

any way up: 69.

basement: double 3.

bottom of the house: double 3.

madhouse: double 1.

fish shop: 22 (an allusion to customers on their way back from a night's drinking and asking for a 'two and two': two portions of fish and two of chips).

tops (also **top of the house**, **upstairs**, **double top**): double 20.

bag o' nuts: a score of 45, apparently from fairground darts games, in which a bag of nuts was the consolation prize for scoring under the target of 45.

lipstick (also **red bit**): treble 20.

bucket of nails: all three darts landing in the 1 segment.

cork: bullseye, usually the double bull.

Shanghai: a turn of three darts that scores a single, double, and triple in the same number wedge, in any order.

three in a bed: three darts in the same number wedge.

T or **Ton**: a score of 100.

ton o' ones: a score of 5 by hitting five 1s.

trombone: a total turn score of 76 points.

Lord Nelson (a score of 111, denoting one eye, one arm, and one testicle).

In play

Annie's room: a lost cause – the player has nowhere to go but double 1. The term has its origins in military slang of the First World War, where someone 'up in Annie's room' was whereabouts unknown.

bomb out: to knock out a loose dart with the following one (not allowed in tournament play, but popular in friendlies).

the brush: the failure to get in a game before your opponent goes out.

double in: starting a game with a double.

double out: winning a game on a double.

break the serve: used when the player who throws second beats the one who technically had an advantage by throwing first.

awkward lie: where a player's sight of their target is blocked by another dart.

The shouts

Cat's on the counter!: shouted when the winning dart strikes home, and signalling that drinks are to be bought by the loser (a 'cat' in the 1800s was equivalent to one quart of beer).

Come out!: shouted if a player in a friendly has scored more than the number required but continues to play, and is now just showing off.

Mind the waiter!/Father's boots!/Webby!/Wet feet!/ Moccasins!: all warnings to a player whose toes are over the oche line.

Game on!: a more polite way of telling a player to stop drinking and get on with it.

Office!: exclaimed at the winning shot. Alternatives include **That's the beer!**, **Hops!** and **Old lady!**

Keep 'em on the island!: shouted by a spectator at a player who only just manages to land on the board.

Ladies and children halfway!: a taunting jibe implying a thrower is making a 'girlie' shot. In the past, women were allowed to stand closer to the dartboard than men.

Mugs away!: used to signal that the loser of the previous match should now start the next.

The throws

JT: 'Just There' – any close shot, but also used mockingly for a very bad one.

Robin Hood: a dart lodged into the shaft of a dart already in the board.

right house, wrong bed: hitting the double or triple zone, but in the wrong number.

iron duke: a fluke, or lucky dart.

scud: a dart that lands way off target.

slop: hitting a number, but not the intended one.

Colditz: any dart that's thrown and falls 'outside the wire'.

cuckoo: a dart that lands in the wrong bed.

PENKERS AND PARPERS

MIBSTERS

Hear the word **mibster** and a nineteenth-century hoodlum might spring to mind, rather than someone whose arsenal consists solely of a finger and a small glass ball. But a few pages into the history of this ancient game, you begin to realize quite how seriously mibsters, as marbles players like to call themselves, take their sport.

Playing for high stakes is not something you'd instinctively associate with this world of glass **muggles** and **mibs**, and yet, some four centuries ago, the prize was arguably one of the greatest in the sporting annals. In 1588, during the reign of Elizabeth I, it's said that a game of marbles was the deciding round in a contest between two young suitors named Giles and Hodge over the hand of a milkmaid. The event, which took place on Good Friday in Tinsley Green in West Sussex, was the culmination of an epic contest lasting a full week, in which the men took each other on in wrestling, cock-throwing, and the intriguingly named Turk's head, stoolball, and tipcat. To this day, the British and World Marbles Championship is played every Good Friday at the Greyhound pub in the same Tinsley Green.

By this time marbles had already been played for centuries. Roman murals are full of images of the game, and marbles were found amongst the rubble and ashes of Pompeii.

If you ask a player today, the jeopardy of that contest in Tinsley Green has nothing on the modern games played out at the Championships, in which rivalry is as intense, tactics as cunning, and spectators as partisan as you'd find in the most brutal of contact sports.

Given its history, you might assume that the rules of marbles would be fixed by now. But not only do different mibsters use different protocols, there is in fact no single game called 'marbles'. Rather there are hundreds of variations, including **cherry pit, bridgeboard, boss out, nine holes, hundred** and **poison**. The one used most commonly for modern tournament play is **ringer**, which involves thirteen ducks arranged in a cross-shape with a challenge of shooting all of them out of the ring (that's the highly condensed version). Venues can be just as varied: ranging from purpose-built playing areas to drain covers, once a favoured marble-playing spot at schools thanks to their uneven terrain and even a corrugated bend or two to up the ante.

There are many myths to be smashed in the marble-playing world. For a start, the players are not nearly as conservative (or old) as you might expect. In pockets of the US in particular, teenagers are choosing marbles over baseball and ice hockey, and taking it just as seriously. The National Marbles Tournament, held in New Jersey in the appropriately named Ringer Stadium, is the ultimate prize, with each mibster playing not just for national honours but often for a college scholarship. Moreover, the competition in the real world of coloured glass is now being matched in a digital one. Online marbles challenges are attracting serious gamers, changing the traditional player demographic even more.

Talk like a mibster

The experienced marbles player has a host of terms for the individual spheres in front of them.

aggie: a marble made from agate.

alley: a marble made of alabaster, but also another term for a taw.

taw: the large marble used to knock around the smaller ones, also known as the **shooter** and, in some dialects, the **scudder**.

duck: a smaller marble knocked by the taw. Also known as a **boodie**.

tombola: a very large marble. Known in Cheshire as a **cheeny** or **crodle**.

stonker: an even bigger marble, sometimes reaching the size of a golf or snooker ball.

deegle: a marble pilfered from someone else.

Smuggins!: an exclamation used at the end of a game of marbles, dating from the 1800s – whoever shouts it first wins the whole lot.

fullock: to shoot a marble by jerking the hand forward.

The techniques

dubbing: the term for taking one shot and knocking two marbles out with it.

lagging: a means of determining who takes the first shot, in which each player rolls their marbles towards a designated line (the **lag line**); whoever comes closest plays first.

dead duck: an easy shot.

plunking: hitting a marble 'on the fly'.

fudge: to step over the line of the ring.

hist: to lift the knuckle from the ground while shooting. The opposite is known as **knuckling down**.

neggy lag: the penultimate shot in a game.

flirt: to flick a marble with your finger and thumb, probably the origin of our modern word, with the idea of flitting from one thing to another.

A different breed altogether are the marble collectors, those with fond childhood memories of 'shooters' and 'taws', and connoisseurs of the beauty of the coloured stones that can be over a century old. Handmade marbles are especially sought after, and each type has an appropriately colourful name, from the **mica** (coloured glass and silver flakes) and **maypole** (with threads swirled on or near the surface), to the prized **goldstone**, whose glass is made with copper crystals. Colours and swirls have their own lexicon too:

onionskin: a marble with swirls of layered colours.

bumble bee: a black and white striped marble.

clambroth: a swirl that has an opaque base with coloured strands along the surface.

slag: an onyx marble. This was the first marble to be mass-produced.

peerie: a small clear glass marble.

spotted dick: a flecked marble.

penker: Geordie for a marble that is more often made of steel than glass, often used by miners. Also known as a **parper**.

THE STRENUOUS IDLER

GOLFERS

If 'Marmite' hadn't become the term for something people either love or loathe, it might have been 'golf'. No other sport seems to attract such extremes of opinion. Either you're an addict, or you find the idea of hitting a small ball into a small hole with a long stick faintly ridiculous.

In arguably no other pastime are the perceptions of the past so persistent. Belief number one is that golf is a game for old fogeys in long shorts and a regimental tie. In fact the golfing demographic is slowly (too slowly for many) getting younger, and plus fours have given way to more fashionable trousers and shorts that still offer the same hip-swivel, knee-snap, and pockets. At the same time, golf's brand image is getting cooler, even positively hip. Hip and, it has to be said, expensive: the game doesn't come cheap, with even a small golf club demanding a membership fee upwards of £600 per year, and that's without all the necessary paraphernalia. The expense is part of the cachet, and partly explains why golf is so popular on the business circuit, where networking on the green is a sure way of getting ahead.

Belief number two is that golf is a leisurely pastime for those who like a potter with a putter. This one is easily dispelled. The game is about as competitive a sport as you're likely to find – not only that, but the behaviour of a player on the green is a pretty accurate reflection of their true personality. From the surreptitious ball-nudger to the wild slasher or silent swinger, what you see on the eighteenth is generally what you'll get at home. 'To find a man's true character,' P.G. Wodehouse observed, 'play golf with him.'

Surreptitious ball-nudging is, it has to be said, a pretty rare event. If there's one thing golf prides itself on, it's honour. There are few games in which the players self-police so extensively for the good of the game. It's a bold player who gives themselves an extra inch of breathing room from the depths of a bunker. And an even bolder one who plays the 'bandit': pretending to be poorer at the game in order to bluff with a high handicap. This all-important notion of moral probity can be carried to the degree that anything designed to make golf easier is positively discouraged. When, in the 1970s, a self-correcting 'non-slice' ball was invented, it was promptly banned.

No one quite knows how golf started, but we do know where:

in the wide open spaces of Scotland, where 'golf' is still a verb (its possible root is the Old Norse word *kólfr*, a 'stick' or 'club'). The earliest record of the term didn't bode well, appearing in an edict issued by James II of Scotland that placed an immediate ban on participation in both golf and football, presumably because they were proving too much of a distraction.

The game, however, eventually won, and even endeared itself to another royal, Mary, Queen of Scots, who is said to have had a team of 'cadets' lift up her long skirts whenever she prepared to tee off. Still, even she ran into a spot of bother herself, when her political enemies accused her of blatant heartlessness for playing a game of golf just hours after the murder of her second husband Lord Darnley.

The origins of the word 'golf' may be ancient, but that has never put paid to the belief that the term is an acronym for 'Gentlemen Only, Ladies Forbidden'. While being patently wrong on the etymological level, the stubborn belief in the myth is entirely understandable. Mary Stuart may have managed it, but other women have been fighting for a level playing green for centuries.

While some clubs today are boldly choosing a female chairman, president or club captain – hitherto an exclusively male domain – it was only in 2014 that the Royal and Ancient, golf's governing body, voted to allow women into its inner sanctum (two years later, in another historic move, it announced it was going to merge with the Ladies' Golf Union). The very public debate over the decision by Muirfield golf club to continue excluding women from membership in 2016 proved just how much of a discriminatory history the game still has to deconstruct.

It's in the members' clubhouse that women will tell you they really feel the barriers. The regimental ties and checked 'slacks' may be disappearing, but it will take time before the philosophies that accompanied them do the same, and before 'golf widower'

becomes as much a staple as the long-suffering female equivalent. In the meantime, if a male golfer hits a rather short 'girlie'
putt or moves it only a few yards up the fairway, you might
hear his male opponent ask, 'Does your husband play golf?'

Flubs, flops and an Arthur Scargill: types of shot

Golfers, particularly seasoned veterans or the competitive types
on a business jolly, love to chat about the technicalities of the
game, which can seem impenetrably complex to the outsider.
Cynics will tell you that if a novice begins a question with 'Am
I allowed to . . .?', the answer will always be no. When it comes
to the types of shot, however, there is little argument. Once
they've performed the golfer's traditional ritual of **milking the
grip** – tightening and loosening their hand grip before taking
a swing – a golfer will know exactly what they've just (mis)hit.

afraid of the dark: (of a putted ball) refusing to fall in the
   hole.
barkie: a ball that hits a tree, in which case the golfer is said
   to have got **a lot of good wood** on the shot.
chunk: where the club hits the ground behind the ball before
   impact, thus kicking up a big chunk of earth. Also known
   as a **fat shot**.
flop shot: one which is hit quite high and stops quickly on the
   green.
flub: a very poor shot; a **whiff** is a complete miss of the ball.
quail high: (of a poorly hit shot) flying low to the ground, like
   a quail. Also known as a **worm-burner**.
rainmaker: a shot with a very high trajectory.
shank: a mishit whereby the golfer fails to hit the ball with the
   club face. It is a shot so poor that many golfers are super-
   stitious about even hearing the term on the course.

yips: a twitch that makes a golfer's hands shake and that can severely interfere with play.

gimme: a conceded putt.

wrong postcode: a shot that is well struck but that travels in the wrong direction.

knee-knocker: a nervy short putt to the hole.

fried egg: a ball buried in a bunker – only the top half is visible.

bisque: an extra shot given to a golfer who may otherwise end up 'in the soup'. The hole it applies to is usually nominated at the start of a game.

ofima: a putt that rolls past the hole to a spot even further away than its starting point. The clean version of the acronym reads 'Oh fudge, it's me again'.

Tread carefully with these ones . . .

Adolf Hitler: two shots in the bunker.

Arthur Scargill: good strike, bad result.

O.J. Simpson: got away with it.

Glenn Miller: made it over the water.

Cuban: where the ball stops just short of dropping into the 'cup', and so 'needs one more revolution'.

Kate Moss: a shot that's a bit thin.

Jean-Marie Le Pen: a ball that goes too far to the right.

The equipment

An expert golfer will tell you that the fourteen-club allowance does not mean you actually need fourteen clubs (or **twigs**). In fact, four will do nicely: a wood, a wedge, an iron and a putter. The same goes for balls – too many and the novice will look as though they're destined to lose. Of course, that doesn't eliminate the need to have some of the proper lingo up your sleeve, whether you're talking **mashie niblicks**, **jiggers,** or **rescue clubs**. And if you really want to get technical, you can always refer to a ball's **dimples**, a club's **flange** and – the new kid on the block – the **smash factor**: the measurement of a golfer's ability to translate club-head speed into ball speed with a particular club.

knife: the 'one iron', a notoriously difficult club to hit properly, and usually only to be found in a pro golfer's bag.

short stick: the putter.

rescue club: also known as a utility or hybrid, with a club head that resembles a smaller version of a wood and that can coax the ball from a variety of lies.

drive for show: the driver, usually carried for display purposes only.

niblick: an old name for an iron club with a sloping face, known today as a #7. Niblicks come in all shapes and sizes, including **forks, spades** and **spoons**.

The players

A skilled golfer needs no particular label: they know they are good, and so does everyone else, which means they tend to command silent respect. For poor players and novices, of course, it's a different matter, and this is where teasing/self-deprecating/ downright cruel nicknames come into play.

duffer: a novice or mediocre golfer.

hacker: a poor player.

lumberjack: a golfer who consistently hits balls into the trees.

mouth wedge: a golfer who intentionally irritates other players by chatting incessantly.

as we lie: a phrase golfers will use to each other when a contest is finely balanced.

as it lies: where a ball comes to rest, and from where it must therefore be played.

sandbagger: a golfer who pretends to be far worse than they are in order to artificially inflate their handicap. Also known as a **bandit**.

The course

beach: a sand bunker. Also known as the **cat box** with an allusion to cat litter.

spinach: the rough. Also dubbed the **cabbage**.

dance floor: the smooth surface of the green.

frog hair: the closely mown grass in the apron surrounding the green.

the tips: the championship tees on a course.

Velcro greens: a putting green on a golf course that plays particularly slowly.

STRANGLED IN COW CORNER

CRICKETERS

Cricket is a romantic sport. It has all the ingredients of a good story, played out on long, hot summer days on picturesque village greens, until the day is done and a drink is shared against the setting sun. The heroic batsmen stand before nefarious bowlers, each attempting to win the day like knights and archers on a medieval battlefield.

The game is, in fact, not quite medieval, being first recorded in the sixteenth century, but that still makes it comfortably the oldest of the established modern team sports. By the eighteenth century, the game was well established in English life, and its basic vocabulary was coming into place, including 'bowler', 'batsman', 'lbw', 'bowled' and 'no ball'. By the end of the nineteenth century, cricket had spread throughout the British Empire and had even become an emblem for it.

It's not surprising then that one of our oldest leisure activities should have a rich and changing language. If cricket represents some sort of rural English idyll, it's certainly true that a sense of the rural can be felt in its vocabulary. It all started off pleasantly enough: in the latter part of the nineteenth century, for example, **barn door** and **stonewaller** began to be used to describe efficient batsmen who were defensive and difficult to dismiss. But eventually the element of the 'hick' crept in, especially when describing unsophisticated batting reliant upon brute force. Today's cricketers will describe, for example, a scything, ungainly swing of the bat as **agricultural**, and a cricketer who plays this way as **having a mow** or playing a **cow shot**; the area of the pitch to which such a shot is aimed is called **cow corner**, there where the fielder is waiting **in the long grass**.

In all sports, the names for positions on the pitch are amongst the most technical and occasionally arcane. Cricket takes both to the next level: its names for positions are often, quite literally, **silly**. Every area of a cricket field has a name, and none of them is remotely intelligible on its own. Where is **slip** or **gully**? Is **mid wicket** closer to the middle of the wicket than **cover point**? In the nineteenth century there was a position called **leg**. It referred to a fielder who was on the leg side, that is, the side of the field lying behind the batsman in his stance. That's almost straightforward: the fielder is on the side of the batsman's or batswoman's legs. Far too straightforward for cricketers then, so 'legs' had to be differentiated into square leg, fine leg, long leg, and short leg. Short leg is in the same position on one side of the wicket as 'silly point' is on the other. Fortunately, no one put two and two together and came up with 'silly leg'.

From the middle of the nineteenth century, cricketers began to create an extensive jargon that is still being used, or re-used today. Different bowling styles and deliveries, batting styles and shots, ways of getting out, qualities of the pitch, techniques, equipment and so on, all had to be described, distinguished and named. An easy catch, for example, has been a **dolly** for some 200 years. If such a catch goes high up into the air, it becomes a **percher**. More recently, if the ball goes up really high (at which point the catch ceases to be quite so easy), it is a **skier**. An unlucky or unskilled fielder might **grass** (drop) any of these chances.

If there's a number cricketers obsess about it is zero, when a batsman is dismissed without scoring any runs. Except they never call it that. Most of the time, it's a **duck**, although **egg**, **duck's egg**, **round O**, **blob**, **balloon**, and **nought** have also featured in the noughtie collection. A **golden duck** is one in which the batsman is dismissed by the first ball he faces. If he is dismissed without scoring in both innings of a match, he **bags a pair**, and if both dismissals are first ball, it becomes a **king pair**. If a batsman is unfortunate enough to be dismissed without facing a single ball from a bowler (it can happen), he can be described as having made a **diamond** or **platinum duck**. All of which sound quite desirable, but are in fact quite the opposite.

Now that ex-players have come to dominate media coverage of the game, more and more professionalisms are entering the vocabulary of sunny social cricketers, only they don't sound so professional. **Cafeteria bowling** is one in which the batsman can 'help himself', while the bowler, or **pie-chucker**, may deliver **left-arm filth**, which can lead to some **pongo** (rapid scoring by the batsmen). Batsmen and -women can still get **strangled** (give their wicket away to a poor ball) or **sawn off** (wrongly given out by the umpire). If the bowler bowls a **good knacker** (good delivery) in the **corridor of uncertainty** (an area outside the off stump where it's difficult for the batsman to judge whether or not to play the ball), the batsman may well **nick off** and be caught by the wicketkeeper or slips. If, however, he **misses his lengths**, he might get **jugged**, **mauled**, or **carted** for plenty of runs.

Cricketers normally need to be made of sturdy stuff. If you are a batsman, your contribution can be over in a single ball; if you are a bowler being carted (i.e. the batsmen continuously hit the ball with full throttle), having to bowl just the one ball would be desirable, but you are forced to carry on for six. It's not surprising then that cricketers are typically somewhat stoic and conservative in outlook, even if the odd bat gets thrown around by a batsman who has yet again been given out lbw (wrongly, of course). And then there's the **sledging**, the strategic taunting of the opposition that takes its name from the image of wielding a sledgehammer. The Australian Merv Hughes famously taunted the England player Graham Gooch with the line 'Would you like me to bowl a piano and see if you can play that?'

Backchat aside, cricket is undoubtedly a sport which allows ample time for reflection even while it's being played ('baseball on valium', as some would describe it). Perhaps that contemplativeness is itself reflected in the game's rich and unique vocabulary.

From jaffas to lollipops: the special deliveries

didapper: a ball that skims across the surface of the pitch like a little grebe across the water.

googly: a ball which breaks from the off, though bowled with apparent leg-break action. Also called a **wrong un** or (in Australia) a **bosie**, after its inventor, Bernard Bosanquet.

Chinaman: a left-arm spin bowler's ball which breaks from the off. Named after Ellis Achong, a Trinidadian spin bowler of Chinese descent.

flipper: a faster, skiddy ball bowled by a leg-spinner.

doosra: a delivery from an off-spinner that spins in the opposite direction of the normal off break. (From the Hindi or Punjabi word for 'second', or 'other'.)

zooter: a leg-spinner's ball that goes on straight without spinning.

beamer: a ball aimed at the head without bouncing; a high full toss (now outlawed).

full toss: a ball which reaches the batsman without bouncing.

jaffa: a superb, practically unplayable ball. Jaffas are usually 'absolute'.

lollipop: a ball off which the batsman can easily score runs.

long hop: a ball that's too short to be of good length, but that also doesn't lift like a bouncer.

yorker: a ball that hits the batsman's feet (probably originating in Yorkshire).

The lucky ones

Surrey cut (also a **Chinese cut** or a **French cut**): an inside edge past the stumps and wicketkeeper.

Harrow drive: an edge through the slip. It first referred to a an off-drive associated with batsmen from Harrow school.

perhapser: any lucky, unintentional or risky shot.

TURNING ON A SIXPENCE

THE FOOTBALL TEAM

Football and obsession have never been far apart. 'I'm off to the temple' was the early twentieth-century fan's way of saying he was going to watch the match at his team's home ground. With that phrase the fans were unwittingly forging a link between the modern game and the Roman mindset, for *fanaticus* was the Latin for 'belonging to the temple' and, by extension, 'inspired by a god'. The term soon encompassed the frantic and manic behaviour of someone possessed by a spirit or demon – in other words, a fanatic was an unhinged enemy of the people.

For today's fans, the god of football inspires every emotion imaginable and, like those fanatics of the temple, usually to the extreme. In fact, if a Roman were to witness the modern supporter's screaming, stripping, and swearing, he might well put it down to a demon. (It so happens that 'profanity' is also linked to the temple – this time meaning 'outside it', i.e not sacred.) The modern supporter is football crazy, they're football mad, and they're not in the least afraid to show it.

To reduce the sport to grown men chasing each other and a ball around some grass is to do it a great disservice. For most it occupies a plane higher even than Cloud Nine, the one regularly referred to after a home win. The playwright J.B. Priestley recognized this early on, observing after one memorable game: 'To say that these men paid their shillings to watch twenty-two hirelings kick a ball is merely to say that a violin is wood and catgut, that Hamlet is so much paper and ink. For a shilling Bruddersford United AFC offered you Conflict and Art.'

The chants

Shakespeare may have been pleasantly surprised by the modern fan's delight in wordplay and jokes, which can spread like wildfire (the Bard's own coinage) amongst the community. Nowhere is this better demonstrated than in the vocal equivalent of the Mexican wave: the stadium sing-song. The terraces are an ingenious lot when it comes to their chants. Topping the list of favourites in a recent poll were **Deep fry yer pizzas, we're gonna deep fry yer pizzas**, sung by Scotland fans to the tune of 'Guantanamera' against the Italian team during a World Cup qualifier. Equally popular was the teasing taunt from his own fans for the Spurs player who just couldn't find the onion bag: **When you're sat in row Z, and the ball hits your head, that's Zamora.**

The idea behind most chants is to get under the skin of the opposition; inspiring your own team is an added bonus. Some are prepared and practised weeks in advance (Liverpool excel at this, with their long, complex, and goosebump-inducing anthems), but the best are unrehearsed, as when Leeds United, under their manager Gary McAllister, were playing the 'Posh' Peterborough at their ABAX stadium and the local council saw fit to park two STI testing vans outside. The result from the Leeds fans was inevitable: **We've got McAllister, you've got chlamydia.**

One of the longest-surviving terrace taunts has to be **Who ate all the pies**? Cue thoughts of Adriano, Gazza, and Newcastle United frontman Mickey Quinn, who even used the catchphrase for his autobiography. The barb was in fact born a century ago, when it was aimed at a Victorian goalie called William 'Fatty' Foulke – the man who came to hold the Guinness World Record for the heaviest footballer.

Swearing

'F★★k' and 'wanker' are to the football fan what 'y'know' and 'like I say' are to their team's manager. These are a badge of identity, a necessary filler, and no matter if you're in the family section of the Emirates or down at Villa Park (recently polled as having the 'quietest' fans) you're going to hear them alongside other unpleasantries.

There is a distinct 'maleness' about the language of the football crowds. Despite the enormous number of women present, and the gratifying advances being made in women's football, the calls are resolutely masculine. An unflattering conclusion would put this down to male irascibility, for at any given time most fans seem to feel a sense of deep discontentment. The ref is always either **a disgrace** or the **wanker in the black**, and all fans can shout about him as much as they like without anyone batting an eyelid. Even the C-word barely gets a stare. This is codified vitriol that is as much a part of the game as the pie van outside the stadium.

But beyond the swears and the prayers, the vocabulary of football is the biggest unifier of all. It's a shorthand that every fan, commentator, player, and gaffer buys into: the mark of the trade, a badge of belonging, and it is utterly tribal.

parking the bus: now one of the biggest footballing tropes, used when all eleven players get behind the ball to defend the goal.
cheese sandwich: a creative player who isn't anchored to any particular position; a riff on the idea of a 'free role' (roll).
the ol' switcheroo: a long pass from one winger to another.
the mixer: the penalty area. To 'put it in the mixer' means to get it in the box.
the false nine: the tactic of deploying a centre-forward in a very deep position.

the magic sponge: the apparently miraculous use of a wet sponge by a medic on a player who has fallen to the ground in agony (usually after securing a booking for the player who allegedly fouled them).

fox in the box/predatory striker: a player concerned less about the build-up of play than the scoring of goals, especially opportunistic ones.

a six-pointer: used in league football to describe a game in which an opposing team's loss is as important as your team's win. Not only do you accumulate three points, but your close rival gets none.

noisy neighbours: a busy rival team. Coined by Sir Alex Ferguson while talking about Manchester City's run of success: 'Sometimes you have a noisy neighbour. You cannot do anything about that. They will always be noisy. You just have to get on with your life, put your television on and turn it up a bit louder.'

Roy of the Rovers: a low-level player or team that is mixing with the big boys.

A few of the moves

Tiki-Taka football: patient and possession-based 'pass and move' football (i.e. Barcelona).

Cruyff turn: a move made famous by Johan Cruyff, in which the attacker quickly changes direction by playing the ball behind his standing foot, leaving the defender facing the wrong direction.

pea roller: a ball with little power that safely ends up in the hands of the opposing goalkeeper.

daisy cutter: a ball kicked hard and low enough to cut the grass.

the Panenka: a penalty kick in which the taker runs up with speed as if to leather the ball, but applies instead a dainty and audacious chip, thereby bamboozling the goalie. Made famous after Antonin Panenka's goal for Czechoslovakia during the first penalty shootout in a European Cup Final.

leathered it: not only scored, but scored by a country mile.

thronker: a term coined by Dan Walker for a rare goal that meets eleven different criteria, including 'Is it hit at full wellie?', 'Is it from at least twenty yards?' and 'Would it annihilate a pigeon?'

The players

Players and fans have a curious and changeable relationship, one that can become turbulent when respect is on the line. Life on the pitch after any exposed 'behavioural' incident can be tough, and a sense of humour can often help to defuse the tension. Ashley Cole chose to laugh with the crowd rather than bridle at them whenever they shouted 'Shoot!' after a much-publicized incident with an air rifle.

Whether affectionate or searing, terrace insults are piled on at most games, not least because the Rolexes, sharp suits, and wild forays of some players or their WAGs frequently take them from the back pages to the front. Some players are simply controversy magnets – like Luis Suarez, who has never quite given the apologies required for leaving imprints of his fearsome incisors on several opponents. (Perhaps that becomes more understandable when you learn that 'remorse' is from the Latin for 'biting back'.)

The language that everyone wants to know usually involves half-time. **Hairdryer treatment** is now a firm linguistic fixture: the half-time rollicking dispensed to an underperforming team by the manager was made infamous by Sir Alex Ferguson's alleged rages at Manchester United. Wayne Rooney was later to say of it: 'It feels like I've put my head in front of a BaByliss

Turbo Power 2200. It's horrible.' The **gaffer's son**, on the other hand, is used of any player thought to receive special attention from his boss.

How exactly does a manager inspire his players when they're 4–0 behind, or maintain momentum when they're riding high? According to insiders, whereas ten years ago you might have heard such phrases as **If in doubt, kick it out**, and **Get in there early doors**, today the team will probably hear **Keep the ball**, **Make sure of your passes** and **Don't go to ground unless you have to**. Perhaps it's not so earth-shattering after all.

The tactics

stand on the keeper: to shadow the keeper so that they can't easily collect the ball during a corner.

the block: a tactic in which a player runs across the path of a marker while his or her teammate makes a free run across the face of goal.

corridor of uncertainty: a term borrowed from cricket and used in football for a pass delivered into the area in front of the goalkeeper and behind the last line of defence. The uncertainty lies in the decision of the goalkeeper and last defender as to whether to leave the ball for the other, or to defend it.

POMO: abbreviation for 'position of maximum opportunity', especially the space inhabited by a striker after pulling away from the goalkeeper the moment a corner is taken.

five-yard frenzy: a strategy in which each player has a radius of five yards in which to run as fast as they can, keep on top of the player with the ball, and try to win it back. This can be effective even if the player isn't an endurance sprinter.

cultured left foot: a player who has the ability to make highly skilful, precisely accurate passes and shots, often with a lot of spin on the ball. A trait typically associated with left-footed players – Arsenal's Mesut Özil has a classically cultured left foot.

turned on a sixpence: pulled off a very tight turn (a lot more plausible than actually standing on a sixpence).

top bins: the art of shooting the ball into the top corner of the net, giving the goalkeeper no chance of saving it.

The verdicts

fluked it: you've kicked the ball and miraculously it's gone in.

missed a sitter: it was harder for you to miss than score, but somehow you managed it.

hospital pass: a dangerous ball passed under pressure, which involves the recipient coming under heavy attack.

taking one for the team: you've made a professional foul, one that was cynical but necessary because it successfully stopped the opponents' pressure play.

hacked down: you've been felled by a malicious or dangerous tackle.

The instructions

On the pitch, there are common phrases that each club will teach its players, no matter which country they hail from.

When it comes to the codes of the game, according to Arsène Wenger (the very articulate manager of my team Arsenal – not for nothing is he called 'Le Professeur'), some will never be revealed and will forever stay on the pitch, while many more 'start with the letter "F"'. But whether a player is from the north or the south of the globe, 'they need to understand a common language soon'.

Clear and concise communication, Wenger believes, is integral to the efficiency of a team: 'When the team is defending a cross, phrases such as: "Behind you"; "Go deeper"; "Come back to me"; "Awareness"; and "Look around" are obviously important. If players can't communicate these simple instructions quickly, it can cost the team dearly. It's vital that every team learns key phrases that can be used in match situations'.

Quick words mean quick actions. Today's teams may play with four or five different nationalities in their defence, meaning that any shout from the goalie can be compromised. This is why Arsenal's Petr Cech already speaks four languages, and why he immediately embarks upon learning another if a new foreign player comes in (he is currently learning Arabic).

Back to English, there are many more shouts for a foreign player to pick up in the heat of play.

Square it!: Pass the ball directly to me.

Line it!: Play the ball forward so I can run on to it (normally used by wingers running near the touchline).

Sid!: the code between players of the same team that the ball should be left for them. Even though the opposition also understands it, it works.

Peno!: the shout for a penalty when you haven't got enough energy to say 'penalty'.

Finish it!: shouted to a player to mean 'I've passed you the ball; now kick it into the net!'

Out!: Normally shouted by the goalkeeper or defender to tell their attacking teammates to stop protecting the goal and push out field in order to clear a congested penalty area.

The post-match interview

One of the biggest clichés in football is that its language is full of clichés. When it comes to the post-match interview, it would be difficult to argue. A manager's reliance on fatigued formulations is often seen as a lack of verbal finesse or a limited repetoire of adjectives, but the reality can be very different. Arsène Wenger explains: 'Football managers' vocabulary is very restricted. But in our defence we are restricted not because we are short of intelligence, but rather because we don't want to cause damage. We are always cautious not to cause huge problems with what we say in press conferences and after matches. Therefore, we are always tempted to use the same words – phrases like: **We were not rewarded; We were unlucky; The ref's decisions didn't go our way; We fought well today** – because if you let yourself go in media interviews you could be in trouble.' Put this way, a manager's responses are the best defenders of a game.

One gaffer who's bucked the trend of saying as little as possible, as unoriginally as possible, is Gordon Strachan, a man who consistently refuses to take refuge in cliché. Of his many famous retorts the best has to be the one given to a reporter who chased after him with the question: 'Gordon, can we have a quick word?' Quick as a flash, Strachan replied 'Velocity,' and then promptly hurried off.

For the most part, however, originality is not the name of the game, and Wenger expresses surprise that, given the predictability of post-matchspeak, commentators still line up to talk to the managers. Nevertheless, there is always the chance of picking up a gem or two, including two firm favourites in the Arsenal manager's own lexicon: the adverb **footballistically** ('footballistically, he's ready for the first team'), and the adjective **handbrakeish** ('I felt we were a little handbrakish today').

When a change in linguistic habits does happen, it is inevitably parroted by fans in thousands of after-match pub-chats and on pundits' sofas. This is a unique kind of English, one in which **quality** and **class** are the adjectives of choice, where **them** replaces **those**, and where **y'knows** are sprinkled liberally throughout conversation. Adverbs lose their endings ('the boy done terrific'), and **like I say** has more caps than Steven Gerrard (even though whatever it refers to was never said in the first place). Meanwhile, performances must be put in **week in, week out**, because **at the end of the day, to be fair obviously**, football is **a big ask**.

In this lexicon, penalties are always **stonewall** or **soft**, and a game has many **situations**: i.e. promising attacking positions from which a chance might be created. These may occur **early doors**: an allusion to premium tickets in a theatre that would allow viewers to get in early and avoid the crowds. As for fouls, managers (including, infamously, Wenger) might say **I didn't see it**, or point out that **it looked for all the world as if** that should have been a red: an unusually poetic formulation borrowed from Shakespeare and other literary giants.

Finally there is the footballing tense, used especially when a manager or player is replaying a 'situation' in their heads: 'The ball's come across; I've gone to hit it, but it's come off my shin and . . .'

All in all, **you couldn't make it up**: one of the most popular formulae amongst commentators, fans, and pundits alike – and one that was beautifully destroyed in a letter to a newspaper editor by an observer called 'Joey': 'I'm sick of sports commentators saying "you couldn't write a script like this". If people can write scripts about dystopian futures in which life is in fact a simulation made by sentient machines to harness humans' heat and electricity as an energy source, they can probably write ones about Gary Taylor-Fletcher scoring a last-minute equalizer against Stoke.'

6

Emergency Services

'As to diseases, make a habit of two things –
to help, or at least to do no harm.'
Hippocrates, Greek physician, 460–357 BC

The 'black' in 'black humour' was put there by doctors, with
the help of the other members of our emergency services.
Tiptoeing on the edge of life and death (or, in the case of
undertakers, around the coffins) can produce a humour so edgy
that, in the wrong hands, it could all literally end in tears. We
don't call them 'sick' jokes for nothing.

Yet the emergency service workers have a unique justification
for such appalling humour, witnessing as they do countless
scenes of pain and misery, every day of their working week
('appalling' itself had the original meaning of 'growing pale' in
horror or fright). And so laughter is their release, meaning that
each of the services has produced its own brand, tuned and
customized for every situation. Should you, for example, ever
decide that you wish to be cryogenically frozen after death, you
will forever, at least until thawing, be known as a 'corpsicle'.
While you're still alive, you should probably hope that you never
require any 'house red' on a hospital ward – that's code for a
blood transfusion. 'Riding the bone', meanwhile, belongs not to
the lexicon of an orthopaedic surgeon, but to that of a firefighter
assigned to an ambulance.

There is inevitably a fair amount of crossover too. As in the
armed forces, there is an empathetic, joshing rivalry between

the services, in which to work together is to banter together. It's a verbal uniform that unites the tribe, and that has laughter at its core.

This is why it pays to focus less on the business end of things (a phrase that signifies something entirely different to most medics) and more on the shorthand swapped amongst and around the acronyms and specialist terminology. It gives a far greater sense of who's doing the swapping, and of the tremendous challenges they and their language must cope with daily. For those in the midst of the suffering it will seem as dark as that house red, but that is its point. One paramedic I spoke to confessed that 'you have to be a little bit crazy to do this job'.

Those in the building trade are a different breed of life-saver, but their lexicon is especially worth recording. Like footballers, they are not exactly famed for their mastery of the word, but their patois proves this to be a gross underestimation of their skills in linguistic as well as building construction. Surely we could all do with introducing the concept of a 'snotter' into our lives, and with announcing 'Job in Guinness' at the end of the day.

BLACK RATS AND KNUCKLE DRAGGERS

POLICE

The first rappers were policemen. For more than two hundred years, 'rap' has been associated with rebuke and punishment. In early twentieth-century America, the law enforcers extended the idea of 'a rap on the knuckles' to mean a criminal charge or prison sentence; they have been delivering the rap ever since, and dealing with a fair amount of it themselves.

Not that their job has ever been easy. To be a 'peeler', in the 1800s, involved the strictest of codes. Early Victorian police worked seven days a week, and their lives were tightly controlled. They were required, for example, to wear their uniforms both on and off duty so that the public didn't feel spied upon, were forbidden from voting in an election, and required permission to even share a meal with a civilian, let alone marry one. Since then, the police have been on the receiving end of countless nicknames. **Coppers** take their name from the idea of 'copping' or nabbing someone; it was the Americans who cut it to 'cop', and added **fuzz** to the mix because they 'make a fuss'. Newer terms on the American streets include the **feds**, **five-ohs** and **po-pos**, all of which buzzed across British social media during the summer riots of 2011. In Liverpool, meanwhile, the police are the **bizzies**, probably because they 'get busy'. If all of these represent the outside looking (uncompromisingly) in, **the thin blue line** is the internal emblem of the police, symbolizing both its camaraderie and its aim of standing between criminal and victim.

Another enduring name for the force as a whole is of course the **Old Bill**, originally a cartoon character of the First World War who was portrayed as a grumbling Cockney soldier with a walrus moustache. The 'police' meaning emerged when the character, this time wearing police uniform, appeared in posters during the Second World War giving advice on wartime security.

Police officers have been dispensing advice ever since. Whether it's asking directions to Leicester Square or reporting a drunk and disorderly, it's a **bobby** (another nickname, based on the name of Sir Robert Peel, the nineteenth-century Home Secretary who created the Metropolitan Police) that we look out for. They're not hard to spot, thanks to their tall, bulbous helmets – designed to make any police officer stand out in the crowd. Psychologists go so far as suggesting that the use of a disarmingly charming helmet – as opposed, say, to a gangsta baseball cap – helps to calm and defuse a tense situation, and so while truncheons may give way to Tasers, the iconic helmet is sticking around. Meanwhile the story told to all pregnant women that they can request the use of a policeman's helmet in an emergency has some truth in it – a pregnant woman is legally allowed to urinate anywhere; it's entirely up to the individual policeman whether he wants to oblige or not.

The language of the emergency services, as we've seen, is all about coping, and that of the police is no exception. Dark humour is a major component – a necessary release valve on the pressure cooker. It is as private as it is sacrosanct, kept in-house at all times. Beyond the uniform, it is the most prominent marker of the tribe.

'Tribe', singular, is in fact a slight misnomer: in the police, there are many groups, and each carry their own nickname, given to them (usually affectionately) by colleagues in the other emergency services.

The Met: London's police force, viewed as solid, grounded and a mirror image of the ambulance crews. On any shift, members of the two crews will always wave at each other – a reflex that kicks in even off-duty.

BTP: British Transport Police, present at railway stations and teasingly known as 'ticket collectors' by the other services.

City Police: situated in the Square Mile of the City of London, and identifiable by their more colourful helmets, known as **tits**. These are frequently ex-squaddies, sporting the telltale sign of a peaked hat pulled down low over the face.

Community Support Officers (or **PCSOs**): those whose main remit is to tackle antisocial behaviour and minor offences, and who bear the unfortunate epithet of **plastics**. They are identifiable by the blue band on their helmets and their slightly oversized uniforms.

Diplomatic Protection Group (**DPG**): those you'll see at access points to Downing Street; otherwise known as **Doors, Pillars & Gates**, since they are usually standing next to at least one of them.

Traffic Police: recognizable by their white hats, even whiter cars, and long bright yellow coats. Also known as the **Black Rats,** allegedly because these are the only animals that will eat their own young. If you ever see a black rat sticker on the back of a car, you'll know that its owner is a traffic cop. The vehemence of feeling they inspire in every other police group (not to say the public) is considerable.

Tactical Support Group (**TSG**): riot control, nicknamed **knuckle draggers**. They tend to be big and muscly, and are generally mocked for having more brawn than IQ.

K9 officer: a police dog.

plain clothes police: ironically, the most easily identifiable of all. Hoodie, body warmer, jeans, trainers, permanent stubble: as one paramedic put it, 'you can't miss them'.

'Get yer trousers on, you're nicked!'

Outsiders are often convinced they know the lingo of the police, thanks almost entirely to the fictional lens of TV. *The Sweeney* casts a particularly long linguistic shadow, even if criminals are no longer **tasty slags** who need to be **banged up**. The police themselves watch these dramas so avidly that the default conversation between two police officers tends to involve the inaccuracy of the latest storyline.

Fictional police chat away about their lives in **the Force**, a term that real police never use: for them, it is simply **the job**. Hence an off-duty officer caught speeding may try 'I'm job, mate' on the traffic officer, while a **job car** is the official one, and **job roll** the sand-papery toilet paper in the nick. Within the London Metropolitan Police, the house journal even goes by the title of *The Job*.

Fictional cops are fond of other terminology that no real police officer would ever draw on. Thus you can forget about their **manor** or **patch** – a police officer's territory will always be their **ground**. The station (and prison) will never be anything other than **the nick**. Anyone **nicked**, i.e. arrested and cautioned, in either is **banged up**. The observation process leading to such arrests is known colloquially as **doing an obbo**.

To us, early and late duties may be 'shifts', but for those in the job they are known as **early worm** and **late turn**, and night duty is plain **nights**. Any single period of work is a **tour** (of duty), for which every officer will need their uniform, including **bonnet** (helmet), **stick** (truncheon), and **PR** (personal radio, formerly known as the 'Batphone').

The past can still be felt in many of the codes used for apprehending criminals. One who's been arrested for carrying equipment designed for theft has been off for **HBI,** the initials refer to the old offence of 'carrying House Breaking Implements by night'. Other offences include **TDA**: 'Taking and Driving Away', **OPD** ('Outraging Public Decency'), and **IPO** ('Impersonating a Police Officer'). These sit alongside better-known abbreviations including **ABH, GBH**, and **ASB** (assaults occasioning 'Actual' or 'Grievous Bodily Harm', and 'Anti-Social Behaviour').

On the job

Inevitably, thanks to the need for speed and secrecy, acronyms and abbreviations feature plentifully in the police force. Most of these are harmless: an **LKA** will be a person's last known address, and **QOA** signifies all is quiet on arrival. Dead bodies (**DBs**) inevitably get a look-in, while **BOLO** is the command to be on the lookout (rather than 'burglars only live once').

Elsewhere, the vocabulary becomes a little mischievous. In-house, for example, suspects are known to the police as potential customers or **pigs**: a sarcastic reversal of the acronym most often levelled against them, only this time standing for Polite, Intelligent Gentleman. **Snitch** remains the term of choice for an informer, a sense it's held since the 1700s. A **100-yard hero** is a member of the public who shouts obscenities at a police officer from a safe distance (as opposed to a **window warrior**, a suspect or prisoner who does the same thing from the confines of their cell), and a suspect is also a **potential** – or, if they've been there before, a **valued** – **customer**. A prisoner is a **body**, one that is always **got** when arrested. An officer may also **feel his collar**, **have him off**, or **get a crime knock**. However he or she came to be arrested, the body will henceforth be referred to as **Chummy**.

Anglers are thieves who use a rod or pole to steal from ground-floor windows – their name goes back four hundred years – and **jumpers** are ones who steal from offices. **Shoulder-surfing** is the act of stealing PIN numbers at a cashpoint, while a **nut** is the expenses incurred by a thief setting up a robbery or theft (you won't publicly hear the term **end** from police: this denotes the share proceeds from a crime). A **twoccer** is someone who 'takes without the owner's consent', particularly cars, while to **spin the drum** has nothing to do with the local police raffle, meaning instead to search a property.

While inside, a **lag** (especially of the **old** variety) is a repeat offender (perhaps at peddling **ice cream**, i.e. drugs), and a **hobbit** a prisoner who complies with the system. Upon release, they may wear a **Peckham Rolex**, i.e. a tag.

Justice never sleeps, and apprehending the language of crime can be as important as nabbing those who perpetrate it. Criminal slang was the first to be collected, and glossaries of the 'cant' of highwaymen, cutpurses, cardsharps, beggars and scoundrels date back to the 1600s. The very premise of its language is secrecy and subterfuge, and hence it moves more quickly than almost any other subset of slang (with the notable exception of teen-talk). In 2009, the UK police were given a list of 2,875 drug-related words to learn, including **abbey habit** (amphetamine), **al Capone** (heroin), **banger** (hypodermic needle), and **zulu** (bogus crack) to help them keep abreast of the continually evolving criminal code.

Working down The Factory

Kremlin: New Scotland Yard.
The Factory: the police station or **local nick**.
guv: an officer of at least inspector rank.
onion: a sergeant (onion bhaji – sargie).
BINGO seat: Bollocks I'm Not Getting Out Seat – the seat at the back of a police carrier where the laziest officer sits.
BONGO: Books On Never Goes Out – an ineffectual police officer who always clocks on but rarely leaves their desk. Also known as the **Olympic torch** (never goes out).
blues and twos: driving very fast on an emergency call.
brief: a solicitor, or a police officer's warrant card.
CSI: Crime Scene Investigator (formerly SOCO).
muppet: Most Useless Police Person Ever Trained. Generally used affectionately.
wooden-top: a person who spends their time dealing with domestics.
strawberries: civilian police (strawberry Mivvies – civvies).
refs: a refreshment or meal break ('What time refs are you?').

Day and night

Numbers belong here too. There are many codes that a police officer can use over the radio to discreetly describe the specific situation they find themselves in, from being followed by a car full of criminals (**11–56**), to finding an abandoned bicycle (**11–26**). **10–12** means there are visitors present and thus the call is being overheard, while in some forces a **10–61** is a request to the officer out in the field to bring a pint of milk when they come back to the office.

Mr Sands

Mr (or **Inspector**) **Sands** is a standard code for fire, used to alert staff or police without panicking customers. 'Will Inspector Sands please report to the men's toilets' indicates the location of the fire. In the London Underground network, a recorded 'Inspector Sands' warning is automatically triggered by smoke detectors. The code for a bomb in the Underground is 'Mr Gravel'.

FATSPREADING ON POET'S DAY

BUILDERS

According to a study carried out by the building industry in 2014, the average British builder is called Paul, Andrew or Dave, will always tune into Ken Bruce's *PopMaster*, and likes a chicken and bacon sandwich for lunch. He (and it is almost always a he) will leave the house at around seven each morning, and clock off at around five. Whoever thought builders spend most of their time chatting, sitting in their van, and drinking tea may need to think again – although the survey did suggest that the average intake of the hot stuff is still six mugs a day (with only one sugar these days, cut down from two, three, or the occasional six).

If this all strikes you as an extreme stereotype, you'd be right, except that most builders will tell you that the portrait is also highly accurate. Above all, the finding that gets them nodding most vigorously is the slog: approximately ten hours a day of hard and unrelenting graft. For sheer physicality, the jobs of the squaddie and the builder have a lot in common. On top of the lugging and the loading, though, and when asked about the hardest aspects of their job, most builders will cite the British weather, finances and, inevitably, the difficult client.

It's true that the profile of your average builder is slowly changing. They are smarter, for one thing. The old habits and rituals are still there but, as one plasterer put it, 'the dummies don't get the big jobs any more, and not everyone on site is hairy-arsed and sweary'. Today, big companies and wealthy clients are entrusting a builder and their workforce with serious money. Not only that, but builds have become significantly more complicated, and planning regulations far stricter. All this means that there is increasingly more expected of a builder, and a lot more money in the trade. More and more professionals are retraining to take advantage of these new opportunities.

But the old stereotypes die hard, and one that perpetually dogs the builders of Britain is that of the wolf: the leering lad who stares after every female who walks past and unfailingly delivers the traditional mating call of the building site – a loud whistle and a Vic Reeves leg-rub. Ask around today, and most builders will maintain that this is one expectation that isn't wholly deserved. They may also cite a recent survey suggesting that three-quarters of all builders, plasterers, roofers, and construction workers consider wolf-whistling to be inappropriate, chauvinistic, and downright sexist.

Yet the same builders will also admit that the legacy of a

century's worth of ogling is not going to vanish in a flash. Which is why, if you find a group of workers on a roof and a woman walks past, she'll probably still get whistled at – even though she is so far away that she looks ant-size, she'll barely hear the whistle because of the traffic, and the whistler is married with kids. 'It's what happens,' one builder tells me, 'you've got a tape measure hanging off you – your "Get out of jail free card" – and the feeling is it's your right to be the "wanker on a roof" because it's happened for the last sixty years.'

One force that will inevitably affect all of this is the influx of women-builders, whose numbers are growing. Admittedly the starting point was low in the extreme, so that today female workers account for no more than six per cent of the total workforce. But for those who believe the market to be unfairly flooded by migrant workers – a fear expressed by many – there are more women in the trade than builders from Eastern Europe.

Whatever the gender and cultural mix, builders seldom work alone: whether on site with a large team or in a small group, the camaraderie is obvious, as is the pecking order. A site-working builder must be thick-skinned, and sharp enough to hit back at the prankers and stirrers. 'It's a "who-can-I-break-today" attitude on some jobs,' you'll hear, 'and the more builders there are, the worse it gets.'The junior will have enough **skyhook**, **glass hammer** and **longweight** jibes to last a lifetime.

There's an unspoken hierarchy within the builder's extended network, too. Electricians, plasterers and plumbers each have very different personalities that, from a builder's point of view, are extremely predictable. Electricians, you'll hear, are highly anal – it goes with the technicalities of their job. Plumbers, meanwhile, for all their hanging around the toilet all day, still see themselves as office workers, even down to ironing their clothes before setting off to work. Intellectually, an electrician and plumber may rate themselves above the brickie or the plasterer – a view that, judging by the words most frequently paired with the profession, the rest of us would seem to share. Common couplings include the terms 'cowboy', 'dodgy' and 'rugged' (we clearly still respect their biceps).

This isn't of course helped by TV programmes like *Cowboy Builders*. In fact, most builders curse the surge in popularity of DIY shows that create entirely unrealistic expectations. Real-life builders will tell you that the side of the equation that you never see is the boring one (especially drying times). So when a customer suggests that you can fit a kitchen in two days, as they saw 'on the telly', their builder will be silently cursing Lawrence Llewelyn-Bowen. Furthermore, for every cowboy builder, you'll find at least two 'nightmare clients'.

Terms for builders from the past, from **upbiggers** to **edifiers,** were often as lofty as their creations. Today the team looks altogether earthier:

chippy/woodbutcher: the carpenter.
sparky: the electrician.
trowel/brickie: the bricklayer.
spread: the plasterer.
brew bitch/Labrador/grunt: the labourer.
hoddy: the hod carrier.
coddy: the foreman.

. . . as do the tools:

muck (also called **pug**): sand and cement mortar.
Painter's mate: the best-known brand of decorator's flexible caulk, and therefore synonymous with it.
screed: a cement-based layer used on a floor in order to level and flatten it.
skim: a thin finishing plaster coat.

Willy Carson box: a small box or platform used by plasterers and painters. When Willy Carson presented *Channel 4 Racing*, he would stand on a box in order to appear the same height as the co-presenter.

muck/bobbo: mortar.

Brummie screwdriver: a hammer.

bark and growl: a trowel.

Gary Neville: a spirit level; also called a **bubble**.

The mechanics

topping out: bricklaying at a high level, such as a gable or chimney.

putting the hat on: completing the roof.

tarting it up: making good something that's in need of attention.

polishing a turd: undertaking a job that is way past the point of minor repair, or trying to make something look good that is doomed to be ugly.

slinging: hanging wallpaper at speed.

going off: starting to set. When plaster, concrete, filler etc. loses its fluidity and pliability, it is said to have gone off. Setting hard takes much longer.

toshing: painting roughly.

spreading the fat: trowelling plaster.

lashing it on: applying plaster or paint as quickly as possible.

firing it up: laying bricks quickly.

doing Lionel Richie's dance floor: plastering a ceiling.

Michael Barrymore: a room that is going to be painted 'All White' (a reference to Barrymore's catchphrase 'Awight!').

The jobs

nose-bleeder: a job that involves stooping low and facing downwards, i.e. any job where the builder's famous bottom is higher than his head for any decent amount of time.

job in the city: a fancy job that is worth doing or that's been done well. The builder has finished a job, it looks great, they're happy, the customer is happy: that's a job in the city.

hospital job: a job that a builder can drop into whenever it works for them, or when there is no other better job available.

shillings and rivets: a builder's wages, often **paid in bangers and mash** (cash).

a rasher: a thin wage packet.

The problems

on the piss: said of an object that's not level, as if it's had a few too many to drink.

straight pisser: a job in which the bonds on brickwork are lined up (stacked on top of each other), rather than broken as they should be.

Wimpey closure: a lazy technique by a worker who won't go to the trouble of making a custom-cut brick for any remaining space in the end of a course, but instead will simply fill up the leftover gap up with mortar. 'Wimpey' is a reference to one of the big housebuilders of the 1970s and 80s, whose standards were considered by some to be on the loose side.

hang your jacket on it: said of a surface, such as brickwork or plaster, that should be level and smooth but isn't – the bricks stick out so far that you could hang your jacket on it.

snotter: anything in paint, plaster or mortar that shouldn't be in there.

a pig in it: used of a wall or footing that has been done badly and consequently has a bow in the middle.

The pub, aka the office

Poet's Day: 'Poet's' being an acronym for 'Piss Off Early, Tomorrow's Saturday'.

Yabba Dabba Doo Time: 'Down tools, it's time to go home' (from the introductory song to *The Flintstones*).

Play my favourite song: a phrase used when one builder asks another to clean out the cement mixer so that he himself can go home. Cleaning involves turning the mixer on and filling it with water and broken bricks. As the mixer spins, the bricks make a clunky rhythmic sound against its sides.

Job in Guinness: The job's done, and it's time for the pub.

The language of the wardrobe

Nothing speaks louder about the changes between the builders of today and yesteryear than what they don to work:

A builder in 2016:

Hard hat.
Goggles.
Face mask.
High visibility jacket.
Heavy-duty work trousers.
Steel toecap boots.
Clipboard and pen.

A builder in 1980:

A rolled-up bobble hat. Pencil shoved up one side, rolled-up fag on the other.
No T-shirt needed for maximum tanning opportunity.

Cut-off jeans: high ('too high in fact. Kevin Keegan high').

Shoes: probably the ones that they were going to wear to the pub later.

Baccy tin and lighter.

BONEHEADS AND LANCELOTS

DOCTORS

If you've ever had the misfortune to sit in A&E, you will have caught some of the code of the emergency room. Amid the bustle of triage and tantrums, the professionals exchange clipped phrases littered with abbreviations and cryptic jargon. Theirs is an utterly private shorthand used for clarity, brevity, and secrecy. It is also practical, creative, and frequently blue.

There has, of course, never been a better time to see your doctor. Doing so in medieval Britain was a risky business, where patients risked the same fate as Alexander the Great: 'I am dying with the help of too many physicians.' This was the age of the itinerant quacks: peddlers of medicines that they claimed could cure everything from a sore throat to infertility. Doctors were guided by the principles of humorism, which posited that an excess or deficiency of any of the four distinct bodily fluids – black bile, yellow bile, phlegm and blood – were the causes of every medical ailment. A medieval prescription might include a cold bath, copious amounts of garlic, and bloodletting; the mortality rate was rather high.

Thankfully, the Age of Enlightenment followed, and between the sixteenth and eighteenth centuries, medical professionals began to understand matters of neurology, the circulatory system, and the body's anatomy. That's not to say that they understood the causes of the illnesses that (literally) plagued the country. Even that most common of Renaissance diseases, syphilis (so common it had a lexicon of its own, including 'copper nose' and 'French withered pears') was thought to be caused variously by punishment from heaven; small worms that floated through the air; Saturn; contact with the New World, or sexual contact between a man and a sick woman.

Medicine held on so tightly to superstition that, as late as the eighteenth century, it was believed that a bite from a tarantula could be cured by music. But by the nineteenth century, the profession had started to take a shape we'd recognise today. The NHS is now the world's fifth biggest employer, behind the US and Chinese armies, Walmart, and McDonald's. It's unsurprising that it's developed its own unique dialect, one that's split into public and private.

The private is characterized by black humour, irreverence, and euphemism. This is never more evident than in patients' notes, which can include more observations than you bargained for. Some are gently amusing: a patient may be **TATT** (tired all the time), an increasing number are **TEETH** (tried everything else, try homeopathy) and some unfortunates are either **PAFO** (pissed and fell over) or **PADE** (pissed and denies everything). Years ago, as the GP and comedian Phil Hammond relates, some were truly pejorative. In the days when patients weren't allowed to read their notes, you might have come across an **OAP** (over-anxious parent), a **SIG** (stroppy, ignorant git), or a **GROLIE** (*Guardian* reader of limited intelligence in ethnic skirt). Such intra-professional jargon would be unthinkable today, as would the letter from a consultant in Bristol who wrote to a referring GP about a patient on whom he had tried and failed to perform a D & C, because she was so large. 'I regret that I'm unable to perform this procedure without the aid of a miner's lamp and a canary.' You can still find traces of fattism and sexism in corners of today's NHS:

any obese patient may run the risk of being privately called a **DTS**: danger to shipping.

Hammond concludes 'These are probably just reflections of the anti-holistic tendency some doctors have to reduce people into labels for ease of intellectual or emotional processing. Or perhaps it's just for a laugh. Either way, they don't sound nearly as funny when they're read out in court.'

Today, quite apart from the fact that patients now have access to their files, such slang is considered unethical, and the omnipresent threat of being sued means its use in hospitals and surgeries is decreasing – publicly, at least. It's still alive in the medical labs and staff tea rooms where patients never tread. Junior doctors and medical students are especially fond of them, not least because they raise a smile at the end of an appallingly long shift. Many patients can see the joke too – not for nothing is 'Doctor Doctor' one of the earliest comedy formulae we learn. Laughter is the best medicine, as they say – backed up by good provisions of blood. When George Best received many transfusions during his liver transplant, he declared: 'I was in for ten hours and had forty pints, beating my previous record by twenty minutes.'

In Joseph Heller's *Catch-22*, we read of Hungry Joe, who 'collected lists of fatal diseases and arranged them in alphabetical order so that he could put his finger without delay on any one he wanted to worry about'. Today that list is spiralling out of control and Dr Google is a frequent visitor to the GP's surgery. Where once there was the medical section of *Pears Cyclopedia*, there sits today a vast reservoir of information and misinformation, and 'hypogooglechondria' accounts for a daily host of worried faces in the waiting room. There are linguistic consequences, too: patients have scaled the wall, and are now in possession of a terrifying arsenal of medical terminology. It's hardly surprising then that, both in surgery and on the ward, the roster of codes designed to elude them keeps on growing.

The diagnosis

For every obliging patient, there are two cantankerous ones. This might explain the hundreds of acronyms for patient types, of which the following is just a smattering. Alcohol is as frequent a theme as it is in A&E. Many are used self-consciously and for a laugh and, as such, are not always kept behind the nurse's screen.

acute pneumoencephalopathy: an airhead.

AHF: Acute Hissy Fit.

AOB: Alcohol On Board.

154: bloodstained urine.

brothel sprouts: genital warts.

DFKDFC: Don't f***ing know, don't f***ing care.

Eiffel Syndrome: a patient with a foreign object in the rectum, i.e. 'I fell on . . .'.

grapes: haemorrhoids (also known as **speed bumps**).

peek and shriek: the result of a patient being opened up surgically only to reveal an incurable condition, whereupon they are immediately closed up again.

PFO: Pissed and Fell Over.

Smurf sign: a patient who goes blue.

spots and dots: the traditional set of childhood diseases – measles, mumps, and chicken pox.

UBI: Unexplained Beer Injury.

VIP: Very Intoxicated Person.

Plumbii pendulosus: swinging the lead (malingering). This has apparently been seen on medical certificates presented in court.

The people

bloodsucker: a member of the medical team that takes blood samples.

bonehead: an orthopaedist, otherwise known as an **orthopod**.

cock doc: a urologist or sexual disease doctor, also nicknamed **pecker checker**.

fanny mechanic: a gynaecologist.

Freud squad: the psychiatrists.

gasser: an anaesthetist.

Lancelot: one who drains abscesses (known in the US as a **Pokemon**).

NFB: Normal For Banbury.

rear admiral: a proctologist.

shadow gazer: a radiologist.

sieve: a doctor who admits almost every patient they see.

bones and groans: the general ward.

pit: the emergency room.

scrape and staple: the burns unit.

stream team: the urology department.

ECU: Eternal Care Unit, i.e. heaven.

Ward X: the morgue.

The treatment

digging for worms: varicose vein surgery.

finger wave: a rectal exam.

digitate: to explore the anal cavity.

eating in: intravenous feeding.

gone camping: a patient in an oxygen tent.

trauma handshake: a digital rectal examination (every major trauma patient gets one).

bury the hatchet: to accidentally leave a surgical instrument inside a patient.

house red: blood.

saddles: maternity sanitary towels, so called both for their size and the bow-legged walk that results from wearing them.

celestial discharge: the patient has died.

Q-sign positive: the patient is dead. The term is said to refer to the shape of the letter Q and its similarity to a face with a tongue hanging out.

PHOENIX MEN AND WOMEN

FIREFIGHTERS

In the New York of the early 1800s, firefighting, still in its infancy, was something of a spectator sport. Enthusiasts would follow the fire engines to the scenes of major blazes in order to be able to witness them at work. These were the 'buffs', the unofficial experts in the profession named after the thick buffalo-skin coats they wore against the icy New York winters. Film, word, and all other buffs owe their label to them.

The earliest term for a firefighter, at least in Britain, was a 'waterman'. Since then, those in the profession have been variously known as 'fire quenchers', 'Phoenix-men', 'pompiers' and 'sapper-pumpers'. 'Fireman', recorded from 1800, is the only label to endure to this day, although the American and gender-neutral 'firefighter' is fast gaining ground.

Like the name, there is much in firefighting that has remained constant for centuries. There's water, for a start, still the number one choice for tackling any major fire. But before any hoses are pointed, the new recruits must quickly know the drill, including how to navigate that unofficial emblem of the fire service, the 'fireman's pole'. Getting up, dressed, and out in a matter of seconds takes months to perfect.

For a new firefighter, acclimatizing to the shift patterns of their **watch** (their station crew), as well as the equipment and the adrenaline rushes, can be a challenge. But it isn't all high-octane drama in the fire service. In fact, for inner-city fire crews especially, many days are punctuated by **AFAs** – Automatic Fire Alarms – the kind found in schools, hospitals, old people's homes, and other large public buildings, and which are set off frequently, by burnt toast, builders' dust, cigarettes, a fault in the system, or a prank. A far cry from the stereotypical kitten-from-tree rescue, these calls often require no more than locating the source, checking the surrounding area, and resetting the alarm.

There is (a) little love lost between firefighters and others in the emergency services. Nicknames for those in the London Fire Brigade are numerous, and include Trumpton, Water Fairies, Pet Rescue, London's Finest Burglars, Drip Stands, and The Borg. That said, the respect they command for their work is never in doubt, either from the public or their colleagues on the ground.

The people

gaffer: the fire chief.

trialman: the new guy. Also called a **probie**, a **subbie**, or a **Womble**.

pipeman: the firefighter on the engine who carries the water-pipes into the fire.

messman: the fireman who buys and cooks the food.

skater: a lazy firefighter who does the bare minimum at the firehouse.

doorway dancer: a firefighter who always manages to have a problem with their air mask or equipment before they enter a burning building.

yard breather: a firefighter who masks up and breathes air from their air packs before they are even close to the actual fire.

Control: the team who answer emergency calls and who direct fire crews from one incident to another.

spark: a fire buff.

The dogs

hooky: an urban search and rescue dog.

Ben: a fire investigation dog.

The equipment

appliance: the fire engine.

set: breathing equipment, as in 'put a set on'.

pipe: the hose, also called **the line**.

nob: the nozzle of the fire hose.

bone box: an ambulance. If you're assigned to the ambulance you are **riding the bone**.

On the job

standby: when someone from another station comes to cover sickness where another fire crew is understaffed, as in 'I'm going on standby', but also 'Hello, I'm the standby'.

Js: when a firefighter is off work due to an injury, e.g. 'he went off on Js'.

stretching: responding to a fire (and thereby stretching the water hoses).

off the run: of an engine, waiting for repairs.

put the bells down: to sound the alarm for a call.

goer: a well-established fire.

running call: one in which the crew is flagged down en route to another incident.

informative: a message giving Control the status of a fire once the attending fire engine arrives.

Stop message: sent to Control if the fire crew are no longer required because another team already has the fire under control.

The calls

bells go down: the term for a fire call, still used even though there are no bells. To be **on the bell** is to be out on a call.

make up: a call for assistance.

persons report: a call indicating that there are people in the building.

mickey: a prank call.

jumper: a person threatening to commit suicide by jumping from a building.

stiff: a dead body.

a shout: a job, also known as a **call**, e.g. 'We were out on a shout'.

CHAOS: Chief Has Arrived On Scene.

BLUE WAVES AND FREQUENT FLYERS

PARAMEDICS

The 'para' in 'paramedic' refers both to their provision of auxiliary medical care and to their original mode of transport, when medics would be dropped from the skies in order to give emergency medical aid on the ground. Today's paramedics are more likely to ride in a **truck** (ambulance) or an **FRU** turbo (fast response unit vehicle) than a parachute, but their mission remains the same: to be the first to an incident and to provide the fastest access to life-saving equipment and skills.

Unlike doctors, most of those involved in the medical emergency services did not answer a vocation. Helping others is the reason most gave me for joining, but beyond that, as one fast responder puts it: 'No one seems to know why they become a paramedic – they just do.' Older veterans will joke that student paramedics are seduced by the idea of a rock-and-roll life of drugs, women, and fast cars – when what they actually get is drug deaths, elderly women, and stripy Volvos.

Recruits come from wildly different backgrounds: at any training course you might find policemen, ex-kick-boxing champions, car mechanics, estate agents, mountaineers, and backpackers. Vocation or not, most of them love their jobs. This is in spite of many reasons not to: each day produces fewer than twenty per cent 'real' calls. The rest are either false alarms or non-emergencies.

It's that twenty per cent that creates the addiction. The euphoria that comes from cheating death, bringing someone back from cardiac arrest, or delivering a baby in the nick of time never pales. Ask a paramedic about the very best part of their jobs, and you'll hear responses like these: 'getting a sick patient to hospital with all the correct treatment and no delays, like a pro team delivering their baton to a runner on a 400-metre relay'; and 'having medics and technicians work together in the silent knowledge that this will save someone's life'.

Topping the job satisfaction list, however, comes something more unexpected: the crowning achievement of a paramedic's day seems to be the successful squeezing of a cannula into a difficult vein – especially if they've managed to make it look like the easiest thing in the world.

Sometimes the peril is less immediate, but the stakes just as high: helping an elderly patient who's fallen down and can't get up, easing them back into their favourite chair, making them some tea and toast and chatting to them for a while – this is the stuff that makes a paramedic's day.

The bad parts of the job are obvious – and death always tops the list. While its frequency inevitably brings some degree of distance, emotion is never far from the surface. 'It's the backstory that gets you,' one fast responder tells me, 'when you have the family and loved ones screaming a genuine, soul-wrenching wail that rips right through you as the bottom drops out of their world.'

To counter this, the black humour of the emergency services is as necessary as it is legendary. The release valve that takes the paramedic away from death, pain, and suffering is triggered by a searing and butcheringly un-PC postmortem of the emergency they've just dealt with. When faced with the unimaginable followed by an immediate mountain of paperwork, they'll tell you they have little choice but to laugh and move on.

This is of course kept well away from the patients. For those they treat, the paramedics reserve a special kind of banter, reflecting the fact that they are unique in being invited into the lives and homes of others. A paramedic sees us at our lowest point, when we have no choice but to place all our trust in another human being. The best, if not the only, way to deal with it is with a bit of cheeky humour, particularly since laughter has been proven to promote self-healing (hence the popularity of India's 'laughter clubs').

As for the banter itself, you need to be there, and in pain, to appreciate it fully. One classic example runs something like:

PARAMEDIC: So, where does it hurt?
PATIENT: All over my head.

PARAMEDIC: Does your face hurt?
PATIENT: No, why?
PARAMEDIC: Cos it's killing me haha.

Of course there's the inside humour too: the secret codes under-stood only by the initiated – like **There We Are Then**, delivered as an apparently harmless response to a reproach from a patient or (more usually) upper management. Take the first letter of each of those words and you'll have the real message the paramedics are exchanging.

For ambulance crews and solo responders, a primary goal is getting through a twelve-hour shift. This means that the day or night will often revolve around caffeine, which in turn means choosing **RVPs** (rendezvous points) located near sources of good, strong coffee. Some crews prefer to stay closer to their station, while bolder ones enjoy mad magical mystery tours just to see how far away from base (**the complex**) they can get. Wherever they go, a lot of their day will be spent in their own linguistic world.

The crew

attender: there are normally two people on an ambulance during each shift – one drives whilst the other **attends**, i.e. talks to the patient, diagnoses them, decides on treatment, and later writes up the paperwork.

HEMS: Helicopter Emergency Medical Service, who deal with extreme trauma cases; they may also operate from a fast car. The team consists of an emergency doctor and advanced paramedics with superior clinical skills. HEMS workers are distinguishable by their (often ill-fitting) bright orange jumpsuits.

technician: a crew member that hasn't yet acquired the skills of a paramedic. An ambulance will normally consist of two emergency technicians or a technician and a medic.

trauma magnet: a crew mate who somehow attracts all the nasty jobs involving traumatic injury or death. As one paramedic put it: 'If you looked at them through fourth-dimension glasses I'm sure you'd see them in a dark hooded cloak with a scythe.'

Central Ops: the solo paramedics, part of the Fast Response Unit in the Volvo estate ambulance cars. Take a close look at their back seats, and you'll see they are equipped for something serious. The primary training of Central Ops is all about Marauding Terrorist Firearms Attacks (**MTFA**). This is the preparation for entering dangerous situations or **warm zones** wearing ballistic armour, with the aim of triaging and treating mass casualties.

The patients

DSS: 'Dying Swan Syndrome'. Used to describe patients whose acting skills are worthy of any B-rated sitcom.

EtOH: In medical terms this means 'ethanol'. In paramedic terms it means 'patient been drinking alcohol', so that a patient's notes might read 'PFO, ?EtOH' (Patient Fell Over, query pissed?).

frequent flyer: a regular caller of the emergency services, of which there are many; nonetheless, a crew must attend every time.

. . . and the rest of us

surfing the blue wave: tailgating an ambulance or other emergency services vehicle in order to take advantage of the clear traffic.

How to save a life

bagging: using a manual resuscitator or self-inflating bag on a patient.

LifePak: a machine that does everything, including measuring blood pressure (BPs) and oxygen levels in the blood (Sats), and taking an ECG.

GCS: Glasgow Coma Scale. The GCS of a patient determines how compos mentis they are. Scored out of fifteen, it charts the reaction of eyes, and verbal and motor skills. If the patient scores one in each they are GCS 3, suggesting a coma (including the alcoholically induced kind). At the other end, a score of GCS 15 is good.

blue call: in a medical emergency the crew will **blue** the patient into the relevant hospital, radioing ahead to ensure the hospital is ready for the truck's arrival. The slower you see an ambulance driving on blue lights, the worse the patient's condition is likely to be: e.g. a shooting victim with a bullet just touching the main artery from the heart. In this case, the paramedics 'take it very slow and steady, and leave it to the junior doctors to kill the patient'.

Death

Death is an inevitable preoccupation for a paramedic. But even the final act is far from black and white: the *degree* of death is also a matter of importance (and curiosity). The term **Purple + –** denotes a patient who is dead, and has been for a while. The more '+' marks you add, the more 'clearly' they are dead. The code is accompanied by such surreal conversations as:

Are they dead?
Yes.
Proper dead?
Yep. Dead dead.
Oh. Dead then.
Yes.

THE CREMAINS OF THE DAY

UNDERTAKERS

The first myth to be dispelled about a funeral director's life is that it's punctuated by sobriety and silence. In fact, for a career that has death at its core, there's also a surprising amount of laughter. Not just the black, tension-relieving kind, echoed elsewhere in the medical professions, but honest, on-the-level humour too. A favourite undertaker joke? 'A woman walks into a funeral parlour, and the man behind the counter asks, "Madam, why the long face?"'

The language used directly to the bereaved, of course, is famously steeped in euphemism. It never used to be that way. In the past, shorter life expectancies and the relative normality of death meant that there was little need for verbal tiptoeing. In fact, many in the Middle Ages were positively obsessed with death, revelling in graphic portrayals of dying and happily consuming manuals that educated their readers on how to go in a graceful and proper manner. Nursery rhymes of the time were packed full of black allusions to dying, telling tales such as 'Who Killed Cock Robin?' ('"Who caught his blood?" "I," said the fish, "With my little dish, I caught his blood"') and, most famously, 'Ring a Ring o' Roses' ('A-tishoo! A-tishoo! We all fall down'), said to refer to the black plague.

Today things look very different, and the undertaker can draw on a lexicon as softly focused as any estate agent's. As one wryly told me: 'We deodorize death to within an inch of its life.' No longer does someone die and be laid out in a coffin, or taken to a cemetery and cremated: instead they **pass away** or **depart**, are placed in a **burial container**, visited in the **slumber room**, transported to the **garden of remembrance**, and **interred in their final resting place.**

The fundamental aim of such terms, of course, is a caring concern for the 'clients'. In fact, the job of undertaker was once listed under the heading of 'caring professions'. A good undertaker, I'm told, will happily give hugs as well as advice. But they occasionally have to dish out warnings too. Alongside Christmas, moving house and divorce, a funeral is one of the biggest causes of family tensions going. That tension, inevitably, may revolve around money. Every undertaker you'll ever meet can tell you stories of barneys and fisticuffs during a service, and some of them are hilarious (for everyone else).

When it comes to caskets/coffins/wooden overcoats, there is a dazzling array of options: from biodegradable to metallic-lined. None but the wackiest, just to make clear, are equipped with bells should the unthinkable happen, despite the myth that such practices lurk behind the idiom 'saved by the bell'. Customization is possible too: whether it be football-flagged, *Star Trek* themed or hot-rodded to look like a Model A Ford. Legend has it that some coffins even set off a firework display in the furnaces – giving 'going out with a bang' a whole new meaning.

Death by any other name

Unsurprisingly, death goes by many names when undertakers are alone. This is where gallows humour abounds.

bag it: to die.

boxed: placed in a coffin; dead. To be **boxed on the table** is to die during surgery in a hospital.

deep six: a burial at sea; a probable reference to the fact that sea interments must take place in depths of six fathoms of water or more.

glue factory: death. The allusion is to old horses whose hooves were often rendered into glue after death.

cremains: a much-derided blend of 'cremated remains'.

O-sign: when a patient shows the 'O-sign' they are well and truly dead, probably with their mouth hanging open to form an 'O'. The **Q-sign** has the same idea, but this time the tongue is also hanging out.

thirty: dead. Said to come from the journalistic practice of appending the number 30 on articles to signify the end of the piece.

The cemetery

black north: the unconsecrated ground where suicides and murderers were once buried, traditionally to the north of the church.

bone factory or **bone orchard**: the cemetery.

Death Hilton: a large mausoleum where memorials can reach significant heights.

The dismal trade: embalming

beautiful memory picture: a photo of an embalmed body displayed in an expensive casket.

dismal trade: the undertaking/embalming profession.

customer: a corpse. Also known as **Mr** or **Mrs Z**.

purge: bodily fluids that are drained and discarded prior to embalming.

belly-puncher: a mortician who practises cavity embalming. The method involves releasing the gases trapped inside the stomach and introducing chemicals such as formaldehyde. The term is an unflattering epithet used by those who prefer arterial embalming.

throat-slasher: the belly-puncher's revenge nickname for an embalmer who practises arterial embalming, in which the body is drained of all fluids and then injected, through the neck and other points, with preservatives.

Coffins and cadavers

coach: undertaker-speak for a hearse.

corpse-cooled: describing a corpse kept cool in an ice compartment.

eternity box: a coffin.

furniture: a collective noun for coffins. Coffins were once made by craftsmen who worked in wood and also made other items of furniture.

meat wagon: an ambulance or a hearse.

nose-squeezer: a flat-topped coffin.

tree suit/wooden overcoat: a wooden coffin.

black tie affair: a funeral.

corpsicle: a body that is cryogenically frozen in the hope of future revivification.

pickles: cadavers. Said to be used by medical schools to camouflage the true content of body boxes.

potted/planted: enclosed in a coffin or urn.

The staff

bier baron: the owner of a funeral parlour, especially one who makes a good profit.

Doctor of grief: a mortician, or a grief counsellor.

Mr Post: a mortuary attendant. Used by hospitals to page the mortuary when a body needs to be removed from a room.

7

The Armed Forces

'As for being a General, well, at the age of four with paper hats
and wooden swords we're all Generals. Only some of us never
grow out of it.'
Peter Ustinov

'Camouflage' first meant a 'puff of smoke', blown into the
eyes of the enemy. It's an image that suits the vocabularies of
the armed forces very well. Honed in the mess hall and on
the battlefield, the slanguage of the armed forces is one that
few civvies can understand. Littered with opaque references
and punctuated by thick, coarse expletives (profanities account
for roughly a third of all words spoken), each of the forces
has its own fiercely protected lexicon, in which the most
colourful lingo is tinged more with humour than concerns of
life and death.

This humour is still a private one. Not all outsiders are the
enemy, but much of what our soldiers, sailors, and RAF pilots
say and do is not for public viewing. It would be hard to find a
community for whom codes are more important, nor such a way
of life.

The first codes are the operational ones. Secrecy has always
been essential to military endeavour, and ciphers require
sophisticated code-breaking by the enemy. During the US
army's Pacific Island campaigns in the Second World War,
Native Americans would employ their own tribal languages
such as Choctaw and Navajo to communicate top-secret

information without Japanese intervention. Codes like these only catch a glimpse of daylight when campaigns are completed.

Then there is the professional side of things, which operates as a speedy and expedient shorthand. Black humour and euphemism flow through it, providing a distancing from horror and giving a respectability to the otherwise unspeakable. In the US army, 'meat-eaters' are the Special Forces soldiers whose mission depends on violence rather than the establishing of peace; a 'kinetic' area is one that sees a lot of heavy fighting, and 'tactical retrograde' is military-speak for a retreat.

Alongside such veiled language are the more open exchanges of the barracks, the subs, and the air. They are no less tribal, and few are completely transparent to the rest of us. But they revolve around daily life, amongst the 'desert lilies' or before 'pit practice', or while sipping a 'bubbly and black' in the pub. This is the banter of the team, and it's integral as much to morale as it is to operations. Any officer or commander will tell you that swapping code is the most telling marker of a team. And team spirit and cohesion are seldom more important than in the military.

It's tempting for outsiders to view the 'Armed Forces' as one big family of happily co-existing soldiers. It's probably no big surprise, however, that the Army, Navy, Air Force, and Marines are fiercely protective of their individual identities, and that mockery (mostly gentle, occasionally not) between each party is standard. Explanations for each force's names are as old as the hills: for the Marines, 'Army' stands for 'Ain't Ready to be Marines Yet', while the revenge acronym for the Marines goes something like 'Muscles Are Required, Intelligence Not Essential'.

TOFFEE WRAPPERS AND FULL SCREWS

SOLDIERS

Military slang is nothing new. Britain's soldiers have always been immersed in a counterculture, in which language plays an important role. Even in the eighteenth century, men in uniform were renowned for their swearing habits, a fact that's borne out by the literature of the time: not for nothing do we use the phrase 'swear like a trooper', an idea first mooted in Samuel Richardson's novel *Pamela*. The chronicler of the language of London highwaymen, card sharps, prostitutes, and cutpurses, Captain Francis Grose, proudly named soldiers as one of the 'most classical authorities' in the preface to his *Classical Dictionary of the Vulgar Tongue*. By authorities Grose meant those wise in expressions like 'betwattled' (confused or bewildered), 'hopper-arsed' (having particularly large buttocks), and 'lobcock' ('relaxed penis', and thus a dull and lethargic man). Having served in the army himself, Grose had first-hand knowledge of military slang. His dictionary referred to terms such as to 'hug Brown Bess', meaning 'to carry a firelock, or serve as a private soldier'; a 'fogey', an invalid soldier; and 'Act of Parliament', a military term for small beer, five pints of which a landlord was obliged by an act of parliament to give to each soldier.

During the two World Wars of the twentieth century, military slang had a profound impact on the English language. This was the first time that civilians – highly literate ones – had been thrown in with the armed forces, and the plethora of words and phrases that emerged from this melting pot were largely a result of the new recruits struggling to come to terms with their strange and horrifying environment. Among the list of everyday terms that originated or spread from the conflict are 'cushy', 'snapshot', 'bloke', 'wash out', 'conk out', 'blind spot', and 'binge drink', while the many euphemisms for death include 'pushing up daisies', 'gone west', 'snuffed it', 'been skittled', and 'become a landowner'. If you're ever feeling 'washed out', 'fed up', or downright 'lousy', then the First World War is also to blame. For all their destruction, wars are surprisingly productive when it comes to language.

If most wars are defined by the slang they produce, then Afghanistan was no exception. The terms that emerged from this twenty-first-century war say as much about British culture as they do about conflict; the main base of Bastion in Helmand is nicknamed **Butlins** thanks to its relative luxuries and facilities (including mess halls, shops, showers, and a Pizza Hut). The Afghanistan war also produced the **Ally**, a battlefield fashionista, the criteria for which apparently involve sporting a no-nonsense beard or significant amounts of tattoos. Special Forces are automatically Ally.

The members

Put simply, the Army is the part of a country's force that is equipped to fight on land. Within it are more than 200 roles, from chaplain and musician to armoured gunners, dental nurses, and household cavalry officers. Of course, they each have a nickname. **Pongo** was once a forces-wide term for a member of the army, and can occasionally still be heard among members of the Royal Navy and the RAF. It may have begun in the seventeenth century as a reference to a large African gorilla (from the Congolese *mpongo*), though others suggest it originates from the nineteenth-century expression used by music hall comedians to get a cheap laugh: 'Where the army goes, the pong goes.'

The modern tribe of soldiers features the following characters:

fullscrew: a full Corporal in the Army.

grunt: an infantryman.

mod plod: a nickname for an officer in the Ministry of Defence Police.

club swinger: the PE trainer.

fang farrier: a dentist.

pusser's issue: a label for any equipment issued by the Service, a corruption of the word 'purser'. Anything done unimaginatively or 'by the book' is done in a **pusser's' manner**, while **pusser's planks** are military skis, and **pusser's hard** is forces-issue soap.

Razzman: a Regimental Sergeant Major.

sneaky-beaky: a member of the Special Forces.

scab-lifter: the medic.

sky pilot: the padre or chaplain.

sprog: a new recruit or someone new to a unit.

terp: an interpreter.

Tom: a young soldier. Also known as a squaddie who **bleeds green**.

wedge: a Royal Engineer. Also known as a **chunkie, field Mouse, field Squeak,** or **toffee wrapper**.

fobbit: a service member who never crosses the perimeter of the forward operating base (or FOB).

fetch: a dog handler.

These are as nothing compared with the individual nicknames given to each soldier: usually a riff on their own name, their personality or their appearance. Smudger, Tommo, Ginge, and Tenko feature quite often, as do **leatherman** (colleagues found him a complete tool); **Del Monte** (always says yes, even to the most unappealing tasks); **thrombo** (a slow-moving clot); and **wings** (a soldier who's always flapping).

Taking it on the chinstrap: daily life

Life in the forces is inevitably very regimented. It also operates at extremes, with preparation and waiting at one hand and full conflict at the other, encapsulated perhaps in the standard Army saying: **hurry up and wait**. Waiting might involve lots of tea, and hence frequent mentions of **jack**: a special term of contempt reserved for those who are looking out for themselves and not their mates. Applied to any number of things, the most heinous crime is the **jack brew**: making yourself a cuppa without making one for anyone else, especially on a cold and wet exercise.

In terms of duty, **GROPE** is Ground Operational Exercise, **stagging on** is guard duty, **yomping** is marching with a heavy load, and **gravel bashing** is marching around a parade square. All training is accompanied by an officer's individual repertoire of 'motivational' shouts. These may vary from 'That's not a stream, that's cover. Now get in it!', 'Swing that arm or I'll rip it off and beat you over the head with the soggy end' and (this one reported by many soldiers) 'It's mind over matter; we don't mind and you don't matter.'

bone: used to describe a thankless task, such as ironing combats. Also known as a **lick-out**.

chin-strapped: utterly exhausted.

desert lily: a urinal made from a tin can or any available object.

scratcher: an Army term for a place to sleep while out in the field, probably in a **maggot** (a sleeping bag).

buckshee: kit and equipment that is 'off the record' and traded away from the Quartermaster's official storeroom. It is an alteration of the word 'baksheesh'.

harry hotters: extremely hot (plain hot is known as being **redders**).

jankers: the official term for a charge or restriction of privi-
leges as a result of a breach of discipline. It may be an
imitation of the sound of jangling handcuffs or prison
chains.

hoofing: a Marine term for something excellent. The opposite
adjective for something bad or annoying is **threaders**.

HTEA: the boring task of 'having to explain acronyms' (from
the BBC sitcom *Bluestone 42*).

brag-rags: medal ribbons.

gong: a campaign medal. A '**rooty gong**' is an old term for a
long-service medal.

Stuffing Frank down your Gregory

The word 'mess', used for the groups within an army unit or
ship's company who eat together, may seem to civvies an odd
choice for the serving of food. Certainly the officers' mess came
first, building on the original meaning of a portion of food (in
Scotland, shopping is still called 'messages'). The idea of an
unappetizing concoction of different foods emerged in the 1800s,
some time after it had become established in the miltary – those
in the forces may draw their own conclusions. The long-standing
terms for their food are **MRE** (officially 'Meals Ready to Eat',
but alternatively known as 'Meals Refused by Everyone'),
mysteries, and **the three lies** (they aren't meals, they aren't
ready, and they definitely aren't edible). Times may be changing,
however: these days, the mess is more likely to be called the
DFAC (Dining FACility), and within it a new kind of military
cuisine is emerging, one in which soldiers are the 'customers'
and rations come with a small bottle of Tabasco, after it was
realized that most soldiers were carrying around their own bottles
in order to pep up their food. Slowly, it seems, the Army's chefs
are feeding morale as well as stomachs; but as the list of 'scran'

and 'scoff' below suggests, they have some way to go before the slanguage of the canteen catches up.

wet: a Marine term for a cup of tea.
battery acid: coffee.
army strawberries: prunes.
cackleberries: eggs.
desecrated veg: dried (desiccated) vegetables.
Gregory: throat (from the rhyming slang Gregory Peck – neck).
slopjockey: the chef.
scran: the Marines' term for food from the kitchen or 'galley'.
scoff: food from the Army cookhouse.
yaffle: to eat; **yaffling spanners** are cutlery.
canteen medals: food stains on a uniform.

The business end

Sometimes speed, not colour, is of the essence, which is why much of a soldier's crucial communication when gearing up for combat is made via acronyms. So the **tock** (TOC) is the tactical operations centre where command elements are located, the **tip-fiddle** is a time-phased deployment list (the blueprint of a military campaign), and an **RPG** is a rocket-propelled grenade.

Every territory of war has a name amongst the troops. Iraq, for example, became known as **The Sandbox**, and Afghanistan as **The Sandpit**. They are home to the **GWOT**: Global War on Terrorism.

There are of course words that are never to be taken lightly, such as **Contact, wait out**: a command that, as one soldier describes it, 'we fear and dream of saying in equal measure'. This is the first communication a soldier must give when engaged by the enemy. **Cleared hot**, meanwhile, means permission to fire your weapon.

PID: positive identification of an enemy.

INS: an insurgent.

KLE: a key leader engagement, one in which a meaningful dialogue is initiated with the key figures of the local community.

atmospherics: the vibe on the ground.

drills and skills: a general shout of encouragement to soldiers to remember their training and expertise.

Dust-One/Wun: a code denoting a missing soldier that stands for 'Duty Status: Whereabouts Unknown'.

Mark One Eyeball: signifying the use of unaided vision to spot something.

battle rattle: the full monty in terms of protective clothing and equipment, including flak vest, Kevlar helmet, and a vest holding ceramic plates to protect the soldier's heart and lungs, itself known as a **sappy** ('small arms protective insert').

mouseholing: blowing an entry hole in a wall of an enemy building rather than entering via a potentially booby-trapped door.

shake and bake: an attack that uses a combination of different bombs.

spin the dit: the retelling (often with a few embellishments) of the battle once it's over.

G-PANTS AND GROWBAGS

AIRMEN AND WOMEN

It would be hard to find a profession with more groups and subgroups than the RAF. From communication to weapons, engineering to logistics, right down to each individual flying squadron, each unit has a distinct identity and, to express it, a closed vocabulary. The fighter pilot's jargon of air-to-air combat is largely impenetrable even to bomber pilots, despite both groups sharing the generic language of fast-jet flying. For each, tribal language is an affirmation of community: a shared commodity that has more value than you might think. As any Flight Commander will tell you, the happier the crew, the more banter they share: it's a vital thermostat for measuring the team's esprit de corps.

References exchanged are usually part of a shared experience, and so a team's language will change as its experiences change. Those who shared duty in the Falklands will still talk about having a **bimble** (a wander around) and of being **bennied** (delayed on duty when due to go home – taken from the irreverent nickname for Falkland Islanders, the 'Bennies'). Rites of passage add further cohesion. When a pilot has achieved combat-ready status, they are permitted to wear the squadron's crest on their shoulder: the badge of being prepared for war. So inextricable is the crest from the identity and spirit of the team that the day a pilot leaves the squadron and relinquishes their command is the day they take their crest off. Years ago, the recipient of the honour was expected to drink a yard of ale – a tradition that health and safety rules have firmly stifled. Champagne is still acceptable though: after 1,000 hours on a fighter aircraft, a pilot will taxi in to the applause of family and friends, and be greeted with a glass or two of fizz. They will also quite possibly be thrown into the nearest available water source.

All of this is preparation for the real thing. Pilots yearn for active duty: to them, not going on operations is like never getting picked for the football team. As a result there is a good degree of disrespect, acknowledged or otherwise, for those who have passed up the opportunity to fight – a team member's standing and credibility is intimately linked with their operational experience. Besides, the spirit of **FOMO** (fear of missing out) is strong in the RAF.

Do the **crabs** swear as much as soldiers? Not really. But that isn't to say that expletives never colour the air: everywhere in the armed forces, **talking a blue streak** is far more evident than in civvy street.

As for inter-force rivalry, when members of the Army, Air Force and Navy used to get together, it was, they'll tell you, a little like the school disco. It took a while, or a lot of alcohol, to break the ice. These days, the forces are far more integrated and, teasing nicknames (like **fishheads**) and media hype apart, they share a healthy degree of respect. Similarly, any rivalry or resentment you might expect to find between commercial and RAF pilots would be hard to find. Many in the Air Force take the commercial route on leaving service. Besides, as Squadron and Flight Commanders will tell you, both groups accept that military pilots are, by necessity, *much* better in the air.

Personnel

auggies (pronounced 'oggies'): auxiliary members of the RAF. Also known as **weekend warriors**.

liney: an aircraft mechanic.

duty-dog: an orderly officer.

fang farrier: a dentist.

conehead: a student. Also known as a **nurkin**.

nugget: a pilot on their first tour.

blunties: non-flying personnel. Those who aren't at the 'sharp end'.

hog dangler: an RAF police dog handler. Also known as a **poodle-pusher**.

body-snatcher: a stretcher bearer.

brain on a chain: an RAF police dog, with the implication that they are more intelligent than their handlers.

god-botherer: the chaplain. Otherwise known as the **sky pilot**.

scuffer: member of the RAF police.

ginger beer: an engineer.

shiny: an administrative employee, said to wear trousers with 'shiny' seats from sitting down so long.

SqIntO (pronounced 'squint-o'): a Squadron Intelligence Officer.

Tiffy: a Typhoon jet-fighter.

tin-basher: an airframe-fitter.

Zobbit: a commissioned officer, especially a self-important one. Possibly derived from the Arabic *dhabit*, 'officer'.

The planes

Double Ugly: an F-4 Phantom.

Turkey: the F-14 Tomcat.

Warthog: the A-10 Thunderbolt II.

Albert (or **Fat Albert**): a C-5 Galaxy.

bogey: an unidentified and potentially hostile aircraft.

lame duck: a damaged aircraft. In US parlance, it is a **wounded bird**.

The equipment

grow-bag: a flight suit or anti-exposure suit, named after the fertilizer sack because of the untidy appearance of flying suits to the eye of the non-aircrew fraternity.

G-pants: nylon trousers that wrap around the legs and abdomen and fill automatically with compressed air in high-G manoeuvres. The aim is to prevent the pooling of blood in the lower extremities and thus reduce the risk of unconsciousness. Known outside the RAF as **speed jeans**.

bat-decoder: a document carried on all flight ops that provides the key to current airborne communication codes.

housewife: an essential sewing kit.

Mae West: a life vest which inflates if the wearer falls into the sea, named after the 'curvy' actress of the 1930s and 40s.

scrambled egg: gold braid on an officer's cap.

shreddies: male underwear.

shufti-scope: a torch.

air raid: a haircut.

thunderbox: a chemical toilet, or any form of field toilet requiring emptying.

The day

jankers: punishment for a minor offence.

pit time: time spent in bed; **pit practice** is taking a nap.

bull: anything related to cleaning, polishing etc. **Bull night** is the weekly clean of the barrack blocks.

dhobi: laundry, washing. **Dhobi-dust** is washing powder.

Mother: the ship on which a flight squadron is based. **Father** is the tacan (navigational aid system) on board a ship. The joke is that there is a father on most mothers.

NATO standard: taking your tea or coffee with milk and sugar, and the usual response to 'How do you want it?'.

Radio communications

Bravo Zulu: a task well performed.

Charlie Foxtrot: 'cluster-f★★k'.

Boola-Boola: the radio call made when a pilot shoots down a drone.

Delta Sierra: 'dumb shit'; describing a stupid action.

FM: 'f★★★ing magic'; very high-tech – used to describe how something you don't understand actually works.

Judy: a radio call signalling that your quarry is in sight and you are taking control of the intercept.

Sierra Hotel: 'shit hot', the pilot's favourite and all-purpose expression of approval.

Tango Uniform: 'tits up'; broken, not functioning.

Cold Nose: radar turned off (Navy pilots transmit 'My nose is cold' before refuelling from Air Force tankers). Also known as **Lights out**.

Zero-Dark-Thirty: a half-hour after midnight, used for operations after midnight or before sunrise.

Say your state: used to ask a pilot how much fuel their plane still has (its **state**). The response is given in hours and minutes until **splash**.

bingo: the minimum fuel required for a safe return to base. Aircraft may fly beyond bingo fuel in combat situations, but at considerable risk.

Goo and gardening: up in the air

clampers: weather unfit for flying. Also described as **dud**.

ginners: as clear as gin; used of a cloudless sky. Submariners traditionally removed diesel oil from periscope lenses with gin until they were 'gin clear'.

goo: bad weather that causes drastically reduced visibility and renders pilots **in the soup**.

angels: a plane's altitude, measured in one thousand feet. 'Angels 12', for example, means flying at 12,000 feet.

catch a packet: to be on the receiving end of offensive fire.

quick squirt: a short, sharp burst of machine-gun fire.

lose the bubble: to become confused in the air.

bat-turn: a tight, high-G change of direction; a nod to the rapid 180-degree Batmobile manoeuvre in the old *Batman* TV programmes.

bug out: to get out of a position or situation rapidly.

buster: full military power; issued as an instruction to go as fast as possible.

saddled up: to be immediately behind a target and ready to attack.

milk run: a mission with an easily accomplished target.

doing a Linda Blair (now dated): on the lookout for the enemy; an allusion to the possessed child Regan (played by Blair) in *The Exorcist* and her 360-degree head rotation.

Naturally there is also a phrase book for ejecting (**banging out** and **hitting the sail**), crashing (**bought the farm, cement poisoning**) and landing (**pancaking** and **hitting the deck**; a **daisy cutter** is a faultless touchdown).

BUBBLEHEADS AND JACKSPEAK

THE NAVY

English is awash with words and expressions from the high seas and those who patrol them, known in British slang simply as **the Andrew**. Quite who the Andrew was no one knows, though one theory is that an Andrew Miller was an over-enthusiastic officer who press-ganged civilians into going to sea during the Napoleonic wars. Alongside Andrew is **Jack**: a soubriquet that is even older and which derives from Jack Tar, the traditional matelot with a glossy black hat and a pair of canvas breeches that have been treated with high-grade tar.

To this day, one sailor can always spot another. Navy men and women will tell you that their entire frame of reference is different, and will remain that way forever. They will automatically use **gash** for rubbish, and **run ashore** if they're out for a drink. And if they're ever overloaded with work, they will talk of being **out to the deck clench**. This applies no matter which Navy they served in. The Royal and the Merchant Navy, rather than having entirely different vocabularies, tend to rely on different nuances – one retired Admiral compares it to the Spanish spoken in Spain (the Royal Navy) versus the one you'll hear in South America (the Merchant).

The new sailors coming into such lexicons are collectively known as **muppets** or **nozzers**. Older sailors have all kinds of complicated teasing rituals, sending them off to look for the billiard table or tricking them into signing up for imaginary and impossible missions, all of which succeed in proving that they don't yet have a clue about life at sea.

Over and beyond the line of duty, the two tent poles of Navy culture have long been alcohol and sex – or at least thinking and talking about sex. In fact, if you had to pick the predominant theme out of the slang exchanged across the deck, it would have to be the coupling of a **mattress mamba** with a woman's **playpen**, and that's just for starters. Euphemisms for parts of the body are more chest-wig than fig leaf. Acronyms such as **BSH** (British Standard Handfuls, a sizing index for female breasts) have long since overtaken the notorious **BURMA** ('be undressed ready my angel'), while political correctness regularly jumps out the porthole with nicknames such as **Cardiff Virgin**, sailor slang for a plate of Welsh rarebit. The encounters such terms describe might result in **catching the boat out**, and a trip to the STI clinic or **pox clerk**.

Drinking

Rations of rum have flowed through the sailor's bloodstream since records of **rumbullion** and **kill-devil** began to emerge in the 1600s. We get the term **grog** from the rum rations prescribed by Admiral Edward Vernon, nicknamed 'Old Grog' on account of his thick coat made of a coarse cloth called grogram. Vernon also introduced citrus juice into the equation, which while diluting the rum also prevented scurvy: from then on British sailors, and eventually all citizens, became known as **Limeys**. Not for nothing does the outsiders' stereotype of sailors speak of 'rum, beer, and baccy'. An **Admiral of the narrow seas**, meanwhile, is not someone any of us should care to meet: this is old Jackspeak for a drunken sailor who vomits all over his friend, while a **Vice-Admiral** of those same seas is one who pees into his companion's shoes.

Today, if a Navy man or woman orders **bubbly and black** in a pub, they're not going upmarket: bubbly is one of the many nicknames for rum – when **neaters** (there's another) is mixed with water, it foams up. Meanwhile a drop of **pusser's** (rum, again) **and sand** was the legendary cure for crabs or pubic lice, much preferred to the dreaded ointment known as 'blue unction'. The theory was that if you applied the mixture to the affected area, the lice quickly became drunk and then threw 'boulders' of sand at each other. To this day, those in the Navy are referred to as **crabs** by the other forces.

Rations of rum were finally stopped on 31 July 1970, known henceforth as **Black Tot Day**. Sailors can no longer speak of the old 'framework of hospitality' in which, as we learn from Rick Jolly in *Jackspeak*, 'two snifters equalled one wetter, two wetters (wet lips) were equivalent to one sippers, two sippers equated to one gulpers, and two gulpers equalled sandy bottoms or "grounders" – the volume of a single tot'.

Where there was rum there were inevitably all kinds of drinking games, and sailors duly produced a whole lexicon for those who couldn't hold their drink. A **pink chit** was once a formal warning to a sailor whenever he came back 'over the brow' looking worse for wear (a second warning was a **green chit**; anything more meant a firm talking to from the Boss). Today, a pink chit is generally used to mean that the 'missus' has given leave for a night out with the boys.

Sons of guns and the showing of legs: what we've taken on board

Hundreds of English idioms have hidden nautical origins. From **A1** to **the bitter end**, **piping down** to being **taken aback**, there is in the Navy a fair amount of pride in the way naval vocabulary has taken over the idioms we exchange every day. When we refer to a **slush fund**, for example, we look back to the fat residues from the salt beef rations that were once the sailors' staple: these would be skimmed off and sold onshore, after which the proceeds would be happily drunk at the local tavern. **Showing a leg**, or getting out of bed, began as an order for male shipmates (with hairy legs) to get to work, while wives and girlfriends snoozed on. Those female visitors may also be behind **son of a gun**, said to be a term for children conceived on board (perhaps beneath the gunwale) who were of uncertain paternity.

Cacklefarts or a baboon's ass: food and drink

A sailor's diet has long been held up as a poor and unappetizing one. In the 1800s, following the grisly murder of a young girl named Fanny Adams, large tins of cheap mutton became blackly known on board ship as **Fanny's**. The unfortunate girl's name eventually became slang for something so insubstantial it was worth nothing at all, and was duly shortened to sweet **FA**, even if today those initials are usually taken for something else entirely.

Adam & Eve on a raft: two eggs on toast.
Adam's ale: drinking water.
baby's head: steak and kidney pudding in a pastry cover.
baboon ass: corned beef.
cackleberry or **cacklefart**: a boiled egg.
elephant's footprints: Spam fritters; also known as **Nellie's wellies**.
floaters in the snow: sausages and mash.
car smash: tinned tomatoes and bacon. A **train smash** is a car smash with sausages.
slide: butter or margarine.
sneeze: pepper.
tits: tomatoes in tomato sauce.
Neptune's dandruff: sea salt.
nooners: a drink as the sun passes over the yardarm at midday. It can also refer to a quick trip home to see a wife or partner.

The personnel

There is no single useful and gender-neutral term for Navy personnel. Which makes things tricky when the force is so hierarchical. 'Sailor' will do for some, and if you see slanting stripes on a seaman's upper arm it's a safe bet they are one. If they are sporting chevrons, 'petty officer' might do, but if there is a **rocker** or inverted 'U' above the chevrons, you're probably looking at a Chief Petty Officer (or a Senior or Master Chief). Shoulder-boards meanwhile signal a Warrant Officer, and a simple 'Sir' or 'Ma'am' will suffice (although if a female officer is in command, she too can be referred to as Sir, especially if preceded by the words 'Aye aye').

All of these are quite apart from the **swabbie** (typically a sailor of low rank), **squid** (what members of other services call a sailor) and **jarhead** (a Marine). As for the distinct roles on board, nicknames are inevitable: once again it's all part of the tribal banter.

bish: the padre (a shortening of 'bishop'). Also known as the **sky bosun**.

bootneck: a Royal Marine Commando, one who has his **green lid** or commando beret, earned by completing an arduous training course.

bunting tosser: a signalman.

jack dusty: the accountant or storesman, formerly known as a 'Jack in the dust' as they worked in the storeroom amongst the flour and biscuits.

muscle bosun: a sailor obsessed with their physical prowess.

Bomber Queen: a member of a Polaris/Trident boat.

Bloke: the XO (Executive Chief Officer) of a large warship who is officially known as The Commander. Other nicknames include **Father** and **Number One**.

cabbage mechanic: a mocking epithet for a chef. Also once known as the **slushy**.

crumb-brusher: a steward in an officers' mess.

outside wrecker: the engineer in a submarine responsible for everything mechanical. **Inside wrecker** is the term of choice for the chef.

cuddy rat: an officer who spends too much time brown-nosing in the 'cuddy' – a cabin set aside for use by either the Captain or a visiting VIP.

nail bender: an ordnance artificer.

pinkie: an aircraft radio mechanic.

scratcher: the second coxswain on a submarine, or the Captain's clerk.

sticks: a Marine bugler.

All at sea: life on the waves

Sailors are used to 'assholes and elbows': it's an expression they frequently hear as an instruction to buckle down to work, the idea being these are the only things an officer should see when hands are scrubbing the deck. They are also all too familiar with their **ABC**s: the code for 'all been changed', and the rather resigned response to any alteration of an official plan of action (**ABCBA** means 'all been changed back again'). Daily life requires them to be **at the dip** at all times, whether in the **donkship** (engine room) or **bombhouse**, ready to take orders from the **bunhouse** (the wardroom) and its **book of words** (any manual whatsoever that lays down the rules **per pusser**, i.e. the official way). This is the sailor's workload: known as their **slopchit**. At the end of the day, hammocks will be **piped down** by means of a high-pitched whistle, audible above the wind, and the signal to go below deck and sleep.

boondoggle: any inefficient or money-wasting venture directed by the government.

scrimshaw: small objects made by seamen in their leisure.

flying the blue pigeon: taking depth soundings with a lead line.

shake book: the book recording the whereabouts and shifts of those who require an early shake in the mornings, e.g. the chef in charge of breakfast.

SWIMMING DOWNSTAIRS

SUBMARINERS

'Hours and hours of boredom with intermittent terror thrown in': thus a description of life as a **bubblehead**: the affectionate nickname that plays on a necessary preoccupation with a boat's water gauges.

Submariners – or **sun dodgers** as the rest of the Navy calls them (the return epithet for them is **skimmers**) – have their own slang that, just like them, operates below the surface. Some of it – like **Battle Stations** – has been played out in hundreds of movies, while much is shorthand for equipment, such as **The Bomb**, the ship's oxygen generator. Other terms are tied up with rites of passage – like the **Bluenose Ceremony**, an initiation for any submariner entering the Arctic Circle for the first time, and involving lots (and lots) of ice. And, as in almost every profession, newbies will be sent on an impossible mission: in the case of the bubbleheads, this can be the order to fetch a **Bulk Head Remover** when the bulk in question is a wall.

Exercises on board a submarine can sound fairly cutesy, but they are usually anything but. **Angles and dangles** is an exercise in which the sub makes a steep dive, revealing anything liable to fall down in the process (the dangles) which needs to be secured. **Bongles and dongles**, meanwhile, refers to the special noise-generating apparatus placed in the water by other Navy or commercial personnel awaiting pick-up by a submarine.

Bubbles in many forms are essential to life under water, and hence they feature large in the submariner's vocabulary. **Chasing the bubble**, for example, is the attempt to level the ship, while a **zero bubble** is an even keel. Higher than zero is still acceptable at **PD** (periscope, or **peepstick**, depth) – it's all about **sea**

state. **Rig for Red** is the instruction to turn the controls to red in preparation for **PD**, but a sudden crisis may necessitate the drama of an **emergency blow**: a blast up through the **roof** and through the surface of the water to **upstairs**.

The Chief's quarters on board a sub are known as the **Goat Locker**, said to date back to the days when livestock were carried on board and when one particular goat became the mascot on the US sub *New York City*. The goat was lucky: juniors have to **hot-rack** it, i.e. sleep in the torpedo room in a bed that's still hot from the previous incumbent; a **rack burn** is the telltale red marks on the face of a sailor emerging from their bed. The **Green Table** is where no mariner wants to go: it signifies they are at **Captain's Mast** to answer a disciplinary matter.

For any feeling those hours of boredom, the sighting of some **biologics** might help: this is animal life, and includes the friendly dolphin companions of the sea. These are not to be confused with **The Dolphins**: the qualification badge for Submarine Warfare that is an important marker of status: without it, you will simply be a **non-qual** or, worse, an **airbreather**. Under the waves, the **saltier** you are, the better.

8

The High Street

'To find extraordinary things, go to the ordinary streets'
Mehmet Murat ildan

The 'high' in 'high street' simply means 'principal'. It was used
in this way by the Anglo-Saxons, who also gave us 'high days
and holidays', days of great celebration, as well as the 'high altar'
of a Christian church. Sadly, there's not a lot to celebrate in the
modern high street, and we are certainly not inclined to worship
it. Supersizing means supermarkets, and there is nothing the
modern consumer likes more than choice and cheapness. It's
an irony perhaps that the original meaning of the very word
'cheap' was to barter and bargain, usually part of the banter
and patter between customer and seller. There's none of that at
your automated checkouts.

It certainly wasn't always this way. The high street as we know
it emerged in the 1860s and 70s, and came of age in the
Edwardian era, when the riches of the Empire made for greater
choice and buying power; even if the gap between the haves
and have-nots became wider. No one captured the London of
this time like Henry Mayhew. A contemporary of Dickens and
author of *London Labour and the London Poor*, Mayhew opened
up the realities of the poverty-stricken city that had never been
charted before. He was the urban anthropologist of his day,
chronicling the language of the streets from the lips of the people
themselves. One of the many tongues he encountered was that
of the costermongers: the traders in London's street markets

who spoke a patois that few had documented and even fewer could understand. Two hundred years on, a lot has changed, although some of the strange tongue that Mayhew eagerly transcribed can still be caught around today's markets if you listen hard enough.

Similarly, if you're lucky you might catch a sentence or two of butchers' back-slang, one of the last survivors of the appropriately named 'pig Latin', a code designed for fun, colour, and private commentary on others (notably customers). A few family-owned and local butchers still relish such patter and, as with the cabbies' cheery banter, it will be a sad day when it disappears.

If the markets offer spontaneous chatter, you'll find the very opposite at the estate agent. Here, codified language makes the difference between a sale and a 'sitter' – a house that simply won't budge. In the end, it's all about shifting the goods, and all pitches, no matter how they're delivered, share the common goal of the sale, right down to the waiter at our restaurant table.

Every high street should have a pub. After all, English loves a drink. The only subjects that get our language working harder are sex, drugs, and money. Our language has over 3,000 words for being drunk, from 'schnockered' to 'spifflicated', 'befuggered' to 'woofled', and 'phalanxed' to 'liquorish'. Benjamin Franklin famously collected 200 more synonyms for a slathered state, including 'cherubimical' (describing a happy drunk who goes around hugging everyone), as well as 'he's taken off his considering cap', 'been to France', 'contended with Pharaoh' and 'been too free with Sir Richard'. Today's tavern-keepers, the pub landlords, inherit a long, lush history. Whether their future remains just as fertile is, sadly, in very big doubt.

KNIGHTS OF THE SPIGOT

PUBLICANS

The story of just one drink reveals the trajectory of our love/ hate relationship with intoxication. In 1736, the first Gin Act was passed. Gin (from the Latin *juniperus*, 'juniper') was first distilled in Holland and brought back to England by soldiers returning from the Anglo-Dutch wars. Cheap to buy and even cheaper to produce, it quickly became the easy ticket out of the miseries of poverty. As a jingle at the time went, you could be 'drunk for a penny, dead drunk for two'. By the 1730s, gin was seen as public vice number one. In the capital alone, there were over 7,000 outlets for what clergymen regarded as the 'cursed fiend'. The Gin Act attempted to stem sales by placing a duty of five shillings a gallon on the spirit. Temperance was advised for all, except 'in cases of extreme necessity' (in this case a medical emergency rather than a relationship break-up).

Inevitably, the black market became awash with gin, and English duly obliged with dozens of euphemisms for tiptoeing around it, including **diddle, sweetstuff, tiger's milk, tittery, royal bob,** and **needle and pin** (**mother's ruin** and **strip-me-naked**, on the other hand, told it exactly like it was).

Cures for the after-effects weren't always too appealing. **Hair of the dog (that bit you)** is about as literal an idiom as you're likely to find. In the Middle Ages, anyone bitten by a stray dog would do their utmost to find the offending animal and pluck out one of its hairs to use in a poultice. This was believed to cure the wound and, later, a hangover. Another remedy of the time involved mixing crab's eyes in wine or vinegar.

Excesses, crustaceans, and canines apart, most of us would assume that the publican sits near the top of the job satisfaction list. The earliest days of the profession didn't bode too well. For the Romans, a publican was a public official, specifically a tax-gatherer and especially one in Judaea and Galilee in the period of the New Testament. These men were universally regarded as traitors to the people, not least because they ran what would today be dubbed a sophisticated extortion racket.

By the 1400s, the sense of 'publican' had shifted, and not for the better. At that time it denoted a heathen, someone excommunicated by the Church. It took another 300 years before the 'public' sense of the word moved to mean 'a Keeper of a publick House, a Victualler or Alehouse-keeper'. Yet even then there was little to be happy about: one eighteenth-century historian pronounced that 'it seems now to be the Business of most Publicans to propagate Vice and Disorder'. On top of everything, tapsters were rarely seen as scrupulously honest: the fun-poking collective noun for taverners was, for some time, 'a promise'.

In the nineteenth and twentieth centuries, as the pub became the pulse of village life, the publican's lot seemed finally to become a happy one. And yet a recent survey has found it to be amongst the most misery-inducing jobs in Britain. Far from a life of pulling a few pints, chatting to regulars, and convivially setting the world to rights, the reality appears to be very different. Instead, today's publicans will tell you that the pressure is relentless, and a sixty-hour week (if it's a quiet one) punishing to both health and family. The average local is open for twelve hours a day, seven days a week, added to which are at least three hours a day for cleaning, cellar work, banking, accounting, maintenance, and deliveries. Few other professionals could hold down such hours. This is all quite apart from the stress of fighting developers who might swoop the moment they detect a failing business. On average, twenty-eight pubs are closing each week, a result both of competition from super-slick chains and of prices going up while income steadily falls – a whole third of the price of each pint pulled goes into the pockets of the Exchequer.

It's perhaps not surprising then that sixty per cent of publicans questioned confess to drinking well beyond the government's recommended weekly units. It's a cruel irony that whichever way you look at it, alcohol is both the raison d'être and the bane of the publican's life. While the tapster will strive to keep up appearances, customers aren't always so obliging, and drunken aggression can mean anything from scratchy cantankerousness to outright violence. Such scenes are thankfully rare, if played up by a media who are sometimes intent on demonizing the British pub culture. What is far less rare are the unsightly messes that turn up with or without a fracas: it's pub law that the loos always get blocked on a Saturday night, when plumbers are probably in a pub somewhere themselves. **Nocturnal upsets** (the mildest of euphemisms on offer) are frequently mentioned as one of the worst parts of a publican's life.

You're unlikely to see any of this dissatisfaction on a pub landlord's face. They are adept at putting on the cheer for their customers and besides, the hours when they serve these customers are the best. The buzz of keeping people happy with excellent food and first-rate beer outweighs, if only for a while, the stress and gruel of the business. And so the publican will smile politely and somewhat conspiratorially when faced with the daily banter of 'Nice to see you behind the bar for a change', or 'Been on holiday again?', knowing full well that slagging off the landlord is part of the game.

There's a role to play outside the pub too. Any publican worth their salt will have knocked on the door of many an old boy who hasn't checked in, or organized a whip round for regulars in need, and even attended a good number of funerals. A good guv'nor is a pillar of the community and doubters are few. As one publican puts it: 'We have the respect of our customers in much the same way a policeman has the respect of the festival-goer – they're having a good time and don't want to get chucked out.'

The establishment

The act of going to the pub has necessitated varying levels of subterfuge over the centuries, and drinking establishments have consequently dispensed a fair number of euphemisms along with their pints. Among the nicknames for one of the few places that, alongside the church, is open to all, are **fuddle-caps hall** and **tippling booth** (1600s); **the good woman** and the **mug house** (1700s); **the tub of blood** and the **Lushington crib** (1800s); **the shicker shop** and the **stagger-juicery** (1900s); and today's **rinky-dink** and **guzzlery.**

Meanwhile the proprietor of a mug house or shicker shop, the pub landlord or -lady, is not without his or her own monikers. Among the earliest labels, in the 1500s, were the **lick-spigot, ale-draper**, and **cove-of–the-ken**. Today you're more likely to hear **the governor** or **mine host**. In the years in-between, and if you were fond of a tipple, you might have encountered the **suds-slinger, groggist**, or **brother of the bung**.

Drinking types

Today, a drinker's choice of beer is as much a window to their soul as their taste in cars. A recent survey suggests that drinkers who espouse a middle-of-the-road politics tend to go for domestic rather than craft or foreign beers, that Heineken-lovers are posers, and Corona-clutchers inveterate partygoers.

Meanwhile, to go with the hundreds of labels for the out-and-out drunk, English describes a few characters that a regular pub-goer will recognize. Beyond the friendly nicknames (surely every pub has a 'Rodge' and a 'Shorty'), you might also spot one or two of these:

shotclog: a pub companion who's only tolerated because they're buying the next round.

snecklifter: someone who peers into a pub in the hope of seeing a friend who will buy them a drink.

tosspot: originally a habitual drinker, one who 'tossed' back his pot and drained the contents.

elbow-crooker: a beerhound, the regular who is rarely seen without a pint in their hand.

Pub talk

In her exposé of the hidden rules of social behaviour, *Watching the English*, Kate Fox examines the social rules that are particular to all drinking places. These are egalitarian environments, where different criteria of interaction apply, and which consequently tell us a lot about British culture.

Nowhere other than the pub bar, for example, is it socially acceptable to approach a complete stranger and strike up a conversation. There the restraints of normal reserve and privacy are entirely shaken off, and it's perfectly standard to ask the person next to you how their day has been, or whether they saw the game last night. Such niceties might be exchanged while waiting to be served, when no one would dream of forming an orderly line at the bar: instead we haphazardly gather at strategic gaps in the counter, still (usually) respecting the invisible queue. At this point the language is non-verbal: a hopeful leaning over the bar and studious following of the bar staff's every move will usually communicate the desire to order a drink oneself.

Once that drink is secured, the pub-goer can engage in a bit of 'openly coded' talk with the publican and others at the bar. 'Put one in for Paul' is a request to get a pint ready for another regular who will surely be arriving soon. 'Have one yourself' invites the bartender into the drinking fold, even if they opt for a Coke. Later on, one drinker might throw in a deliberately subversive comment just for fun, and to get a bit of banter and backchat flowing alongside the beer. 'The pub-argument,' Fox concludes, 'is one context in which the quintessentially English gentlemanly edict that "it is not the winning, but the taking part" that matters, still holds true.'

The ensuing conversation rarely follows the typical logic of exchange. As regulars come and go, content might be duplicated, or take off in entirely erratic directions in a form of free-associating whimsy. In essence, the pub offers a conversational lockdown: once inside, anything goes, and we are all beyond the reach of linguistic law.

HASH-SLINGERS AND HOT POTATOES

WAITERS

In the course of a conversation about the British waiter, the French will usually pop up somewhere. In France, we'll say, a waiter has cachet. And ambition: theirs is a *proper* career. At this point someone might also mention the word 'arrogance' – the imperious attitude of the *garçon de café* has become so notorious that national measures have been put in place to give him a cheerier makeover, after which such phrases as 'Pas possible!' or 'Ah non Madame!' will be cleared away forever. But whether revered, maligned, or simply misunderstood, a French waiter has that je ne sais quoi which few would question: he is *someone*.

The attitude towards the British waiter or waitress (or **waitron**, if you prefer the new and hopefully transient gender-neutral term) couldn't be more different. Much like the bartenders, they are frequently there *en passant*, on their way to another, better, different job. Not that this applies to all: rising to the top to work in one of London's top restaurants is an entirely different kettle of gravadlax. Here a head waiter or maître d' relies on years of experience and savoir faire, doubling up as a mathematician, social engineer, and loyal confidant, knowledgeable enough about their clientele to place business rivals at separate ends of the dining area, and discreet enough to welcome a regular's new girl- or boyfriend as though they are the first companion ever to step through the door. These masters of the front of house require tact, discernment, and considerable skill.

Such finesse is matched up and down the land by those waiters who know the way it works. Yet the fact remains that many of them are seen as part-timers without much dedication, and are thus frequently given a difficult ride by some of the customers perched on their velvet banquettes. The 'battle' between server and servee is as ancient as it is disguised, and it follows therefore that waiters have developed a private lingo that is deliberately blocked to outsiders, one that allows them to mock, complain, or simply entertain themselves.

This code is particularly hard to crack because it's not universal: each establishment has their own version. While in one café the signal for the desire to escape a particularly irritating/boring/obnoxious customer might be 'Kenilworth' (from the film *Glengarry Glen Ross*, in which that place name is the cue for action), in another it might be as simple as 'Dave's asking for you' (Dave being of course entirely fictional). Waiting staff turn out to be experts at creating their own secret slang, and it's one that's regularly updated, for as soon as someone scales the wall and decodes it, they must move on to another.

The journalist Simon Usborne is one of the few people to have been granted an insider's ticket to the language of what the nineteenth century contemptuously called the **hash-slinger**. Usborne managed to penetrate the secret lexicon served up at some of the country's top eateries, and the lingo is as finely tuned as their champagne flutes.

The customers

job du jour: waiter-speak for a fit-looking female customer. 'Job du jour' has shifted from one staff member's daily duty, such as cleaning the hob, to 'hot' customers, sometimes becoming shortened to **JDJ** in the process. If word gets round that there's a JDJ on table 5, waiters will make a **drive-by** to take a look. Occasionally a Job du Jour is known as a **rush job**, because the waiters must rush to have a look before said hot customer leaves.

WKF: 'Well-known face', i.e. a celebrity. The far subtler alternative to 'VIP'. Also known as **TI** (*très important*). WKFs are always assured a good table and special service.

Assisi: one of many codes used by one head waiter at a top London restaurant for customers waiting at the bar for a table. When things get busy, first names simply won't cut it – no waiter is going to remember who Stephen is and which one is Sam or Sarah. Assisi, a reference to the tonsure of St Francis of Assisi, is a typical epithet for a bald customer, and certainly more PC than 'slaphead'. The same waiter is fond of putting two zeros, 'oo', for a female customer who's well endowed.

camper: the universal term amongst waiting staff for a lingerer – one of those who caress a single espresso for two hours, depriving the restaurant of revenue, and waiters of their tips.

flea: a bad tipper – one whose arms are too short to reach their pocket, and of whom their waiter may say out of earshot, **I've been stiffed**.

chewer and screwer: the 'dine and dasher', aka runner, who walks out without paying. This happens far more than you might think in busy restaurants.

chimneyfish: a customer who smokes like a chimney (now outside) and drinks like a fish.

ground control: the diner who stays sober enough at dinner to keep an eye on their over-indulgent partner.

The tactics

postcode filter: the selection process once used by top restaurants for choosing the wealthiest customers. So, for example, one caller from Chingford or Lewisham would be told the waiting list is four weeks, while a resident of Hampstead would get in that same evening. Mobile phones have thankfully put an end to this.

Mr Save: in restaurants with a long waiting list, Mr Save is the name given to a fictitious customer for whom one table is always held in reserve, just in case a WKF shows up.

upselling: a tactic used by waiters and sommeliers of suggesting something more expensive than the customer may have bargained for. If, for example, a diner asks for a G&T, the waiter might say: 'Bombay Sapphire?' It takes a bold customer to say they'll just have the bog-standard. The bigger the bill, the bigger the tip.

The orders

all day: the total of identical dishes being prepared; e.g. 'I need two more steaks. That's six all day.'

fire: to start cooking. As in, 'Table 5 have finished their starters. You can fire the main course now.'

on the fly: used to indicate an order is needed immediately.

Hot behind!: a warning called when walking behind others to prevent them stepping back into a tray of hot food.

bussing: cleaning tables; a term that crossed over from the busboys and busgirls who once collected fares on a bus.

top: the number of people at a table. A two-top has two guests.

86: when the restaurant runs out of something, the staff will say it's '86'. This code is also used for other situations. If Andrew the waiter is conspicuously missing one day, he may have been '86'ed', i.e. sacked. Customers can also be 86'ed if their behaviour warrants it. The phrase seems to be American in origin, and one theory places it in the Prohibition era, when the maximum capacity in a restaurant was 85 and the 86th customer would be turned away.

soldier: a beer bottle. A **dead soldier** is an empty one, and a **wounded soldier** one that has been only partially drunk and then left. In seventeenth-century naval slang, someone 'down among the dead men' had passed out drunk on the floor of the pub.

the line: the crucial point between kitchen and dining area where food crosses over from the back-of-house and is prepped and garnished for immediate serving to the customer.

jizz: sauce, or gravy ('Don't forget the jizz').

marrying: combining two or more bottles of condiments. Marrying has even been known to be carried out on wine. When it comes to ketchup, marrying is technically illegal.

BRINGING OUT THE FLASH

MARKET TRADERS

The chat of the marketplace of nineteenth-century London still survives in pockets of our cities and, if you catch it, its riffs and rhymes are as engaging and welcoming as ever. It may seem strange, then, that its roots are murkier than the mud of the Thames.

Cockney rhyming slang is believed to have sprung up as a tribal code amongst the thieves and cutpurses of seventeenth- and eighteenth-century England. At that time, its aim would have been to pull the wool over the eyes of the police and anyone else who stumbled into the criminal underworld. It seems a far cry from there to the sellers of apples and pears (the literal, rather than climbing kind), but street hawkers had a reputation for trickery and small-time deceptions: hardly surprising when it was hard to make even a penny's profit on the goods they were selling to the equally poor.

Whatever its roots, rhyming slang will forever be associated with the banter of the market. If today it's giving way to the influences of other cultures – the ethnic mix of craft, farmers', Christmas, and produce markets has resulted in a patois as rich as any you'll find elsewhere – the old **Lady Godivas** (fivers) are still exchanged, in the mix with newer linguistic currency in the form of **Pavarottis** and **Ayrtons** (tenors/Ayrton Senna/tenners).

For all this, cries of 'a paahnd a paahnd' of brown-bagged apples for your **cows and kisses** (missus) may, if you believe the papers, become as immobilized in aspic as the Cockney's jellied eels. Back in the 1800s, Mayhew offered a buzzing account of the clamour and bustle of a typical Saturday night in the capital, when hundreds of traders competed to sell their wares: 'Chestnuts all 'ot , a penny a score'; 'Real Yarmouth bloaters, two a penny'; 'Now's your time! Beautiful whelks, a penny a lot'. Take a walk down Soho's Berwick Street market today, you might yet recognize the formula of any one of these cries, and more. If the rhyming slang may have gone all Mockney, and the sing-song volume been turned down, you can still catch a Cockney rap from a gravelly-throated trader: 'You won't find this perfume at this price anywhere: it's the real thing, come up and smell it. I'm tellin' it straight!'

Meanwhile, flying in the face of giant, anonymous food halls are the artisans' and farmers' markets, bringing about a conversion of minds towards sustainable produce. With that conversion goes conversation, back again as money and news are swapped in equal measure. This is where you'll find the street equivalent of the office water-cooler.

Below is a slow stroll through some of the language of the market. There you'll find some rhyming slang, some back-slang (watch out for the **esclop**), and some words with a heavily Yiddish influence thanks to the rich history of the Jewish cloth trade. If you imagine yourself as a flâneur (one who strolls, observes and enjoys), you might almost hear its sounds.

Setting out the stall

the flash: the display of goods.
joint: a stall.
tilt: the stall's roof or cover.
toby: a market stallholder or superintendent.
packing: putting everything out for sale.
pitch: a trader's allotted space at the market.
punter: the customer.
bat: price.

billig: cheap.

bunce: profit.

kite: a cheque.

nause: a complaint or problem.

casual: a new trader.

demmer: someone who demos the goods to the crowd.

spiel: the patter.

north and south: mouth ('close your north and south sunshine').

grafter: a seller of speciality goods.

knocking-out time: the selling off of perishable fruit and veg at bargain prices at the end of the day.

The good days

burster: a great day's trade.

fiddle: a fair day's trading earning a decent profit.

flyer: something that sells like hot cakes (may include hot cakes).

getting an edge: drawing a crowd.

. . . and the bad

kipper season: the low season when little money is to be had.

esclop: back-slang for the police.

ganiff: a thief; from Yiddish.

fence: a buyer of stolen goods.

plunder: goods sold at below cost as loss leaders.

The goods

reem gear: quality goods (a term coined long before Joey Essex, who was later to propel it back into fashion).

swag: the cheaper lines.

snides: the unserviceable goods.
demic: broken.
shmatty: poor quality.

FULL OF CHARACTER WITH SOME ORIGINAL FEATURES

ESTATE AGENTS

Of all tribal lingo, that of the estate agents is arguably the biggest open secret. We are all wise to its euphemistic sidestepping and elastic imagination, and yet our desire to believe means that we buy into its verbal mollycoddling too. After all, nothing is as important as home, and estate agents have built an entire lexicon around that simple recognition.

Even though this shorthand is more public than private, polls suggest that estate agents come second only to politicians on the scale of those we mistrust. The stereotype is of flashy, commission-driven twenty-somethings who roll up in their hatchbacks with a grin, a leather clipboard, and a set of keys as shiny as their teeth.

The best estate agents slip you the nod when they hear about the perfect house that just may come on the market, and let you conduct viewings at your own pace and without itemizing the house's virtues every ten seconds. These are the quiet professionals who have been at it for a long time, and who can sum up a prospective buyer in a matter of minutes. They also know you won't be fooled by such fig leaves as **compact** (broom-cupboard size) or **unique** (quirky to the point of downright eccentric).

No matter what the calibre of the agent, however, euphemism will always find a home (unlike their audience), and that home is usually the glossy particulars that beckon online or that are handed out to house-hunters with a flourish. But, as Saki once put it, 'a little inaccuracy sometimes saves a ton of explanation', and we recognize the motivation behind the guff. After all, few of us would consider a house described as 'minuscule and in need of help', although reports suggest that somewhere in Britain is a handful of agents who deliver it entirely spin-free, opting for a bit of dysphemism, euphemism's rude sister, instead. One such in London was apparently fond of such descriptions as 'suitable only for troglodytes and mushroom-growers'.

The journalist and language blogger Steven Poole offers a nifty description of estate-agent lingo. He refers to their 'strangulated syntax, peculiar vocabulary, and breathtaking in-souciance', one that dances 'on a rhetorical knife-edge between salesmanship and fraudulence'. It's an irony perhaps that the US term for the 'housemonger' is 'realtor', a word whose very first meaning was 'having a basis in reality; true and honest'.

Essentially, over-egging the pudding is in the job description. The equation may be a little bit like the one offered by the novelist Tom Holt: 'Telling lies is a bit like tiling bathrooms – if you don't know how to do it properly, it's best not to try.' Tiling bathrooms is clearly on the estate agent's list of skills.

Lifting up fig leaves

Full of character: hasn't been renovated since the 1950s, or alternatively, falling down.

Imposing: stark and scary-looking.

Bijou: no bigger than a postage stamp. **Compact** means a postage stamp cut in two.

Convenient for: within loud earshot of a motorway/airport/ railway station.

In need of modernization: has narrowly escaped demolition.

Viewing essential: we can't get a nice photo of the outside.

Original features: beams full of woodworm; fireplaces may be crumbling.

Priced to sell: we really want to take this off our books.

Charming: hard to find any other adjectives to suit.

Range of storage: no matching cupboards and shelves.

Conservation area: forget all hopes of home improvement, including a washing line.

Popular area: particularly with the police.

Up and coming area: don't venture out at night just yet.

Partial sea view: if you stand on top of a wardrobe.

Garden flat: damp and definitely dark.

Light and airy: has large, draughty windows.

Ideal investment: you wouldn't dream of living there yourself, but desperate tenants will rent it.

Potential: expect at least a year of building work.

Purpose-built residential development: large housing estate.

Easy-to-maintain: so tiny you can get a Hoover round it in five minutes.

No onward chain: the previous elderly tenant has died and the house probably needs a lot of renovation.

In our opinion: you can't sue us if it's not true.

Style over substance

There is a particular kind of phraseology in estate-agent-speak, one with flourishes and embellishments that are all part of linguistic inflation. **Benefits from**, for example, is a formula usually reserved for the entirely predictable, such as a bath in a bathroom, or an oven in the kitchen. Nouns are frequently turned into adjectives for added grandeur – houses are **four-bedroomed**, **beautifully-gardened** or **impressively-fronted**. Archaically formal language helps too: **whereby** is frequently chosen above 'where', for example, as in 'walk into the dining room, whereby you'll be met with a delightful view'. Similarly, **comprises** is used interchangeably with 'consists of', simply because it sounds fancier and enhances the linguistic decor.

BACKCHAT ON THE HEL-BAT

BUTCHERS

John Camden Hotten was one of the first and foremost lexicographers of slang. He was also an authority on 'back-slang', a category in which words are pronounced backwards. In his *Dictionary of Modern Slang, Cant and Vulgar Words* of 1859, he (like Henry Mayhew) wrote of the costermongers of London and their secret tongues, observing that 'the new dead-meat market' was 'strongest in the way of pure . . . back slang'.

It seems entirely appropriate that 'pig Latin', as back-slang is often dubbed, has such a clear connection with the butchers' trade. It's a complicated business: words aren't just spelled backwards, but extra syllables are tagged on, letters are jumbled up, and other letters added to aid pronunciation. Thus 'hat' becomes **tach**, and 'half' is turned into **flach**. Among the costermongers of the 1800s, regular market-goers would have encountered phrases such as **yennom** for money, **dab tros** for 'bad sort', and perhaps even **cool the delo nammow**, meaning 'look at the old woman' and secretly conveying the fact that she's an irritating customer. **Fil-heath** was code for a thief, while a **hel-bat** was a table, including the bloody benches that once served as the butchers' stalls and which were known as the **shambles** – today's disordered messes hark back to those tables of flesh.

You might think all of this is quaintly irrelevant to today's meat trade. Yet there are still some butchers who use the code that goes by the name of **Rechtub Klat** ('butcher talk' reversed). 'We use it mostly to avoid swearing in front of customers,' one butcher tells me, giving the anagrammatic **tish** ('shit') as an example, as well as **kay-cuff foo** ('f★★k off'). Others might use **Who traffed**? ('Who farted?') and other riffs in a similar vein, only cruder. Such talk has been defined as 'competitive workplace comedy', for which butchers go to extreme lengths to learn entire sentences so that they can both dazzle and discombobulate their colleagues the next day. As a customer, it pays to know at least one surviving example of back-slang: **dee-loo**, a signal asking butchers to offer an older piece of meat. Let the buyer of chops beware.

Elsewhere in the butchers' lexicon, there is comedy to be had in its nicknames and teasing terms. Another pioneer of slang lexicography, Eric Partridge, wrote in the 1930s of a butchers' annual dance which went by the name of the **Blood Ball**. Any women attending it would do well to avoid wearing crimson, lest it be considered 'too trady'. Partridge also made note of one gang in Victorian London made up of butchers from the Clare Market of Lincoln's Inn Fields, who went by the name of the Clare Street Cleavers. They were, by all accounts, 'a tough lot: great fighters and boasters, *cleavin'* becoming a synonym for braggart'.

What of the butchers' slang today? Is it as meaty as it clearly once was? The answer seems to be a partial yes: a typical day of lugging around freezing meat and breaking down animal carcasses is bound to produce some raw vocabulary. But if the language is sometimes rough, the skills are not. Butchery is an exact science, requiring the anatomical knowledge of a surgeon, the triceps of a Trojan, and the culinary nous of the latest celebrity chef. When a client comes and says, 'Could you cut me a 3.5 pound blade roast next to the first rib?', there can be no hesitation. Should a different customer request a long-fibred cut of beef for an Asian stir-fry, any butcher worth their salami will know that a piece of **flap-meat** (or, more elegantly, a **bavette**) is called for, and that the same cut should *never* go near a stew. From **tri-tips** to **flat-irons**, the nation's **meat-men**, as they were once known in the 1600s (when one collective noun was 'a goring of butchers'), are the supreme masters of meat. For a time, they were also an endangered species.

Between the early 1990s and the beginning of the noughties, the number of traditional high-street butchers fell from 15,000 to fewer than 6,000. This was largely down to the proliferation of supermarket meat, presided over by **meat-cutters** rather than butchers, with far less experience than those who take an animal right through from slaughter to table. The outlook was grim, and the poor pig wasn't the only one likely to kick the bucket (a bloody idiom that refers to the wooden frame or 'bucket' used to hang animals by their feet for slaughter).

But then horsemeat happened, or rather it made a surprise appearance all over British plates. The result was a marked upturn in concern for locally sourced, high-welfare, and sustainably produced meat, a boon to the traditional butcher. Put that together with the current desire of TV chefs to introduce exotic cuts of meat like short ribs, rump medallions, or the Tomahawk steak, and the future looks bright again. The supermarket shambles may be bringing the real kind back to every high street once more.

The jargon of meat can be a baffling business. If you find it hard to distinguish between a brisket and a biscuit, it would pay (as one butcher punningly puts it) to do some 'boning up'.

marbling: small flecks of fat in the meat, which usually make for juicy and succulent cooking.
pluck: the heart, oesophagus, liver, and lungs from an animal, which must be passed for human consumption by a meat inspector.

sweetbread: the pancreas or the thymus gland from the neck of an animal, distinguished respectively as heart or belly sweetbread, and gullet or throat sweetbread.

lights: the lungs of a sheep, pig, or bullock.

bags o' mystery: a term from the 1800s for sausages, because no one knew quite what was in them.

TALKING RUBBISH

BIN COLLECTORS

Known for years as binmen, the collectors of our household detritus now go by such official terms as **waste disposal technicians**, **garbologists**, and **sanitary operatives**. Whatever name they go by, their job frequently tops the 'Jobs I'd least like to do' list.

A typical day for a rubbish collector begins at 5 a.m., where a team of men (and we are talking almost exclusively about men) gather in their national uniform of quick-dry, fluorescent-hooped trousers, steel-capped boots, orange sweatshirts, woolly hat, and industrial gloves. Together, they prepare to face a day of physical aches, the risk of injury, and the occasional public abuse.

But they are a team, and if you ask most dustmen what they love about their job, they will invariably speak of the camaraderie it offers and the feeling, as one put it, that it's 'us against the world'. The world or, he added with a wince, 'the maggots'.

The worst bits of the job are the stuff of nightmares. They include rats, burst nappy liners, those maggots, and unspeakable human waste. Above all other evils though, and as anyone caught behind the open jaws of a bin lorry will testify, is the stench.

Some binmen will tell you they've never got used to it, but that only lightweights wear masks.

One of the earliest meanings of 'dustman', back in the nineteenth century, was as a personification of sleep. As with the sandman, the image struck was the rubbing of eyes as if they were gritted with dust. But the definition of carting away dust and refuse has been there since the beginning, and its depiction has never been very positive. As John Gay, writer of *The Beggar's Opera* and a poem 'The Art of Walking the Streets of London' put it, 'The dustman's cart offends thy clothes and eyes, When through the street a cloud of ashes flies.'

The subject of waste has attracted many story-writers. For Dickens and Wilkie Collins, dust and detritus are linked with powerful but repressed human impulses. In those times there was money to be made from dirt. The dust mounds of Victorian London scarred the landscape; described by Dickens in *Our Mutual Friend* as a 'suburban Sahara, where tiles and bricks were burnt, bones were boiled, carpets were beat, rubbish was shot, dogs were fought, and dust was heaped by contractors'. Those contractors, who sold on their material for the manufacturing of bricks and the farming of manure, became men of considerable wealth.

Perhaps because of this history, there is a common misconception, indignantly shouted from the headlines, that today's dustmen earn a great deal. While it's true that they can pick up valuable overtime, dust is no longer the 'filthy lucre' it once was. Just occasionally, the team will discover discarded items of value, a few of them still in their original packaging, and trading can bring in a nice bit of cash on the side.

Another popular belief is that refuse collection is straightforward menial and unskilled work. That particular myth can be busted the moment you see the 47-page induction document that each new recruit must absorb, along with the map of their lorry's route which details the myriad of cul-de-sacs and narrow streets that have to be manoeuvred down in good time, regardless of awkwardly parked cars and recalcitrant drivers.

But should you ever choose to join the crew, you'll find laughs, companionship, and larger-than-life personalities. Plus some lively lingo:

air mail: rubbish thrown at the truck from a window.

chucking on: the duty of those who walk behind the lorry and throw the rubbish in.

fetching out: the duty of picking up the bags from household bins.

sitting bull: the driver, if they're not helping with the chucking on.

tissue: someone on a desk job, usually because they have a **LODI**, a line-of-duty injury.

death march: an extremely long and onerous route.

disco rice: maggots.

urban white fish (US): used condoms floating in water.

getting it up: successfully clearing the street of rubbish. Saying a dustman can 'really get it up' is high praise.

junior flip: a newbie.

laying pipe: working extremely slowly.

mungo: items rescued from the rubbish. 'To mungo' is to take discarded items for personal use. Also known as **scalping**.

rip: to get rubbish off the street quickly. To **rip both sides** is to clear both sides of a street at once.

Tiffany: a particularly good shift that leaves the streets on the route sparklingly clean.

9

The Powers That Be

'Laws are like sausages. It's better not to see them being made.'
Otto von Bismarck

Money has always talked, right from its beginnings in the Roman Republic when, from about 300 BC onwards, coins were made near the temple of the goddess Moneta, located on Rome's citadel, the Capitol. The name Moneta eventually came to refer both to the place where the coins were made, the 'mint', and to its product, 'money'. Such mythical beginnings might account for some of the wonder that has always surrounded what in the 1500s they called the 'oil of angels'.

Like all tribal lingos, that of bankers works in two ways. It keeps outsiders out, and it's a shorthand with which to communicate with speed and precision. Before the 'crisis' (a word that in 2008 became the number one pairing with 'banking' in English language databases), most of us neither wanted nor needed to know what the money-people were saying – bankers' 'bafflegab' was as unthreatening as it was unimportant. But as the climate began to change, so did our perception of such words as 'deleveraging' and 'standard deviations'. The bankers were no longer on our side, and we resented it. The private language ceased to be innocuous, and seemed instead to be elitist, secretive and dangerous. This was the age of the 'bankster'. With the word 'bailout' inevitably went 'government', and the power of the banks became inextricable from that of Westminster.

Ridiculing the state – and especially its politicians and civil servants – is a national pastime. This might explain the extent of the tribalism in the vocabulary of each group: a united lingo is clearly necessary when the world is full of hecklers, and even more so when those hecklers are on the opposite side of the House ('Save the prawns!' is a three-word shorthand that will speak volumes to a lunching politician). As for the law, it too has its detractors: even Shakespeare wanted to kill its proponents, while the American judge Hiller B. Zobel famously described it as 'asking the ignorant to use the incomprehensible to decide the unknowable'.

For the barristers and politicians on whom we rely so heavily, but whom we are ever-keen to criticize, a private lingo is a matter of survival. In the end, it's all a game of risk and chance, something the goddess Moneta must have known all along – 'monere' can also mean 'to warn'.

DOOMERS IN BUM-FREEZERS

BARRISTERS

John Mortimer, author, QC, defender of the Sex Pistols, and habitual drinker of a glass of champagne before breakfast, offered a useful definition of the law for those outside it. It is, he said, 'in another world; but it thinks it's the *whole* world'. These words he gave to his best-loved creation Horace Rumpole, a whimsical but principled barrister who loves to perform, both in court and in the wine bars of Fleet Street. Rumpole is ever ready to place himself as a buffer between the underdog and the establishment, spurning the fine wines and cigars of his colleagues in favour of cheap plonk (Chateau Thames Embankment) and stinky cheroots. He is wise to police shenanigans and the powers of the establishment, and yet can also be resistant to change. When told he must move with the times, he responds: 'If I don't like the way the times are moving, I shall refuse to accompany them.'

Many barristers will tell you that, for all its claret-stained desks and well-fed pomposity, Rumpole's world gave a pretty accurate depiction of the legal profession. While today there may only be two or three Rumpolean figures left at the bar, Mortimer's character offered us a glimpse into a closed shop, and explained its terminology and traditions to the uninitiated. From him we learned the difference between Chambers and the Inns of Court, and between being **called to the bar** and **taking silk**. Mortimer himself maintained that his protagonist stood for the 'great legal principles', namely 'free speech, the idea that people are innocent until someone proves them guilty to the satisfaction of twelve ordinary members of a jury, and the proposition that the police should not invent more of the evidence than is absolutely necessary'. Few in the profession would take issue with that.

Mortimer was a playwright as much as a barrister, and he often remarked upon the irony of leaving the artificial construct of the courtroom to enter the 'real life' of the theatre. The notion that the stage of the law is more removed from normal life than the fictional boards of the playhouse is one that many outsiders would share – for a period in the nineteenth century barristers were even known as 'actors'. The wigs, robes, and briefcases tied up with ribbons only confirm the belief that the courtroom is a cathedral to spectacle and egomania.

In reality you're more likely to spot a barrister from their aircrew-style push trolley than anything more lavish. These will be full of the files needed for the case: wrapped in blue ribbon for the defence, and white for the prosecution. For the men, a collarless shirt and collar studs are the other giveaways, together with (for both sexes) huge and tatty handbags. Before the trolley, lawyers traditionally carried a bag of green cloth in which to carry their **briefs**. They are heartily tired of the inevitable joke, though it's worth noting that one slang dictionary from the eighteenth century remarked that 'those gentlemen carry their clients' deeds in a green bag; and, it is said, when they have no deeds to carry, frequently fill them with an old pair of breeches . . . to give themselves the appearance of business'. These days, barristers carry their wig and gown in a blue bag until given a red bag after being **led** by a Queen's Counsel.

Positions in law are very much reflected in dress. A **junior**, a lawyer of any experience who has completed **pupillage** (an apprenticeship) but who has not **taken silk**, are attired in woollen court dress; there are some very old juniors. A silk is a barrister who has been appointed Queen's Counsel on merit by Her Majesty The Queen. Here, as the name suggests, the court dress is very expensively fashioned from silk. (The Queen, as it happens, has absolutely no idea who the QC is. She might, however, send the occasional invitation to her Garden Party where, along with hundreds of other personages, the silk might glimpse HM The Queen at a distance and from behind a barrier. The silk will thereby understand that they are not terribly impor-tant at all really, although they do get to park in The Mall on such occasions.) A **bum-freezer** is the short, black, and tail-less decorated silk jacket worn by Queen's Counsel, in preference to the stuffier frock-coat. Occasionally, disappointed juniors and chippy solicitor advocates can be seen affecting a similar but plain-style woollen version, an affectation that is universally despised.

The profession finds itself today in a moment of flux. When legal aid was reformed in 2014, some areas of the law became entirely inaccessible to state funding, and for the first time in their history barristers walked out in protest. Solicitors were dramatically affected too, with the traditional distinctions between their role and that of the barrister becoming so blurry that a solicitor-advocate can now appear in high court to represent their own case, rather than handing the brief on (to a human brief, i.e. a barrister). This decimation of legal aid, or **Lucozade** as it is still known, has meant that many workers in the profession have had to seek new specialisms in order to navigate the commercial turbulence.

Much is new in the language of the barrister's world, too. Not too long ago, they could get by without using much English at all, for the predominant tongue of the profession was Latin. Among the phrases that befuddled clients was a profusion of terms involving the Latin *res*, meaning a 'thing' or 'matter': *res ipsa loquitur, res judicata, in re, mens rea* and *actus reus*. Whether or not such terminology was specifically designed to obfuscate rather than impress, it operated as a shorthand of division that few could penetrate. Its entrenchment had lasted centuries.

When the Normans rebuilt English society after 1066, their French vocabulary became the language of privilege and of the law. If the Vikings' term *law* itself resisted replacement, the language of its practices and enforcement was rapidly engulfed. The new language was made up not just of Norman French but also Anglo-Norman, a hybrid of Anglo-Saxon and French (much of which was descended from Latin), seen in such words as 'impeachment', 'assault' and 'suit'. These were unique to William the Conqueror's new land, and were for the most part incomprehensible to its citizens. To many modern outsiders, not a lot has changed since. The Yale professor Fred Rodell spoke for many when he declared that there were two problems with legal writing: 'One is its style. The other is its content.'

But a new broom came in the guise of Lord Justice Woolf, whose work in modifying or excising legal gobbledygook led directly to the Civil Procedure Rules of 1998. Above all, the

Procedure swept away the Latin of the past, so that, for example, *ex parte*, *plaintiff*, *writ*, and *in camera* became 'without notice', 'claimant', 'claim form', and 'in private' respectively. Many terms named after **precedents**, rulings set by previous cases and the mainstay of English law, were also reformulated. Thus an 'Anton Piller order', one that gives the right to search premises and seize evidence without prior warning, will today be called a **search order**, while a 'Mareva' injunction is now a **freezing** one (the two are often combined; an observer could be forgiven for thinking that with a 'Piller Mareva' a judge was ordering an artisan beer rather than the freezing of assets seized in a search).

The Civil Procedure Rules (known inevitably, and without irony, as the **CPR**) codified civil law and gave rules to a language that, to use the Latin of the old school, had become all too ad hoc. The effects have been widespread and dramatic, and yet 'old school' is a term still associated with the law. The outsider's view of the London Inns of Court might be summed up by a definition offered by Dickens in his excoriating take on the legal profession, *Bleak House*: 'old school – a phrase generally meaning any school that seems never to have been young'. The novel's long-running legal case, Jarndyce and Jarndyce, crawls along in a London smothered in fog: a none-too-veiled swipe at pea-soupers of the legal kind. The outside perception of an elite profession trading in secret and deliberately opaque jargon persists to this day.

Despite the move to linguistic transparency, barristers consider their profession to be, in some ways, more remote than ever, albeit in different ways. They will cite prominent judges and QCs who never got degrees before they took the bar exams, and who would never make it today. In those days, some twenty-five years ago, academic prowess mattered less than shrewdness and determination. Today, as 600 applicants compete for one pupillage, academic achievements (including a Masters and

PhD) count for everything, and taking a chance on a candidate without them is rare. The result is an elitism of a different kind from before – one that is defined by education and funding rather than ancestry or wealth.

But these academic and commercial imperatives within the law are profoundly important to the status of the British legal system. It is regarded as the best judiciary in the world, to the extent that major cases which have no British involvement whatsoever may still be tried here, while contracts between large companies may stipulate that any failure to meet obligations will be tried in the jurisdiction of England and Wales.

Inevitably, given its multiple components, the legal profession contains tribes within tribes. Criminal lawyers and their lingo will differ from those in both commercial and traditional Chancery, who deal with probate and land cases. These will be different again from the exchanges you might hear at the Old Bailey.

Inevitably again, each niche within a niche has attracted its own stereotype. According to the 'rule', Chancery lawyers are super-bright and full of academic excellence. It is in Chambers that you may still find tea being taken at 4 p.m., and the senior clerk addressing their barristers as 'Miss' or 'Sir' (a veneer of deference from a position that is actually enormously powerful). You may also catch old-fashioned phrases like **going to the winders** when a company is about to be liquidated.

Those at the criminal bar, as the stereotype has it, tend to be performers. This is chiefly by necessity – a young practitioner with only three years' experience will have chalked up more court appearances than a barrister with twenty years at the tax bar. Criminal lawyers move in groups, and are collegiate in nature; prosecution and defence counsels on the same case will happily lunch together or take a drink in **The Annex**, their preferred watering hole. Theirs is a fight over justice rather than

money, and the joint pursuit brings with it a degree of camaraderie. These are the barristers who refer to themselves as
hacks: dealers in everyday, knock-about crime.

At the Old Bailey, sitting at the bar mess, the language may
become decidedly more 'old school'. The vibe is of a gentleman's
club, and its phraseology reflects it, with a touch of distancing
black humour thrown in: so 'manslaughter' becomes **man's
laughter**, while **How long are you good for?** might encourage
the response, 'Not long, it's just a **murderette**'. **Prize-giving**,
here, is a term for sentencing, in which a defendant is **weighed
off** for their crime. It's said that the expression derives from the
historical need to assess the condemned prisoner's weight, so
as to indicate the length of rope needed for hanging; great care
had to be taken that, in the course of the drop, the deceased
was immediately dispatched but that the head was not detached
from the body.

In the end, of course, judges are as individual as the personalities beneath the wig. The same goes for their reputations:
barristers quickly know which names will send their stomach
lurching and which inspire delight. In truth, there are few **nightmares**, although some **doomers**, as they were once known
(along with **deemers**, **dempsters**, and **triers**), clearly have a
greater preference for custodial sentences than others. District
Judge Cooper, for example, has a reputation for putting people
away rather than granting them bail, or sending them down to
the cells to 'help' them change their plea. Far from being reviled,
Judge Cooper is known for his charm and wit, and his moniker
'Custody Cooper' seems to be more matter-of-fact than mocking.

Using the correct terms of address is crucial in law. A district
judge, or **DJ**, will expect **Sir** or **Madam**; a judge in a Crown
Court will be **Your Honour**, and a High Court Judge **Milord**
or **Milady**. In the Chancery Division and Queen's Bench
Division, it is a **Master** who presides over the more routine

cases, and barristers must address them as such whatever their gender.

Other formulations are occasionally used to convey an underlying contempt. Most barristers are well aware of the correct 'translation'. **May it please your Lordship . . . ?**, for example, is an interjection to the effect of 'Listen up, I'm about to say something'; **with the greatest of respect** equals 'are you really that stupid?'; while **Mr X, in a succinct submission, argues . . .** is tantamount to 'Mr X knows perfectly well that his submission is worthless.'

Such niceties, together with the inevitable complexity of a language that deals in the finest details of statutes and regulations, enforce the distance between the lawyer and the layperson. Today that distance harbours far less resentment than of old, when lawyers went by such names as 'limb of the bar' and 'pettifogger', even if it remains true that the root of the word 'barrister' – the bar that separated judge from prisoners – still seems fitting. The barriers between the legal world and those outside it persist, but they are eroding slowly, and its language may well be the first bastion to fall.

TWATS IN THE BULGE BRACKET

BANKERS

The gap between those who understand money and the rest of us is big. Those with the understanding inevitably also hold the power – as the saying goes, 'we live by the Golden Rule: those who have the gold make the rules'. When it comes to bankers, the rule-makers' gold has become tarnished, and there may never have been a time when learning their language was more important.

Part of that language is full of promise, including for the bankers themselves. For the junior recruit, seduced by the chance to **execute transformational multi-million transactions**, the reality can be dull, with the only true executions involving **pitch books** (presentation formatting) and Excel spreadsheets that take up all day and most of the night – junior bankers can work anything up to twenty-hour days. In the revenue-generating departments of a global bank, the one thing that matters is the generating of revenue.

On her banking blog *Game of Clones*, 'Arrivederci' relates how, on a Friday evening, a 'sit-down to discuss a deliverable due on Wednesday' is far from unusual, and the intense work to get there will be presided over by the terrifying triumvirate of the MD/ED/VP (managing director; executive director; vice-president), 'who have been put on earth with the sole purpose of ruining your personal life'. This is the time when all warnings about selling your soul may start to stick in the throat.

For a group that is thrown together for the best part of day and night, it's unsurprising that there is a common lexicon, one that's not always designed to deceive, for it rarely steps beyond the walls of the banks. The tropes exchanged between managers and juniors are particularly formulaic, operating as a kind of complicit masquerade in which both parties know *exactly* what is being asked. If, for example, an associate wonders if an analyst has any **capacity** or **bandwidth**, usually late on a Friday after-noon, it will mean that the job about to land on their desk will require working all evening and into the weekend. Occasionally this will be dressed up with faux-empowering phrases like **Why don't you run point from here?** Or **I'm going to let you hold the pen on this**.

The rest of bankers' lingo, particularly on the international trading floor, is a mix of Cockney rhyming slang (emanating from the quick-thinking 'barrow boys' who were able to make a City fortune without any Harvard MBAs), market banter, and expressions picked up from horse racing. Currencies in particular attract a good nickname, such as **Bill and Ben** for the yen, or **Loonie** for the Canadian dollar (which displays a picture of the loon bird on its front). Presiding over it all is the **Old Lady**: the enduring moniker of the Bank of England.

Such chit-chat may be fading away as electronic communication takes over, meaning that there is now such a thing as a quiet dealing room. Nonetheless, some of the old slang seems impermeable to change: a **yard** will always mean a billion (short for the French *milliard*) and a **cable** will forever signify the currency pair rate of the British pound and US dollar, a throwback to the transatlantic telegraph cable that once transmitted prices between the London and New York Exchanges.

At the desk

bulge bracket: the collective noun for the world's largest and most profitable multinational investment banks.

face time: staying in the office until late to prove that you're incredibly busy and to prevent your boss from giving you more work.

spinning: the art of making yourself look more successful than you really are.

fire drill: an emergency task that needs to be completed yesterday.

bake-off/beauty pageant: a pitch whereby several investment banks compete for the same business. This may result in several **fire drills** and tens of presentation **rewrites**.

STARR: Strategic Try-hard with Awesome Reputation & Relationships. A US acronym for a socially adept, outward-looking employee who works well with others and is good at 'submitting deliverables'.

TWAT: Technical Wizard with Antisocial Tendencies. The complete opposite of a STARR; this is a banker who is both relentlessly competitive and financially astute, but who is not a team player.

killer bee: an investment banker who helps a business resist a predatory takeover bid.

The green stuff

In *How to Speak Money*, his exploration of financial lingo that manages to explains this alien world to the rest of us, John Lanchester relates a typical conversation amongst bankers that an outsider might catch: 'When you hear money people talk about the effect of QE2 on M3, or the supply-side impact of some policy or other, or the effects of bond yield retardation, . . . or sub-prime and Reits and CDOs and CDSs and all the other panoply of acronyms . . . it's easy to think that somebody is trying to con you.' In fact, Lanchester concludes, it's not as sinister as all that. This is the social aspect of language, and its power lies in its giving its community a shared experience. If it excludes others, that may not be a bad thing, for it can only enhance that sense of belonging.

This isn't to say that smokescreens aren't also erected – arguably the language of finance accounts for more glazed eyes and switched-off minds than any other, particularly within politics. But beyond **decoupling** and **sequestration**, the vocabulary can be both vibrant and inventive – and sometimes a little dark. Perhaps it all started with the coining of **mortgage**, a word whose literal meaning is 'dead-pledge', not because it might kill you to pay it off, but because the loan becomes 'dead' once it is repaid.

Money talks

bear hug: an approach a company makes to the board of another company, indicating that an offer is about to be made for their shares.

bed and breakfast: an operation on the London Stock Exchange in which a shareholder sells a holding at the end of one day, but makes an agreement with the broker to buy the same holding back again the next when the market re-opens.

corset: a government restriction on the growth of bank deposits.

dead cat bounce: a temporary recovery on a stock exchange after a substantial fall. It doesn't mean that everything will go back to normal, just as a dead cat bouncing off the ground won't come back to life.

living dead: a company that has received venture capital funding, but is unlikely to meet its growth targets.

Valium picnic: a colloquial name for a non-trading day on a stock exchange or other commercial market; a market holiday.

haircut: a term in investment bonds whereby the bond holders – those who have lent money to a company or government – won't get all of their money back; everyone loses the same amount of 'hair'.

bar-bell: a portfolio made up of short- and long-term obligations, the idea being that it is **weighted** at both ends like a bar-bell or dumb-bell.

The crisis of 2008, known to all as the **credit crunch**, was at least highly productive in terms of language. Some of the terms to come out of it remain with us still:

Ninja loan: a loan or mortgage made to someone who has 'No Income, No Job, No Assets'.

jingle mail: the practice of sending back one's house keys to the mortgage company because of negative equity, or the inability to keep up with payments.

IPOD: acronym for 'insecure, pressured, overtaxed, and debt-ridden'.

exploding arm: a variable-rate mortgage with rates that soon rise beyond a borrower's ability to pay.

home debtor: a homeowner with a very large mortgage, particularly one that they are unlikely to ever pay off.

going underwater: falling into negative equity.

stagflation: stagnant growth and rising inflation.

funt: someone who is Financially UNTouchable.

BERSERKERS IN WHITE TOGAS

POLITICIANS

'Being in politics is like being a football coach. You have to be smart enough to understand the game, and dumb enough to think it's important': so wrote the American Democrat Eugene McCarthy in 1968. The analogy between the occupants of the Commons and a bunch of people who spend ninety minutes fighting over a ball might strike a chord with anyone tuning into Prime Minister's Question Time. The mob-like squawking and frantic paper-waving of usually genteel individuals is a uniquely British tradition that leaves outsiders either perplexed or highly amused. There's not much sympathy for the underdog here either; as the columnist Simon Hoggart once put it: 'Sometimes the house is like a medieval village green where cruel boys throw insults and fruit at the local idiot, who shouts back and waves his arms like a broken windmill.'

Few are the tribes whose reputation sits as low as that of politicians (bankers may be the one exception). In this business, as Churchill noted, you can be killed many times, and not just by one's fellow workers. The public views its constituency and country leaders as at best slightly odd, and at worst downright fraudulent. In Roman times, candidates would don clean white togas as a symbol of purity and integrity – the very word **candidate** is from *candidus*, meaning white. The journalist Martin Bell once tried this, in suit form, when standing against the candidate Neil Hamilton, embroiled at the time in allegations of high sleaze. Bell became 'Mr White', and duly won.

But the white suit failed to catch on, and such is the current level of esteem held for politicians, you'd think that securing major change by bringing in a new MP at voting time has worse odds than the National Lottery.

Yet however much one might criticize MPs, very few of them are slackers. Sixteen-hour days and seven-day weeks are pretty much the norm. Outside the demands of Parliament, time is spent on constituency casework, appeasing querulous customers at the weekly surgery (at which, as the unspeakable murder of the MP Jo Cox proved, the threat of violence can also loom), and attendance at local events requiring hours of small talk and a continuous smile. The ex-MP Gyles Brandreth remembers a fellow member's sighing utterance at the end of a long day: 'Happiness is the constituency in the rear-view mirror.'

A job so demanding and yet so maligned must have something going for it. And it does, summed up in the word power – not, as many believe, the elite sort of power that goes with the rank and ritual of Parliament (though there is some of that), but power to make a difference. The ability to influence can release all kinds of professional endorphins. Simply put, politics has good intentions in its heart and egotism in its head.

What an MP can and can't say in the Commons is tightly circumscribed and laid down in the bible that is *Erskine May: Parliamentary Practice*. Here you'll find the law on everything from appropriate attire and legitimate expenses to what is acceptable language in the chamber (versus what will get you immediately thrown out by a sergeant-at-arms). Importantly, this does not mean that gentility and decorum are the governors of parliamentary speech. You only have to study the heckling teams on either side of the house to realize that politicians are not always politic, and certainly not always polite. To take the sentiment of the late backbencher Julian Critchley, 'the only safe place for a parliamentarian is a bag of boiled sweets'.

In fact, if you ask a member of the public what they think of a Commons debate, you might catch the term 'fishwives'. The public perception of a group of politicians (for whom past collective nouns have included **equivocation** and **odium**) is one of unruly clamour and a frenetic hurling of insults. In many ways this din is encouraged, with each party organizing heckling teams that could outbark any professional sledging on the cricket pitch. The journalist Alison Hardman demonstrated in the *Telegraph* how the PM has their own political version of the A-team, known fondly amongst themselves as the **berserkers**, whose job it is to issue roars of support at their leader and snarls of vituperation at the opposition. The **Q-team** are said to meet before every PMQ to agree the specific lexicon for that day, which is why the ex-Shadow Chancellor Ed Balls once notoriously heard the words 'weak' and 'nightmare' repeated ad infinitum during one beserker challenge. The word 'berserk', incidentally, is from the bear-shirt put on by Viking warriors before performing a frenzied war-dance: associations clearly known to whoever coined the political nickname.

Such apparent mayhem is at odds with the rest of the language of the Commons, which includes the insistence (again by Erskine

May) on using the correct title of respect for other members. Thus one MP must address another as 'the (Right) Honourable member for X'. The distinction between **Honourable** and **Right Honourable** is crucial, the latter reserved for members who have been admitted to the Privy Council, including cabinet ministers and the Leader of the Opposition. Each Commons newbie is allowed only a few slips before the Speaker will come down hard on any aberration.

Questions in the Commons will frequently follow various patterns, and include code formulations that are recognizable to all but the unseasoned newcomer. When, for example, a Tory backbencher asks about the **jobs fair** that has been organized in their constituency, everyone present will know that the said member is deliberately taking up valuable Commons time by asking a totally pointless question, thereby saving 'their' minister from potentially awkward ones. Such patsy questions, organized by whips or private secretaries, will usually include such openings as **Will the minister join me in congratulating . . . ?** or **Does my Right Honourable Friend agree with me . . . ?** The MPs behind the questions quickly gain a reputation amongst commentators as hired plants, but such behaviour is as entrenched in parliamentary debate as the snoring member in the back row.

Considerable euphemisms are also required if comments are to escape the Speaker's censor and censure. Those that catch on are endlessly recycled and become standard fare, and include many that originated in the satirical magazine *Private Eye*. Thus **tired and emotional** will always mean falling down drunk, while **enjoying Ugandan relations** (or **playing an away match in Uganda**) is disguise in plain sight for having a sexual relationship with someone you shouldn't be. (The term is said to have referred to an incident at a party at which a journalist allegedly had a **meaningful confrontation** with a former cabinet minister, later claiming that they were 'upstairs discussing Uganda'.) An **exotic cheroot**, meanwhile, is *Private Eye*-speak for a cannabis cigarette.

Moving from print to TV, every politician and civil servant will tell you that Antony Jay and Jonathan Lynn managed to skewer their lingo perfectly in the comedy *Yes Minister*. In the world of the Minister Jim Hacker and his staff, fancy linguistic footwork is everything. This is where **under consideration** means 'we've lost the file', and **under active consideration** means 'we're trying to find it'. Euphemism abounds, as in this dialogue between the Minister and his Permanent Secretary Sir Humphrey:

> SIR HUMPHREY: The identity of the official whose alleged responsibility for this hypothetical oversight has been the subject of recent discussion is *not* shrouded in quite such impenetrable obscurity as certain previous disclosures may have led you to assume; but not to put too fine a point on it, the individual in question is, it may surprise you to learn, one whom your present *interlocutor* is in the habit of defining by means of the *perpendicular pronoun*.
>
> HACKER: I beg your pardon?
>
> SIR HUMPHREY: It was . . . I.

Governments today will no longer speak of 'public spending' but of **public investment**, and an issue is always **nuanced** rather than complicated. When he was Chancellor, Gordon Brown spoke of **post-neoclassical endogenous growth theory**, a phrase coined by his Chancellor Ed Balls who later explained that all it really meant was that the government could make a difference to the economy.

Political nicknames are what one MP describes as 'Commonsplace'. Margaret Thatcher had a whole bevy of them attached to her in the course of her career, including The Blessed Margaret, Attila the Hen, The Iron Lady, The Milk Snatcher, and Tina ('There Is No Alternative'). David Cameron went by the soubriquets of 'Call me Dave', or Flashman, while Tony Blair before him was dubbed Bambi thanks to his youthful appearance, only to morph later into Teflon Tony, when nothing seemed to stick.

Such epithets can occasionally make or break their owner. When Ann Widdecombe, as Home Office minister, stated that her then boss Michael Howard had 'something of the night about him', the phrase hung around his neck for years, and newspaper cartoonists had a field day with their representations of a Howardesque Dracula. Similarly, when Vince Cable stood in at PMQs at the tail-end of the Brown government and said that the 'bungling Brown' had gone 'from Stalin to Mr Bean', many would say that Brown's authority never really recovered.

Sexism still simmers in parliamentary language, of the kind distilled in David Cameron's infamous 'Calm down, dear' to Labour's Angela Eagle – words traditionally used whenever a woman becomes 'hysterical'. More recently, a journalist reported to the police a Member of Parliament who had approached her with the opening gambit 'I want to talk to the totty'. The writer Allison Pearson decided a decade ago that she 'would rather be a lap dancer than a woman MP – the hours are better and unruly male members are shown the door'.

Politics is home to some unlikely metaphors. One such was the 'prawn cocktail offensive', which had nothing to do with our national fondness for crisps and everything to do with workers in the City of London, whom the Labour leader John Smith set out to charm in the early 1990s. The rather surreal image ran and ran, culminating in the clarion cry 'Save the prawns!' and the response from the then Deputy Prime Minister Michael Heseltine: 'Never have so many crustaceans died in vain.'

Dog-whistle politics, meanwhile, is a relatively new kid on the block, imported from Australia to signify the kind of politics that will rouse a very specific portion of the electorate, just as a high-pitched dog whistle is audible only to some dogs. So, for example, the subtle reminder by US Republicans that Barack Obama's middle name is Hussein was designed to prick up the ears of those desiring what was euphemistically termed an 'Anglo-Saxon heritage'.

In the end, political language is all about promise and persuasion. This is true whether it is expressed openly and publicly, or kept under wraps – at which point the folds of a Roman toga might occasionally come in handy.

10

The Power of Words

The trouble with words is you never know
whose mouth they've been in.
Dennis Potter

I can't roll my 'Rs'. For years I thought this would stop me becoming a 'proper' linguist, blurring in my head the distinction between the spoken word and the written one. Years later, that distinction is all but gone. Current language is all about the written-spoken word, and as the linguist John McWhorter pithily put it, today we 'talk with our fingers'.

The consequence of this fundamental shift in the way we communicate is that our word industries, including journalism, lexicography, teaching, and even the Church – find themselves straddling two worlds. Their audiences like words on paper, and they want them online, and the two are far from mutually exclusive: in essence, we want it all.

It's an irony that while there is no limit to how much information can be presented and stored online, the consumers of that information want it more concise than ever, to the point of breaking the sound-bite barrier. We have become used to ingesting every form of news in short chunks or 140 characters. As a result, modern language needs to be pithier and punchier, supersized not in wordage, but in power, and today's communicators must choose their words accordingly. It comes as a surprise, then, that even in the midst of the revolution, they don't always need to dip into an entirely new lexicon.

Despite the fact that, over the course of a millennium, English has proven itself to be amazingly adept at adapting to change, much of the language of the media is still happily entrenched in the past. Editors still 'spike' a story, even though the lethal-looking contraption on their desks is long since gone. Typesetters of books will still talk about 'galley proofs', and an advertising creative will still attend boxloads of 'tissue meetings'. Terms like these are far from relics: in fact they remain as current a part of the professional patois as a publisher's 'flywheel' or a tabloid's 'sex romp'.

The reason for such adherence to traditional language is probably twofold. Firstly, change has happened quickly, and even if English is ready to adapt, its users may not be. Secondly, consumers love the solidity of history, to the extent of preferring cosy, reassuring names like Kindle and Nook for their latest high-tech e-reader. We may be hungrily embracing novelty in technology, but through language we are clinging on to the permanence of the past.

As for lexicographers, we are traditionally seen as the oldest fogeys of the lot. Images of robed and bearded scholars poring over dusty tomes in a silent library tend to spring to mind. Apart from the silence, none of this is true. Today's diction-ary-making is as technologically sophisticated as you'll find in any part of the word business, and it has a vocabulary to match. Like English itself, a dictionary resists change at its peril.

Meanwhile, vicars always keep a word bible alongside the real one: it helps them with their wordplay. And as I found out, there is plenty of that.

RAPS, ROMPS AND BASEMENTS

JOURNALISTS

Journalism, according to G.K. Chesterton in the 1920s, 'largely consists in saying "Lord Jones Dead" to people who never knew Lord Jones was alive'. A lot of journalists will concur, and add that not only do they need to say it, but they need to say it quickly. The first **deadline**, back in the 1800s, was a line drawn around a military prison, and any prisoner who dared to cross it was liable to be shot. Most journalists can relate to this; the nicotined fingers and haunted eyes of old may be disappearing, but scrambling under the hot breath of time limits remains a constant demand, never more so than in the world of digital copy.

Arguably journalists understood the idea of the military deadline so much that the word crossed over into the printing lexicon, where it meant the guide-line marked on a printing press. From there it was a straightforward step to our modern meaning: a time by which material must be ready. Many more expressions in English have their inky fingers in the printing profession. Lots of them are **clichés** – quite literally, for today's stock phrase was originally, in the 1800s, the French name for a stereotype block, the cast obtained by letting a matrix fall face downward upon a surface of molten metal on the point of cooling, known in English type-foundries as **dabbing.** Within fifty years the metal **stereotype** had been extended to embrace any commonplace phrase that had set in its ways.

Despite the fundamental shift in the way we view journalistic copy these days, the language of newspapers and magazines sticks closely to the old printing presses, run by the **inkies**. Online news may never sleep, yet journalists will still talk about putting copy **to bed** when it's ready to go **to press** – a practice which once involved physically locking up the type form of a publication in the press before it went to print. Some of that old language slipped so deeply into the mainstream of English that its beginnings are long hidden. **The dog's bollocks** began as a joke amongst printers for a colon followed by a dash (:–) before being propelled into stardom alongside 'the bee's knees' and 'the kipper's knickers' as metaphors for excellence.

Old methods die hard too, at least in journalistic language. None more so than when a story is **spiked**, a reference to the foot-high (and very lethal) metal spike that once sat on each desk on the editorial floor. For reporters it was their crucial filing system: once a paper news release had been written it would end up, with great force, on the spike. For subeditors, the spike was used either to keep a copy of a story or to kill it. Larry Lamb, the editor of the *Sun* in the 1970s, famously impaled his forehead on a spike after junking a piece of copy with rather too much relish.

The chapel

Newspaper unions, both print and journalist, were traditionally organized through **chapels**: associations of the **journeymen** in a printing office which laid down rules on working practices and who settled disputes as to the price charged for work etc. Within each chapel were the **companionships**: groups of writers or compositors who worked as a team, while the leader of each chapel was either the **father** or **mother**. Much in the style of a masonic lodge, reference would be made to the **Laws of the Chapel** and to its **secrets**. As the name suggests, the chapel involved a great deal of ritual, particularly when it came to initiation. Perhaps it was these rituals that prompted the name, though some say it is connected to the location of early printing offices in or near churches, and the fact that many of them made their money through the printing of religious books and bibles. Whatever the origin, to this day NUJ members organized in a single workplace are said to belong to their chapel.

Positioning the story

Today each journalist will refer to their newspaper as **the book,** and each page of that book has its own geography. A story can be referred to as a **back-of-the-book** one or, if it's less significant or less visual, a **downpager**. Similarly, a weaker story that runs along the bottom, often without a picture, is **the basement,** and the one running down the side is **the wing**. A basement might become a **nib** (news in brief); the **lead nib** is usually where, as one journalist has it, 'the boring stories by specialist correspondents go'. However short, it still gets a **byline** and a **dateline** (the date and place of writing). The other nibs are often filled with **wire copy**: stories taken from those news agencies with which the paper has contracts.

The best stories compete to make the **splash,** a term for a prominent or sensational story that can also function as a verb; 'What are we going to splash on?' is a regular question asked by a paper's senior staff, known as the **back bench**. A good story in the book may be worth **puffing** on the **skyline,** the panel up high on the front page between the **masthead** (newspaper title) and the splash. Below it are the words the subeditors use to explain the content. It's a golden rule of newspaper journalism that reporters only ever file the copy or the 'body text'. The headline, the byline and the **standfirst** (the explanatory introduction to a feature) are all provided by the subs, who occasionally (at least from the journalist's point of view) get it wrong. It can even happen to John Humphrys, self-confessed language pedant, whose sub once headlined his article 'Work Comes Second for Tony and I'.

The caption to an article may contain a **kicker** – a two-word phrase, usually a laboured pun – following a colon and the actual caption, while **sidebars** and **pull quotes** are displayed to draw the eye. Collectively, these things are known as a story's **furniture**.

The scoop

Getting the story to begin with involves a host of tactics, from the **phoner** (phone interview) to **doorstepping** (confronting someone at their home by surprise) and **hosing down** (taking a bombardment of photographs as the subject comes into sight, sometimes curiously known as **hosing the Doris**). This will be done by a **monkey**: reporter slang, along with **snapper**, for a photographer, who in turn will call the reporter a **scribe**.

If the scoop is really juicy, the paper might run a **spoof**: a weak first-edition front page that fools the opposition.

The newsroom

It would be hard to find a profanity not uttered in a newsroom. Journalists love the C word, which is used there as liberally as 'hell' is in headlines. This may be the last bastion of old lingo that survives in the new, digital arena. On the web and in content management systems, page layouts have other, less evocative, words. As the journalist Simon Usborne comments: 'It's hard not to look at words such as **content** and become nostalgic about basements and splashes and spikes.' At today's 'digital desks' you are more likely to see rows of twenty-somethings in headphones staring at screens than gathering in noisy huddles or waving bits of paper.

One consequence of this new journalism came in March 2016, when the *Independent* decided to fold its print newspaper. At the end of their last day, journalists **banged themselves out** by drumming their desks with their hands. It's a tradition that began as a ceremony for those finishing their printing apprenticeship, in which the apprentice would be paraded around the machine room (often in a state of undress) while colleagues banged the machinery with whatever they had to hand. Banging out was also, occasionally, employed on the editorial floor for the departure of a time-served colleague.

The art of the headline

Sex, sensation, pets, heroism: the four ingredients of headline news according to the former *Daily Mirror* columnist Donald Zec. So much for the subjects, but what about the art?

A good headline isn't determined by stylistic devices alone. Headline writers draw on a special vocabulary that, though determinedly pithy, by no means follows ordinary speech. Above all, journalese, a term first recorded in 1882, loves a monosyllable. These are the words that allow the reporter to say a lot, loudly, and in very little space. Three-letter words are the favourites: all journos seem partial to **axe**, **wow**, **yob**, and **bid**, while **rap** and **romp** sit alongside **spate**, **spree**, **bash**, and **shame** as words you will only ever encounter on the news stand. **Tsar**, like **union baron**, is the fictional job title of choice when the real one is too boring or doesn't adequately convey a newspaper's editorial prejudices, and there are plenty more phrases that have little or no life outside the pages of a paper, such as **shock verdicts**, **death plunges**, **love rats**, and **murder bids**.

Wordplay and jokes are another essential. You would be forgiven for thinking that there's a house rule at the *Sun* that ninety-five per cent of all headlines must contain a pun. Frequently, these puns stretch both credulity and the English language to near breaking point. Of the best, the reporting of the Queen's 'annus horribilis' as 'One's Bum Year' bears comparison with Shakespeare. If a pun proves unmakeable, it's always worth throwing in a rhyme, especially if that rhyme involves either popular slang or words that don't actually exist. In 2004, the *Daily Star* responded to a judicial report's criticism of the Home Secretary's plans for extending the use of electronic tagging with 'Judge slags tag-a-lag'.

Headlines like 'Where's there's a Wills . . . There's a Wey Hey!', used above a picture of Prince William clubbing in Bournemouth, could scarcely be further away from the sober deliveries of newspapers a century earlier, which included such splashes as 'A Judge's Wife Cured of Pelvic Catarrh'. (Even then, sensationalism was finding its way in, as in a headline from the rowdy streets of 1900s San Francisco: 'Man punched by his son and horsewhipped by his wife'.) In the same edition, we hear that 'exercise for a businessman past middle age is detrimental'. Note the lack of **screamers** – a journalistic word for exclamation marks, alongside **pling**, **shriek**, **gasper**, **Christer**, and **slammer**.

Ultimately, a headline is just that. It's a seller, and the story below it frequently bears little relation. As Andrew Marr pointedly put it: 'The classic *Mail* headline which begins "Is this the most Evil/Depraved/Shocking . . .?" can almost always be answered "actually, no".'

WIDOWS AND BASTARDS

PUBLISHERS

The old saying is wrong: you *can* judge a book by its cover, or at least that's what publishers believe. If you see someone surreptitiously rearranging the displays in bookshops making sure that their titles are as prominent as possible, ideally **face-out**, odds on it's a publisher. Proof positive comes when, rather than reading a few pages, they look at the **spine** to check who published it, or fondle the cover to assess whether that deep black **jacket** is actually **soft touch**. And if they're with another person (publisher or not) they'll criticize the look of each and every book, discussing everything from colour scheme to text design. In the book trade, every conversation has the tendency to become a mini focus group.

For a group of people whose business is words, it can be surprisingly difficult to understand what publishers are saying. If you were to overhear a discussion between two editors, the industry might sound a rather brutal place. You might, for instance, be alarmed by how casually (often over a glass of warm Prosecco and cake at a **carpet shuffle** – not an obscure 1950s dance move, but a get-together to welcome an author) they might discuss **breaking a spine** or how much **bleed** they need. Let alone the forensic examining of **dummies**, or debates over the importance of avoiding **widows** and **orphans**.

In fact, somewhat unsurprisingly given that the industry is eighty per cent female and packed with English graduates – publishing is for the most part exceedingly polite, perhaps overly so.

How to make No sound like Yes

According to one editor, the essence of publishing is the ability to say many nos as nicely as possible. Accordingly, the language of the **turndown** letter has turned into a gentle art form with its own euphemistic code:

> **strong** = wrong-headed.
> **literary sensibilities** = pointlessly polysyllabic.
> **regretfully** = with enormous relief.
> **fascinating** = rather on the long side.
> **expert** = know-it-all.
> **needs a more powerful platform** = no one has ever heard of you.

Prospective authors who don't want to get stuck on the **slush pile** should be warned to avoid brightly coloured ink: **green-ink** has become shorthand amongst publishers for the frothing of a lunatic. It's rather harder to spot a bestseller in waiting. While anglers spin tales about the one that got away, most publishers have several. The first *Harry Potter* book was famously turned down by every publisher in London before it was taken on; each of them have spent the intervening years spinning a variety of stories about how they managed to miss it.

The naming of parts

Today, most books are published electronically as well as physically, which means that many publishers are widening their focus to **IP** (intellectual property) and thus to any way and anywhere the words can be read. Consequently, as in the other word industries, the language has become rather bipolar: electronic publishing is full of robotic acronyms like **DRM** (digital rights management) and invented words like **EPOS** and **e-readers**, while the language of physical books remains rather regal, featuring **Royal hardbacks, Crown Quartos** and **gold foil** (it is all about **royalties** after all, a term that's developed from its sixteenth-century use for any rights granted by a sovereign).

Many of the words for the art, production, and editorial aspects of publishing have been used for centuries, and, as in journalism, they sometimes refer to processes that no longer exist. The terms **upper case** and **lower case**, for example, still have their feet in the printing press, where letter blocks were stored in specially organized boxes called cases – the cases for capital letters were stored higher than the smaller letters. William Caxton's impact on the English language was enormous, and it seems fitting that it's in the lexicon of the book trade that his revolution is at its most tangible.

recto: the right-hand page of a book (pages 1, 3, 5 etc.). The left-hand is the **verso**. They have been called this since the 1800s.

folio: the page number printed at the bottom of each page.

bastard title: the first page of a hardback carrying nothing but the title of the book, usually preceding the title page. Also known as the **mock title**, **fly title**, or **half-title**.

dust jacket: a hardback book's detachable outer cover.

flaps: on a hardback book, the part of a book jacket that folds over and onto the inside of the boards. The front flap tends to be used for the blurb, and the back for the author biography.

widow: a paragraph-ending line that falls at the beginning of the following page, separated from the rest of the text. An **orphan** is the reverse, a paragraph-beginning line at the bottom of a page.

gutter: the inner margin of the leaves of a bound book.

bleed: an extra allowance at the edge of printed pages (especially pictures) to avoid any white space from imperfect cropping.

deckle: the uncut edge of the page left deliberately rough and untrimmed.

running head: the line which commonly appears at the top of each printed page, typically showing the book title on the left-hand side and chapter title on the right. Despite the publishing flurry around deadlines, the term has nothing to do with headless chickens.

dummy: a book mock-up.

double daggers: the symbol that marks the third footnote on a page (it follows an asterisk and a single dagger).

blad: a short sample of a book.

yapped: refers to the cover of a paperback book when it extends beyond the edges of the book.

The genres

A decade or so ago, a new wave of romances featuring smouldering Scottish heroes was dubbed the **plaid-ripper**, one step on from the **bodice-ripper** (and many steps on from the **bodice buttoner**) which itself joined a long line of inventive epithets for literary genres, dating back to the **dime novels**, **penny dreadfuls**, and **shilling shockers** of the early twentieth century.

The 1990s brought us **lad lit** and its opposite **chick lit**, a pairing otherwise less elegantly known as **prick lit** and **clit lit**; travel novels, meanwhile, were **trip lit**. They joined **dad lit** (books about fathers and children), **biker lit**, **git lit** (for and about 'yobs') and **grit lit** (gritty realist novels). Historical epics (looking further back than **Vic lit**) are alternatively known as **sword-and-sandals** novels. Some saw the unsung genre of the twentieth century as being the **sex-and-shopping** (or **S and F**, for 'shopping and f***ing') novel, not to be confused with the lighter **bonkbuster**, a genre preceded (in a purer fashion) by stories under the famous **Mills & Boon** label.

Those detective stories with a traditional setting and a lady detective are now fondly known as **cosies** (a term reminiscent of the **Aga saga**). By contrast, if dealing with gritty urban themes, they can be **hard-boiled**. They sit alongside the categories of **TOT** ('Triumph over Tragedy') stories, **HIBK** ('Had I but known what I know now . . .', a term coined by Ogden Nash), **fem-jep** ('female in jeopardy'), or **WIP** ('women in peril') fiction.

In some cases, **genre** has become an umbrella term for science fiction, fantasy, and horror writing. And under that umbrella are a host of other terms for particular scenarios. **Speculative**, for example, is generally used to describe books that contain science-fictional elements but that are not marketed and sold as science fiction. Other stories may be **high-concept**, in other words, they deliver an easily described and marketed idea, as in *Jurassic Park* being 'a Disneyland with dinosaurs'.

The suffix **–punk,** meanwhile, suggests something disruptive, modern, a little dystopic, and fast. Alongside **cyberpunk** sits **steampunk**, a Victorianesque setting where all technology is run on steam, as well as **atom punk**, where nuclear energy runs everything and the world resembles the 1930s.

Diving into the world of genre fiction can, for the uninitiated, feel like you've fallen down a rabbit hole. Sub-genres of SF include **new weird** (urban fantastical, including monsters) and **alt history** (alternative history, where the fiction imagines that a certain point in history has been changed); **space opera** involves big human emotions against a space backdrop. Fantasy fiction will offer you anything from **epic fantasy,** with quests and a life/death ultimatum, to **grimdark** – violent fantasy with very dark antiheroes. For such an unobtrusive word, 'genre' has become a thrilling place to be.

FLYWHEELING OVER THE DUMPBIN

BOOKSELLERS

Given their trade, publishers have inevitably borrowed many a term from the bookseller. These include **dumpbin**, a promotional cardboard display unit sent to bookshops in order to display a particular book, and **flywheel**, the word online retailers give to a self-perpetuating seller that needs no added prompt from them (flywheeling books are the stuff of dreams). Not forgetting the **halo effect** – the knock-on sales after a promotion has gone live.

Meanwhile, a particularly striking lingo is shared amongst second-hand and rare book dealers. As you would expect, these bookmongers draw on a large lexicon to describe the condition of their wares. They also delight in sprinkling suffixes like *-ianas* (Sherlockiana, Dickensiana etc.) liberally around the name sections of their shops. Bring booksellers together, and you'll hear them revel in tales of magical **house calls** to private homes or estates of the deceased, ones that have produced wonderful hauls. Those for whom such riches remain elusive may attract the unkind epithet of **teabag bookseller**: one who spends a lot of time mug in hand, reading their rather less than valuable stock.

The condition

We all know books can be dog-eared, but in the trade, that's just for starters:

dog: an unsellable book. Also known as a **woofer**.
foxed: the word for a book which displays a degree of spotting

on its pages, resembling a fox's footprint. Booksellers will often refer to volumes that are **slightly foxed**.

God's copy: a particularly fine example of a book. A **hospital copy**, on the other hand, is a defective version of a canonical book held in stock only so that it can be cannibalized to improve another defective copy that may come along later.

koshered: a borrowing from Yiddish to indicate a book or a signature that has been pronounced authentic by experts.

cocked: a condition that results when a book has been leaning too long against another on the shelf.

married: said of a book that's sporting a dust jacket taken from another copy of the same book.

shaken: showing some loose pages.

inky: short for 'incunabulum', a book printed in 1500 or before, when printing was in its infancy.

Sexton Blake: a fake (rhyming slang).

sleeper: a book whose immediate value is not obvious. London's Any Amount Of Books cites as a classic example *No Decency Left*, written by one Barbara Rich but which in fact is known to be by Robert Graves and Laura Riding, with a chapter by T.E. Lawrence. The French word for a sleeper is apparently *un Chopin*.

LEARNING JOURNEYS AND CARPET TIME

TEACHERS

Evolving English, an exhibition at the British Library in 2011, demonstrated the failure over many centuries of every attempt to standardize English. The exhibition charted the multiple efforts to impose conformity and rule upon on an apparently chaotic tongue. Hornbooks – wooden paddles with texts affixed to one side and covered in a thin layer of transparent animal horn – would be hung from a girdle worn by each pupil, who would then be required to learn, by rote, the alphabet and the Lord's Prayer. The results were occasionally surprising, as in the case of the character '&', designated the twenty-seventh letter of the alphabet and therefore part of the compulsory recitation of letters. The symbol was chanted as 'and per se and' (and, by itself, 'and'). So laborious were these chants that children raced through them, mangling the final letter in the process to produce the word 'ampersand'. Some say this is the only good thing that came out of drilled learning, parrot-style.

Fast forward some 200 years, and the differences are startling. Not only are multi-ethnic and multicultural classes the norm, but parrot fashion and prescriptivism – in English at least – are politically unacceptable, despite the government imperative that children learn the rules. It's through this minefield that today's teachers must gingerly tiptoe. And it's partly thanks to the conflicting pull of liberalism and 'proper' education that disillusionment is rife. Endless changes of curriculum, daily mandates from government, and a lack of empathy from the rest of us are all taking their toll. Like junior doctors and nurses, many teachers have had enough. Yet that same disillusionment is paired with a stoicism and humour that is as essential as it's unexpected. The core of the job – training minds, and enabling discovery – remains as compelling as ever, and seeing a disengaged child suddenly look excited can vindicate every hour lost to stress and doubt.

Thirteen-hour days are typical rather than occasional. Observations, reviews, inspections, evidence-gathering – quite apart from eight hours of teaching and the marking and lesson-planning at home – are the meat of a teacher's day. Many of the so-called 'holidays' follow the same pattern; a teaching career is not for the faint-hearted.

The lingo

A visit to the staffroom of a twenty-first-century school can be surprisingly overwhelming, particularly if you have an aversion to acronyms and abbreviations. From **SAT**s and **AfL** to the dreaded whisper of **Ofsted**, the teaching profession – one which puts good communication at the top of its priority list – positively teems with bureaucratic terms and phrases that have no easily discernible meaning. In at least one school, pupils are referred to as **individual data points**.

And yet the community of the staffroom, like any other, has its own shorthand that is both efficient and necessary. It is characterized by a substantial amount of jargon, a good many euphemisms, and a healthy dose of self-deprecating humour.

Key to acceptance in this world is the liberal use of the terms **achievement** and **attainment**. While these sound broadly similar, don't be fooled: the distinctions between them are crucial. Achievement relates to the rate at which pupils make progress, and is usually categorized according to 'more than expected', 'as expected', or the grim initials **L.E.**: 'less than expected'. Attainment, on the other hand, signals the level at which a pupil is currently working: the hope is that they are at least 'meeting age-related expectations' (which fortunately is never turned into the acronym MARE).

Armed with this new-found vocabulary, you will now be welcome at the coffee machine. And here the fun really begins, because the new recruit must get to grips with the curriculum. At seven years old, children in England are now expected to explain what an **algorithm** is in coding, and know how to **subitize** numbers – a term borrowed from American psychology to denote the ability to immediately apprehend the number of things contained in a small sample without needing to count. Furthermore, today's teacher must ensure that their young charges vary their sentence openers by throwing in the odd **fronted adverbial**, and form complex sentences using the notorious **subordinating conjunctions**.

Often, it's the children who are readier with the lingo than their tutors, to the extent that the distinction between roles becomes slightly hazy. One of the key aims of AfL (Assessment for Learning) is that children know what they are learning, and why. As a result, visits to classrooms will involve conversations about 'Learning Intentions' or the **WALT**, short for 'We Are Learning To'. WALT's partner is **WILF**, 'What I'm Looking For' – in other words, WALT is what the child is learning and WILF is what the teacher is looking for in order to show that learning. Children will talk about their **word-rich environment** and about the **I can statements** that they have **met**, while the heavily promoted **growth mindsets** – whereby mistakes are rebranded as **learning opportunities** – are in the lexicon of both teacher and pupil. Linguistically speaking, the lingo of the classroom can rival that of any company boardroom.

Nor does the business terminology stop there. **Non-negotiables** is the intimidating term for a list of things that each child must remember in order to complete their work correctly. Before they even start, they must consider the **success criteria**, which may be posted on the **working wall** alongside a **WAGOLL**, i.e. 'What A Good One Looks Like': a model of the level children should aim at.

All of this is part of the **learning journey**, a phrase that can be heard in many a planning meeting, as school leaders ask teachers to plan the learning journey with an **entry point** or **jumping-off point**, a **hook**, a **knowledge harvest**, right through to a worthwhile, real world outcome which, according to the International Primary Curriculum, is called an **Exit Point**.

How will children know how well they have done? Their teachers may gather together for moral support with tea and biscuits for a **marking party**, offering mutual support as well as the sharing of rude spelling mistakes.

As for that marking, it will often include **2 stars and a wish**: shorthand for two positives followed by one area requiring improvement that is otherwise known as a **Tickled Pink and Green for Growth** thanks to pink and green marker pens.

If children are in on all of this industry vocabulary, it also pays the teacher to absorb some of the lexicon of their charges in turn. They will learn that films are no longer good; they are **epic** or **sick**, and that children no longer have close friends, but **BFFs**. Any teacher needs to be at the top of their game to keep up: by its very nature, slang is meant to evade, and by the time a teacher has mastered **on fleek** the pupils have already moved on.

The acronyms

PPA: planning, preparation and assessment time, for which all teachers are entitled to take ten per cent of their overall teaching time. You will often find teachers hiding in the PPA room.

EYFS: the Early Years Foundation Stage, covering the year groups up to and including reception children. Many KS2 teachers fear to step into this unknown realm where contact with snot, slobber, or worse is inevitable.

INSeT: In service training. Schools have five INSeT days as well as other training opportunities. This training is also known as **CPD** or Continuing Professional Development. As one teacher puts it, they tend to be either really exciting or the longest, most tedious hours of a teacher's life.

twilight: not another teen movie but an after-school CPD session, in which teachers may spend the time wondering what they could have been doing instead.

Types of teacher

edutainer: the teacher that stands at the front of the class and performs; the children in their class are excited to learn and are often noisy whilst working together.

child whisperer: the calm and quiet teacher, whose class is always silent, and who never needs to raise their voice.

mood hoover: a teacher who continually moans, whether over changes to break rotas, children in their class, children in other classes, parents, or their own home life. Their nickname reflects the fact that they will suck the cheer out of even the most positive teacher.

The instructions

Talk to your elbow partner: Talk to the person sitting next to you.

Talk to your face partner: Talk to the person in front of you.

That bell is for me and not for you!: Do not rush out of the room just because the bell has rung.

Carpet time: group discussion on the class carpet.

Time for a brain break!: permission to children to stand up, shake their bodies or get a drink. Also known as **brain gym**.

Time for a thought shower (or **ideas rain**): the PC way of referring to a 'brainstorm' that word now being deemed offensive to those suffering from epilepsy.

Golden time: for teachers, this is usually 2:30 on a Friday afternoon when all energy is spent. For children, it's a time when they can choose any activities they want as a reward for working hard all week.

FISH AND CHIPS AFTER POTTY TRAINING

VICARS

'More tea, vicar?' Surely one of the most reassuringly British phrases, born in the music hall, beloved of 1980s sitcoms, and sister of 'How's your father?' Old as it is, the phrase crystallizes two truths about most clergymen and -women: they drink lots of tea, and they laugh a lot. As G.K. Chesterton put it: 'It is the test of a good religion whether you can joke about it.'

The term 'vicar' is first recorded in the early years of the fourteenth century, where it was applied to those in the Christian Church who acted as the earthly representatives of God or Christ. 'Representative' is the operative word there, for 'vicar' is from the Latin *vicarius* meaning 'substitute', also the root of 'vicarious'. In its earliest use, the term described a person who acted as a priest in a parish in place of the real parson. Today, it has become a catch-all term for members of the **God squad** (a term that many vicars themselves will freely use), and 'vicar' is simply a working title for someone in the Church of England who has the cure of souls in a modern parish.

On the practical level, this cure encompasses many things. First and foremost is pastoral care – pastors being once inter-changeable with vicars, and whose name is linked to 'pastoral' as they were originally those who tended a flock of sheep rather than parishioners. Today's vicars tend to the ill, the grieving, and those in material or spiritual need.

Then there is the planning and preaching of the weekly sermon from the pulpit (or 'cackle-tub', as they liked to call it in the nineteenth century, in which the preacher was the 'tub-thumper'). The sermon is the source of endless jokes and sore bottoms – as Prince Philip once quipped: 'The mind cannot absorb what the backside cannot endure'. Alongside these duties is the almost endless admin associated with the parish, from the renting of the church hall to the arranging of marriage certificates. These are the services that are paid for as distinct from a vicar's other duties within the mostly 'non-prophet organization'.

Vicars will tell you that the happiest part of their job is weddings – not just because they are there as the bringers of joy, but also because of the many mishaps that occur, the things that add both difference and laughter as well as the anecdotes for the next clergy dinner. Humour aside, weddings and funerals account for those times when they are needed the most. The ceremonies attached to such services are equally important: steeped in history and ritual, they too have their funny side. In the closing moments of Baroness Thatcher's funeral service in 2013, the journalist Quentin Letts described the Archbishop of Canterbury's sign of the Cross as having 'something of a window cleaner reaching into every last crevice'.

The influx of female vicars in the past few decades is inevitably having an impact upon language. One poll has estimated that by 2025 women priests will match males, a very different situation to the one in 1994, when the comedy TV series *The Vicar of Dibley* was first aired. Some of those joining are keen to dispense with the male imagery that dominates services and sermons, and eagerly debate whether God should be referred to as He or She – much to the horror of those continually opposed to 'vicars in knickers'.

As for a collective personality, the modern clergy houses a host of different characters. Perhaps this is partly down to the introduction of sector ministries over the last fifty years or so, which has brought a definite shift in the type of person being selected for the clergy. The one requirement is what's known as

potty training, short for the **Post Ordination Training** that takes up three of the total six years involved in preparing for a vicar's role.

Away from the dog collar, one telltale sign of a vicar might be exceptionally soft hands. Plus a liberal sprinkling of the phrase 'Bless you', and not just for sneezes. The shorthand of the vicarage combines such blessings with a good deal of affection and, ironically, a great deal of devilry. Like paramedics and doctors, a little black humour in the face of suffering and death goes a long way: far better to talk of **pushing up the daisies** than a 'negative health outcome'. Not to mention **ash cash**, the money received for signing a cremation form which, of course, should be collected from a nearby **ash point**. Some vicars also like to give their parishioners nicknames, although these they would never share publicly. One vicar confesses to choosing Pontius Pilate for a churchgoer who consistently mispronounces 'crucifer' (the bearer of the cross in processions) as 'crucifier'. Meanwhile, The Poison Dwarf seems to be another regular customer at parishes up and down the land.

Nicknames aren't just reserved for parishioners, either.

archdemon: archdeacon.

orgynist: organist.

serviette: a female altar server.

rural queen: rural dean.

Archie: Archbishop.

Guild of Serpents: Guild of Servants of the Sanctuary (an association of altar servers).

Mothers' Onion: Mothers' Union.

Jezebel's Trumpet: *The Church Times.*

supermarket trolley: a wheeled funeral bier.

Complain: the late Evening Office of Compline (prayers at the end of the day).

As for the hymns, this is where a vicar's chuckles really come into their own. **Fish and Chips** refers to two hymns that are regularly paired together at funerals, namely 'The Lord's my Shepherd' and 'Abide with Me'. 'Loving Shepherd of thy Sheep' is known as **Shoving Leopard**, and 'Conquering Kings' as **Kinquering Kongs**. Local allegiances play a role too: thus 'City of God, How Broad and Far' can suddenly feature the **City of Leeds**, while 'There's a Wideness in God's Mercy' may morph into **There's a Widnes on God's Mersey**.

THE FINGER-TALKERS

THE ONLINE TRIBES

Shakespeare knew a thing or two about popularity contests. In his works he used the word **unfriended** several times to mean someone who has lost the hearts of everyone around them. Four hundred years before the arrival of Facebook, he already knew what it meant to be rejected from the tribe.

In the early days of the computer, the screen seemed the ideal haven for the unfriended. The new technology was seen as the beginning of social isolation and the end of conversation as we knew it. For a while, it seemed that the computer keyboard was to become the refuge of both society's rejects and techno-babbling nerds.

In some respects this wasn't too wide of the mark – this was indeed the end of social interaction as it had existed over a millennium and a half. But just a few decades on from the first computers, those same keyboard bandits were looking up their classmates and establishing new friendships in another universe. This was social networking, a force behind the largest tribal membership in this book. According to the *Daily Telegraph*, if

Facebook were a country, it would be the third most populated one in the world.

A country is not a bad analogy. This is not one tribe but many, and Twitter, Instagram, Facebook, Reddit, Tumblr, and Buzzfeed all have their own lexicons. But common to all is the most singular characteristic of the new spoken-written language of social media: brevity. This is a land where vowels are dropped, phrases condensed to acronyms, sounds reduced to numbers, and most punctuation forgotten. All of these require a re-engineering of the conventions of normal conversation. (Not that all inflation has disappeared: 'YAAAAAAS' is an expression of excitement that can never have too many vowels.)

The acronyms born in the early days of MSN Messenger are now so well known (and largely defunct save for deliberate irony) that it would probably be harder to find someone who *doesn't* know what **LOL** means, apart from David Cameron. Terms like these belong to the 'old school' of social media, but there is an even older one. A love poem from 1876 contains the following lines, 130 years before the arrival of the text message: 'He says he loves U 2 X S, / U R virtuous and Y's, / In X L N C U X L / All others in his i's.'

As for the newer codes, you probably wouldn't have encountered **NSFW** in the 1800s, signalling that something is Not Safe For Work, i.e. contains adult words, themes or images, and therefore not something that you want on your work computer's search history (**NSFL**, on the other hand, is Not Safe For Life: in other words, the content might scar your eyes). **IRL**, In Real Life, is another fairly recent addition to the list, and is often used with an ironic awareness of how little communication goes on face-to-face. Meanwhile, **FOMO** (Fear Of Missing Out) has become **LOMO** (Love Of Missing Out), and LOL has morphed into **LULZ** (as in 'doing it for the lulz'). **Dafuq** is the latest way of saying **WTF** (What The F★★k?), which is now considered far too uncool; **ELI5** is a request for a dumbed-down explanation of something (Explain Like I'm 5). On Instagram, you'll probably be more concerned with **TBT** (ThrowBack Thursday) and **FBF** (FlashBack Friday), two days when you have a chance to post photographic blasts from the past. By the time you read this, those will probably sound archaic too.

Another key aspect of online language is wordplay. If you remember the grammatical craziness of **LOLcat**, you will know all about it. These viral jokes tend to follow a certain pattern which other memes then follow, for example: 'When you're out with the **squad** and . . .', 'When you're chilling with **bae** and . . .' .They are the verbal equivalent of identity badges, and they define their tribe.

Not all of the emerging words of online communities are new. Many, including those same baes (the people in our lives who come 'before anyone else'), and squads (cliques of friends) are borrowed from elsewhere, especially hip-hop.

New senses of older words keep emerging, too: **status**, **tag**, **poke**, and the ubiquitous **on fleek** (on point; perfection) have been given new nuances by Facebook and the rest of social media. A **friend** is now any acquaintance and your **fam** your close circle of friends, while in this world **like** revolves entirely around a thumbs-up icon or a Twitter heart. But in the online world, allegiance is only ever temporary, and all such friendships can be reversed, especially if someone looks **sus** (suspect, i.e. shady or false). Just as nonchalantly, **Netflix and Chill** is a coded invitation for casual sex.

When words aren't sufficient, it may be time for an **emoji**. In 2015, the Oxford Word of the Year was a pictogram (Face with Tears of Joy) for the very first time. Love them or loathe them, emojis are one of the fastest-growing forms of language, and they serve the medium of digital communication extremely well. Whether or not they are considered 'words', they offer nuances that traditional language can't always convey. Besides, in some cases the descriptions of the emojis are creeping into conversation too: **small aubergine** became a euphemism for 'penis' after the emoji was removed from Instagram searches, and you might find **grimacing face** after an embarrassing post. The word **smugshrug**, a falsely humble shrug ¯_(ツ)_/¯ , is today's code for a swift dismissal.

So integral are such language conventions to online and digital communication that Mark Zuckerberg, founder of Facebook, even defines what his service does in terms of language. It began, he has explained, with a 'limited vocabulary', before 'nouns' were added with the introduction of the Open Graph. The latest addition is 'verbs': 'We're going to make it so you can connect to anything in any way you want.'

Don't forget the blogrolls

Beyond social media, the new generation of **bloggers** and **vloggers** (video bloggers) also have their own words and phrases, including self-referential ones. A **haul vlogger** is one who posts on fashion – typically a teenager in her bedroom just back from a major shopping spree. A **nourishing** or **blessed vlogger** reports on matters of lifestyle. Any one of these will probably need **blogrolls**: a list of hyperlinks to other blogs or websites.

Speak like a superfan

One of the thriving online communities is based around **SFF** – science fiction and fantasy (think *Twilight* or *Game of Thrones*). Here, a **fan favourite** is a book, character, or setting that is particularly loved by fans of that property. **Shipping** is a not-so-new spin on 'relationship', and is generally used to talk about an affection someone has for two characters who are either in a relationship, or whom the speaker would like to see in one: 'I ship Han and Leia' means 'I am invested in their relationship'. The hope is of an eventual **OTP**, 'One True Pairing'.

Han and Leia's relationship, having been established in the second and third *Star Wars* films, would be **canon** – established in the canonical text. **Fanfic**, on the other hand, is a non-canonical text using the characters of a particular work but written by a fan.

Superfans are highly dedicated ones, but not as dedicated as **trufans**, who are generally unwilling to accept any alternative interpretations of 'their' characters. **Fangirl** and **fanboy** now have a slightly disdainful tinge. All three tribes may get together at a **con** (convention) and, if they're lucky, may even get to meet their favourite author or actor, producing an inevitable **squee**: an excitable word that mimics the sound of a super-enthused girl fan.

THE WORD NERDS

LEXICOGRAPHERS

A lexicographer is 'a harmless drudge, that busies himself in tracing the original, and detailing the signification of words'. Not my description, but that of the most famous of lexicographers, Dr Johnson, in his celebrated *Dictionary of the English Language*. I suppose it was only natural that the Great Cham as he was known – 'cham' being a form of *khan*, suggesting that the man ruled over words like a Mongolian emperor – would offer a telling definition of, in effect, himself. It's certainly a definition that resonates with anyone who's undertaken the task of writing any sort of dictionary. There's little glory in lexicography; you're not going to win glittering prizes and see your name in lights on the basis of your definition of 'walrus'. Indeed, the editor who wrote the original *OED* definition of 'walrus' was one who realized that and swiftly focused his efforts elsewhere (he was called Tolkien).

What lexicon there is would go some way to confirm most people's expectations of a lexicographer – a term than in itself doesn't lend itself to high excitement: even pronouncing it correctly is a challenge. Words for the key components of an entry in a dictionary, and the different types of word (**compound, derivative, etymology, sense**) have been around for generations and are now virtually standard. More recent developments speak to finer details. For example, an **entry** will today contain a **headword** and probably several **lemmas**, any of which might have a **label** and most of which may require the lexicographer to furnish an **antedating** and **postdating**. These are not as dry as they seem: this is the difference between placing 'OMG' in the 2000s or tracing it back to 1917, when it was used by a British Admiral in the exact same way teenagers would use it today.

Today's lexicographer has lived through a revolution. Whereas for centuries records were made on pieces of paper known as **slips** (based on a lexicographer's **reading**: a word that has an entirely different sense in dictionary-making), they now study vast language databases to discover the current meaning of a word as well as the terms it tends to be partnered with, and whether it's used politely, offensively, ironically, or not at all. These databases also allow dictionary-makers to chart the changes in the histories of our words: to note, for example, that it was men who were originally 'buxom' (obedient), that 'baffling' originally meant stringing a knight upside down by his ankles and jeering at him, and that the caustic 'sarcasm' originated in a Greek verb for 'tearing flesh'. Then there are the **eggcorns**

– a term that sprang from an exchange between the linguists Mark Liberman and Geoffrey Pullum about the mishearing of the word 'acorn'. An eggcorn is a word that is mistakenly substituted for the standard one, but that still sounds logical. We all know about **damp squids**, but Oxford's databases now show that **trending towards** and 'tending towards' are neck and neck, that **putting the cat before the horse** and **like a bowl in a china shop** are both doing the rounds, and that curling up in the **feeble position** is just beginning its journey. Meanwhile, **lack toast intolerant**, to me, makes all the sense in the world.

Lexicographers love these and laugh at them regularly, but their laughter is of the quiet kind. It remains fair to say that lexicographers' offices are not the loudest places in the world. Lexicographers are (very) quietly proud of the work they do, of their scholarship, and of the fundamental usefulness of the dictionaries they write. Not only that, but it's a job in which you really do learn something new every day. Be wary of taking a lexicographer to a pub quiz.

Most importantly of all, dictionary-writers are never linguistic purists or pedants; they wouldn't be able to do their job properly if they were. If you have a particular language bugbear – perhaps the split infinitive, or the dangling preposition – don't tell a lexicographer, because they'll simply sigh and explain that the offending item has been widely used in English for donkey's years (they'll show you the evidence) and suggest very, very politely that you are completely and utterly wrong.

11

Top Secret

'See all your best work go unnoticed.'
2005 advertisement for MI5

Daphne Park was the Principal of Somerville during my time at Oxford. She was a Margaret Rutherford kind of figure: stout, bespectacled, plummy-voiced, and utterly charming. That she was also in possession of a steely intelligence was never in doubt, and the few encounters I had with her were marked by verve, precision, and real kindness. Students referred to her affectionately as 'Daffers'.

Some years after I left, I discovered another truth about her. She was a spy (or rather had been, but as insiders will explain, you stay a 'friend' for life). And an enormous part of Baroness Park's success was that, had she been part of an identification parade to spot the secret agent, you'd have taken her for the tea lady. She herself later said: 'It's been a huge advantage during my professional career that I've always looked like a cheerful, fat missionary. It wouldn't be any use if you went around looking sinister, would it?' Any student who visited her sunlit office was entirely unaware that she stored a small, bejewelled revolver in her safe.

The first collections of secret language were also the first glossaries of slang – in this case, the vocabulary or 'cant' of criminals in the sixteenth century. Its secrecy meant that collecting it wasn't easy: one magistrate, so intent on exposing the patter used to dupe honest citizens, threatened to whip those who came in front of him if they didn't reveal their code.

In recent years, small chinks of light have been cast upon the languages of priesthoods, including that of espionage. Thanks to TV, film, and literature, what John le Carré called The Circus has become something of an open secret. But few could penetrate the active operational codes swapped on the ground, a fact equally true of the Freemasons, who actively promote open exchange and yet whose codes and handshakes are closely guarded. These are the circles who depend upon a closed tribal language for their success. Not that it will seem anything like this on the outside, where life carries on as normal. As Margaret Atwood put it in *The Blind Assassin*: 'The best way of keeping a secret is to pretend there isn't one'.

The Magic Circle has an equally secretive reputation, and the success of its members also depends on what is unseen and unheard. You may find rabbits in their pockets rather than daggers, but their language is still rooted in camouflage.

LEG-UPS AND WIDOWS' SONS

THE FREEMASONS

Few communities invite such suspicion and on-the-fly assumptions as the occupiers of a Masonic Lodge. Look up 'Freemason' in any search engine, and the terms that pop up most regularly are 'handshake', 'secrecy', and 'leg-up'. It wasn't always thus.

In the 1300s, freestone was a type of sandstone or limestone, the kind that could be sawn in any direction, or readily shaped with a chisel. The person wielding that saw and chisel was a freemason, a member of a class of skilled craftsmen who worked in stone. The kinsmanship and fraternal traditions of those medieval stonemasons are the foundation of modern Freemasonry.

Rituals were there from the start. Like other craft organizations of the Middle Ages, the associations of masons developed special rites for imparting the knowledge of their craft to others, and for the initiation of new members. These ceremonies were both elaborate and well guarded, designed more to encourage fraternity and education than to intimidate outsiders. Seven hundred years on, today's Freemasons will tell you that this ethos remains unchanged.

One of the first questions non-Masons want to ask is 'Who are they?' The answer may surprise: Freemasonry attracts all religions, all ages, and all professions. It tends to run in families – it's not uncommon, for example, for a father and son to be members of the same Lodge. But genes are not the key. Nor is money. In fact, there are only two entry requirements for admission into the brotherhood, and it involves neither wealth nor ancestry: you must be an adult male, and you must believe in a higher being.

Contrary to popular belief (a phrase that pops up a lot in a discussion with a Freemason), that higher being need not be of a particular religion; it need not in fact be of any religion at all – the Freemasons are a secular society. But the would-be member must embrace the belief in a Great Architect of the Universe, a benevolent power that presides over human destiny. What form that power takes is unimportant: it's the belief that, somewhere, it exists that counts.

If you pass that test, then today's would-be Mason no longer needs to be invited to join. Walk into the Freemason's Hall in London's Great Queen Street, and you will be given as much information about the fellowship as you could possibly want. You'll also be put in touch with a Lodge considered to suit you best. 'We welcome everybody,' one Mason explains.

Not quite everybody. The elephant in the Freemason's Lodge is, of course, women. There are two women-only Grand Lodges, as well as a form of Freemasonry known as Co-Freemasonry, but the latter has no formal recognition from the major Masonic orders. UGLE, the United Grand Lodge of England, maintains that the society simply follows the example of medieval stone-masons and so is, and always has been, restricted to men.

Back to myths, and Rick Wakeman, world-renowned keyboard player and member of Chelsea Lodge No. 3098, tells me: 'I spend my life saying to people, "That really isn't true at all."' One of the biggest associations with Freemasonry is secrecy and, as Wakeman concedes, it certainly exists, though not to the extent outsiders expect. Not, certainly, as much as it used to: in the past, membership of a Lodge was so clandestine that two members of the same family might not know about the other. Today, it's a more open affair, with numerous YouTube videos offering the curious some tutorials on what the organization is really all about.

Masons may 'verify' each other with such well-known formu-lations as **Are you a travelling man?** or the even odder **Are you a widow's son?**, both of which refer to lines in the script of the Master Mason ceremony. Then there are the handshakes. A Freemason will tell you it's not enough to know **the tokens** (there are more than one): you also have to know what goes with them – the particular words and phrases that connect the brotherhood. And they are as closely guarded as the three rituals involved in becoming a Master Mason, ceremonies that are full of pageantry, historical references, and resonances, at which each Mason will wear particular regalia displaying his individual rank. Wakeman describes them as 'short playlets with many actors, telling a story that's entirely relevant to the Mason-to-be'.

The story about a noose being put over the applicant's head is, it seems, quite true, but the rope is intended to represent the umbilical cord rather than anything more sinister. A trouser leg is indeed rolled up – but only for five minutes. As for proper leg-ups, that may be another myth. Part of the Masonic code is that membership of the brotherhood should not entitle you to undue favours, and that includes parking tickets.

Despite attempts to be more open, conspiracy theories will keep piling up, in numbers greater even than the assassination of JFK – an event they've also been blamed for, alongside Watergate and 9/11. An irony then, perhaps, that the phrase **on the level** has special significance in Freemasonry, meaning that all Masons are brothers, irrespective of class or income. **On the square**, meanwhile, is used both to describe mutual trust and to indicate when something is private, akin to 'between you and me'.

All this speculation about handshakes and jiggery-pokery means curiosity is rarely directed elsewhere, to what Freemasons consider one of the primary roles of the fraternity. It is one of their biggest ongoing frustrations that their organization's considerable charity work goes largely unrecognized. That work addresses a wide spectrum of causes, from children's hospitals and air ambulance services to fishing trips for disabled children and concerts in care homes. Most Masons will quote the opportunities for such charitable giving as one of the main catalysts for joining the brotherhood.

The language of the Freemasons – the exact phrases used within the ceremonies – is never revealed. What a Mason will tell you is that it is lyrical, and steeped in the past – in words rooted in Anglo-Saxon or with Latin ancestry that are as weighty as they are old. Thus you will hear about **ardour** rather than fiery passion, and **benediction** rather than a simple blessing – one that will be **beseeched** with **zeal**. You will hear references to things **seraphic**, **celestial**, and **consecrated**, **endued** (endowed) upon all **diligent** Masons who show **rectitude** and

reverence, spurning **superficies** (trivialities) and weathering **vicissitudes**. The rules that govern behaviour and thought are the **precepts**, and the place of worship the **tabernacle**. Finally, you will probably encounter **prudence** more than once: it is a word cherished even more by Freemasons than by Gordon Brown.

Freemasonry strikes me as being a little like Janus, the Roman god with two faces: one looking ahead, and one looking back (in whose honour January, the month that straddles the new and old year, was named). It combines openness and secrecy: a keenness to talk and to be inclusive, but also intensely private. What is certain is that the community continues to attract more myths than almost any other – the inevitable conclusion, perhaps, of outsiders looking in through a very misty window.

AN HONEST LIAR

MAGICIANS

If the saying goes that prostitution is the oldest profession, magicians might argue otherwise. The cup and balls routine, still part of the street performer's repertoire, was a favourite even for the ancient Greeks. It was one of the tricks played by the *Acetabularii*, a group of magicians who took their name from the small vinegar cups they used for it. Today's 'thimble-rig' trick ('rig' being a swindle) owes everything to these early magic-makers. 'Magician' itself is an even older word, looking back to Persian priests or 'magi' considered wise and skilled in eastern enchantment; its ultimate roots may lie in a prehistoric word meaning 'to have power', also at the heart of 'machine'.

While today's magicians aim to entertain, magic for their predecessors was a far weightier affair. Together with alchemy and astrology, it was held to be an essential part of an all-round education, one component of 'grammar' within the 'trivium' designed to teach the elite how to learn.

Thanks to this system of learning, 'grammar' encompassed an education that included 'the occult sciences'. In fact it remained rooted in this fourteenth-century idea of 'magical' learning for some four centuries, until rationalism and the age of reason demanded that magic and enchantment be split off and be given a new term – 'glamour'.

Magic may seem inherently glamorous, but much of today's variety is the opposite, especially on the street, where the gimmicks and bedazzlement of vaudeville theatre are replaced with (outwardly) rough and ready spontaneity. But who chooses it as their profession? 'We're talking loners,' the magician Paul Zenon explains, 'focused, often only children, and similar to tech-geeks and nerds.' In other words, he expands, 'the sort of people that would have played *Dungeons & Dragons* for unhealthy lengths of time as kids'. Spot one in a pub, and they're likely to be alone in a corner, fiddling with a deck of cards. In summary, Zenon concludes, most magicians are 'anally retentive'.

As for their motivation, for the quieter practitioner, the draw of magic is its compelling mix of lateral thinking and puzzle-solving. But for the entertainers, magic can offer a power trip, a means of impressing others and a kind of social leverage. A magician will always be the most hounded person at a party – if they show one trick they'll end up performing all night. If most comedians are ever-prepared for the 'tell us a joke' line, the pressure is notched up a gear for the magician, who needs real tricks up his sleeve at all times: you'll rarely find one without a deck of cards.

No matter how introverted, the skin of the professional magician is necessarily thick. Like a preacher, their audience will always be divided into believers, agnostics, and sceptics. The latter will always assume that a trick is the work of a camera, and never anything more than jiggery-pokery of the highest order. In fact, and as the stage magician James Randi famously said, 'magicians are the most honest people in the world: they tell you they're gonna fool you, and then they do it'. (Randi did not, categorically, include spoon-benders, escapologists or mediums among such honest liars.)

The motto of The Magic Circle, established on a summer's day in 1905 by twenty-three amateur and professional magicians, is *Indocilis Privata Loqui* – 'not apt to reveal secrets'. It's a neat description of the history of magic and its hold over the public and private imagination since society began.

Members of The Circle (always use the capital M and T) meet each Monday evening at their London head-quarters to swap ideas and to learn from visiting magicians. To most outsiders, the century-old institution is assumed to be as full of codes and secret rituals as any Freemason's Lodge. In reality, there are no passwords or masonic-style ceremonies: the only pledge asked of members is to advance and promote the art of magic wherever possible, and to guard its secrets closely, lest any **muggles** (non-wizards) or **laymen** (punters) penetrate its walls.

The tricks

Numerous words and expressions used in mainstream English started life in magic. Some of them, like **phoney**, are unexpected. The fraudulent practice of the **fawney-rig** was first recorded in the USA at the end of the eighteenth century. In 1823 Pierce Egan, a chronicler of popular pursuits and low life in England, described how the trick worked. 'A fellow drops a brass ring, double gilt, which he picks up before the party meant to be cheated, and to whom he disposes of it for less than its supposed, and ten times more than its real, value.' It's a street con that is still around today. 'Fawney' is from the Irish word *fáinne*, 'a ring'.

Ultimately, magic is a test of skill and illusion, with a bit of cunning thrown in: the 'sleight' in 'sleight of hand' – manual dexterity in the performance of tricks – is related to 'sly'. Prestidigitation, meanwhile, has its roots in the idea of being 'nimble-fingered', reflecting what is a common misconception: in fact, magic isn't necessarily quick, and is far more about psychological than manual skill.

angles: the lines of vision of particular audience members which will determine whether the mechanics of a trick can be spotted. If a trick is **angly** it can only be performed to certain viewpoints.

misdirection: the deliberate manipulation of the spectator's attention to prevent their spotting how a trick is done.

ditch: to secretly dispose of an object without the audience knowing. Also known as **going south**, as in 'he went south with the extra card and no one spotted a thing.'

palm: to conceal an object in the hand (though not necessarily in the palm). There are many types, including a **back-palm**, concealing one in the back of the hand, and a **thumb-palm**.

cold deck: a deck of cards that is secretly switched in for another one during a trick.

woofle dust: an invisible 'substance' that supposedly makes tricks work, but which is really an excuse for secretly picking up or getting rid of an object.

gaffed: used of a prop that's been altered in some way.

load: to secretly introduce an object or objects into a location, e.g. a ball underneath an inverted cup which the audience believes to be empty. Taking an object away is **stealing**.

monte routine: a gambling routine in which the audience has to guess where a specific object is hidden; in other words, a rigged guessing game.

The audience

burn: what an audience member does to a magician when they continue to stare at the performer's hands no matter what misdirection is thrown at them.

fry: to hugely impress an audience.

flash: to accidentally expose an object or part of an object momentarily during a secret move.

confederate: an audience member planted to act in a co-operative manner; a stooge.

sucker effect: a trick where the spectator is led to believe they have worked it out, only to be proved wrong.

The patter

The words spoken by a magician as an accompaniment to a performance – part and parcel of 'misdirection' – is known as the **patter**, a word that began as a shortening of 'paternoster', referring to the rapid mumbling of prayers. The first record of it in this sense is from a glossary of 1758, when its home was the cant language of thieves and beggars.

The formula we all know and love is **Abracadabra**. This incantation, once made with great gravity, was held to be part of a gnostic spell that had special powers against fatal diseases and was commonly recited to ward off evil. Many Roman emperors are said to have worn amulets bearing the word written in a triangular pattern, with the first line reading ABRACADABRA, the second ABRACADABR, and so on, until the last line which was simply A.

Hey presto, another, now stereotypical magical command, began as 'Hey Presto, be gone', and was the customary accompaniment to the repertoire of street performers. They also liked the phrase **hocus pocus**, the opening of an absurd string of mock Latin used by jugglers in fairs and markets in the 1600s that may also have given us the word 'hoax'.

Today, along with **Pif paf pouf!**, it's mostly kids' entertainers who deliver the traditional patter. Those on the street and on stage are a little less formulaic.

Talking props

A magician's number one prop is a pack of cards. So much so that the sorcerer's apprentice will often plough the small amount of money they earn straight back into buying more packs to replace those that have been ripped, manhandled or over-shuffled.

profonde: a large pocket in tail coats that can be used for vanishes or productions.

slicks: highly polished cards used for flourishes.

talking: inadvertent noises made by the props which can give away the trick ('He might have got away with that if the coins hadn't talked at the vital moment').

gimmick: a word with a special meaning in magic, used for a small object or piece of equipment that facilitates the magic and of which the audience is unaware.

feke: an item which looks like a regular, everyday object, but which has been adapted (or **gimmicked**) for the trick, e.g. a drinking glass which has had the bottom removed, or a coin with a magnet embedded in it.

DANGLERS AND DISCARDS

SPIES

When, in 1915, a heavily armoured combat vehicle rolled into military service (nicknamed, rather incongruously, Little Willie), Britain's secret weapon was finally revealed. For months it had been under construction in separate locations and listed in paperwork as a 'water carrier for Mesopotamia'. This code name gave rise to the eventual name of the machine: the tank.

Such subterfuge (from the Latin for 'escape by stealth') was a typical example of the workings of military intelligence, with one exception: the truth was finally made public. In the world of espionage, secrets generally never make the light of day.

When it comes to spies, intrigue has a double meaning, combining undercover scheming with a sense of curiosity and excitement. For the public, there is no shortage of the latter. Myths and rumours abound – forever fuelled by 007, John le Carré and *Spooks* – as do implausible conspiracy theories. The latter are the inevitable by-product of a secrecy so tightly held that even an agent's closest friends and family have little or no idea about what they do. The public face of the spy is that of a civil servant – no more, no less. Theirs is the life of the **mole**, a term that's described someone working underground in darkness and secrecy since 1601.

As for recruitment to Box 500, as MI5 is affectionately known by civil servants thanks to its official wartime address of PO Box 500, there is no mysterious tap on the shoulder at university. Instead, most agents apply themselves online. If accepted at this stage, they face gruelling tests and interviews that probe everything from their sex life to compromising situations of the cannabis kind. Disclosure, of course, is all.

Once through the door, there are any number of different jobs available, none of which – officially at least – go by the actual word 'spy'. When MI5 was first established in 1909, its enemies were fascism and communism. Today, the number one opponent is terrorism, and there is now a major emphasis at Number 12 Millbank on digital surveillance and computer network forensics. The proliferation of electronic communication, and the need it creates for intense scrutiny, has inevitably had a profound effect on spy operations and their language.

That language, together with the highs and lows of the job, can only really be exchanged within select groups. It is part of a secrecy that defines the job but that can also make it lonely at times. When there's a need to talk – shop or not – there is always the MI5 watering hole, formerly known as the Pig and Eye Club when it was set up by spies during the Cold War, and later renamed (for reasons of political correctness) as the **Eye Club**.

Like the intelligence it describes, much of the shorthand of espionage will never emerge. But there is a hybrid, open-private lexicon that is publicly known and that collectively gives us a glimpse into spydom – that state which the *Morning Star*, in 1862, declared 'so abhorrent to the English feeling'. A hundred and fifty years on, the debate over a Big Brother surveillance society continues to rumble.

The friends

C; the director of MI6. The first of these was Captain Sir Mansfield Smith-Cumming, who would always initial his papers 'C' in green ink, thereby creating the nickname for all successive directors.

asset: a person or thing that has value to intelligence. Usually known as an agent.

bagman: an agent who pays spies and bribes authorities.

birdwatcher: a spy.

agent-in-place: a spy who, instead of openly defecting, is now operating with a foreign government and so working on both sides.

bridge agent: one who acts as a courier.

cobbler: a spy who creates false passports, visas, diplomas, and other documents.

cut-out: a person used as a conduit between the members of an operation to allow them to pass material or messages securely.

dangle: one who approaches a foreign intelligence agency in the hope of being recruited as a spy, so as to become a double agent.

discard: an agent allowed to be arrested in order to protect more valuable agents. A **throwaway** is an agent deemed expendable.

floater: a person used just once or only occasionally within an intelligence operation.

friends: the collective term for members of the Secret Intelligence Service.

raven: a male agent employed to seduce people for intelligence purposes. The female equivalent is a **swallow**.

sleeper: an agent living as an ordinary citizen in a foreign country, who acts only when a hostile situation develops.

walk-in: the act of a potential asset simply turning up at the embassy door.

going rogue: said of a spy who decides to act outside the rules and stop following orders.

The operations

rabbit: the target of an investigation.

in the gap: those brief moments in which spies may meet each other without any kind of surveillance.

bang and burn: a sabotage operation.

eyewash: a false entry made in files in case they are ever found, or hacked into by an enemy.

chicken feed: genuine, but not at all compromising, intelligence knowingly provided to an enemy intelligence agency through a double agent, in order to establish their credentials.

blowback: a deception that is planted abroad by an intelligence agency but later returns to the originating nation with unfortunate consequences.

black bag job: secret entry into a building in order to steal or copy materials.

black operation: a covert one that can never be linked to the organization performing it. **Black propaganda** is disinformation that will always be denied by its source.

brush pass: a brief encounter in which information is passed between case officer and agent.

dead drop: a secret location where materials or messages can be left for another party to retrieve.

dry cleaning: actions that agents take to determine if they are under surveillance, such as making everyday errands.

music box: a clandestine radio. The **musician** is its operator.

The kit

legend: an agent's claimed background and life history supported by forged documentation (the **backstop**), which is always memorized. Also known as **window-dressing**.

parole: a password that identifies intelligence personnel to each other.

pocket litter: items in a spy's pocket (such as receipts, tickets etc.) that add authenticity to their identity.

shoe: a false passport or visa.

L-pill: a poison pill used by operatives to commit suicide.

Hello number: a number used to indicate an emergency. The
agent in trouble will deliver a coded message for help, such
as 'Hello. It's freezing in London today'.

Spies seem a particularly fitting group to end on. On the one
hand, their codes sit at the farthest corner of tribal conversation,
where secrecy is as essential as it is expedient. But even they
may not be as remote as that secrecy suggests. Our fascination
with espionage may stem from the fact that we are all, to some
degree, conspiratorial, living our lives in secret, if only in our
heads. Our world is full of priesthoods, packed with ritual and
terminology designed to bind, bamboozle, and impress. Put like
this, spies are simply an extreme version of ourselves. And
whether the double agents are amateur or professional, the game
will go on. As le Carré noted, it's a lot like the wiring in a
building – 'it's just a question of who takes it over and switches
on the lights'. That those lights will always be illuminated is
never in doubt.

How to Eavesdrop

If *Modern Tribes* has left you just a little more curious about the secret conversations going on around you, it will have done its job. There is so much more to tell.

I've never really liked the term 'fag-ends' for those bits of information you occasionally pick up when other people are chatting. It's a term that actually has nothing to do with the burning embers of a cigarette, and everything to do with the odds and ends of cloth in textile-making, those fragments that 'hang loose'. All of which suggests that these are flabby, conversational inconsequences that don't lead very far. In my experience, the opposite can be true.

Curiosity is innate in all of us, and so it follows that eavesdropping comes quite naturally. That said, there is a knack to doing it efficiently: to becoming an expert at listening as though you're not listening, and sitting in on other people's lives if only for a minute or two.

Here are a few tips as to how to tune in effectively, reflecting my own personal habits should you want to try them. I should, of course, add that this is for picking up secrets of the linguistic, rather than the gossipy, kind.

1. Be curious. An obvious first rule, but curiosity will take you to places and conversations that you wouldn't normally pay any heed to. If a trainspotter shares his memories of 'using

the bedpan', don't write him off as an old dear: what he knows may surprise you.

2. Filter out the trivial. Part of the art of 'hearkening', as they used to call it, is to siphon off the white noise and focus on the main event.

3. Write it down. Have a pen and paper with you at all times. I carry my notebooks with me everywhere, even on my bike or in a rowing boat. You never know when you might hear something that tickles your fancy or positively intrigues you.

4. Listen out for new senses of words you already know. A vicar talking about a 'supermarket trolley' is actually discussing the transport he's laid on for a coffin.

5. Always investigate new words. Word spies will take their catches home for further investigation. You may not yet know what a 'snotter' is, but you might stumble across one later.

6. Consider what these words mean about the group they came from. Being an armchair anthropologist is as much fun as being a closet linguist.

7. Love your dictionary. And if the word you hear isn't in there, let others know, it might catch on. English is a democracy in which usage, and only usage, rules.

8. Be tribal. Appreciate the lingo of your group and profession as well as that of others. Not only will it help you to fit in, you will become multilingual in the process.

Happy hunting.

Acknowledgements

'Characterized by a lack of modesty; barefaced or brazen'. Thus the dictionary's definition of 'shameless', which is what I became in the writing of this book. I enlisted the help of almost everyone I know, and hundreds of people I didn't, which makes *Modern Tribes* as much the result of their endeavours as mine. If the following list looks enormous, it could have been a great deal longer had I been able to thank all those anonymous people whose conversations I've tuned into over the past few decades. If any book could be dedicated to eavesdroppees, this would be it.

Many of the following have offered so much valuable information that a single mention can't possibly do them justice. To them I would say that I owe you a lot more, and that I hope one day I can return the favour – especially if it's language you're after. To borrow (one time only) the words of Donald Trump: 'I know words. I have the best words.'

In addition to the following consultants, I must thank my editor Georgina Laycock, who has gone over and above the call of duty to be unfailingly positive even when deadlines looked likely to overtake us and grin in the rear-view mirror. Her intelligence and instinct inform much of this book. John Murray's Kate Craigie also delivered smiles, support, and many great examples for the text. I wouldn't have met either of them without my brilliant (and patient) agent, Rosemary Scoular. I should add that the bad puns in the section titles are all my own: I didn't study under Richard Whiteley for nothing.

My family have borne with great patience my scribbling down any titbit I've 'happened' to overhear, and the embarrassment of my approaching complete strangers with random requests for vocabulary. They have also uncomplainingly put up with my disappearing into the computer screen for hours on end. This includes my mother, who was quite ill in the course of my writing and who nonetheless always encouraged me to keep scribbling.

Above all, I'd like to thank my sister, Nicky, to whom I owe some of the best material in here, and a lot more besides. This book (and my life), would be a lot poorer without her.

My Consultants

Pete Allen
John Anderson
James Anderson
Janette Anderson
Arrivederci
Nihal Arthanayake
Paul Atkins
Andrew Ball
Julia Bradbury
Jo Brand
Gyles Brandreth
    (and his wonderful *Oxford Dictionary of Humorous Quotations*)
Catherine Burton
Nicky Campbell
Fleur Clarke
John Cockerham

Matthew and Paul Coleman
    of Coleman's Butchers,
    Salcombe
Colin @theabingdontaxi
Luke Collyer
Dave Craigie
Charlie Croker and his legal
    representative Mark Mason
Matthew Dales
Ruth Davidson
Malcolm and Vicki Dent
Shirley Dent
Denise Else
Nicola Garfield
Bobby George
Jamie Gilbert
Jonathon Green
Julian Gregory

Phil Hammond
Luke Henderson
Nick Hewer
Andrea Hill
Ollie Howe and *Daniel Surf Ltd*
John Hulse
Natalie Iyayi
David James
Lee Joseph
Jim Kempton
Jake Knott
Elizabeth Knowles
Tom Knox
Christopher Layden
Sarah Ledingham
Robert Lordan
Alistair McGowan
Laura McNeil
Jack Manuel
Sally Ann Matthews
Andrew Menniss
Richard Molloy
Rebecca Morgan
Christopher Mulvey and the English Project
Naga Munchetty
Dave Myers

Joe Namadh
Chris Packham
Terry Payne
Anne Perry
Steven Poole
The Rev. Norman Price
Nicholas Rhodes QC
Alison Root and *Women & Golf Magazine*
Rachel Riley
Greg Rusedski
Roger Sharp
Rob Smith and the *Literacy Shed*
Peter Souter
Neil Stuke
Simon Usborne
Aidan Vine QC
Rick Wakeman
Dan Walker
Dean Webb
Arsène Wenger
Admiral Alan West
Brett Westwood
Joe Wilkinson
Jonathan Yardley
Paul Zenon

Index